Bad Guys In American History

BAD GUYS  IN AMERICAN HISTORY

GEORGE CANTOR

BARNES & NOBLE

NEW YORK

ISBN-13: 978-0-7607-9077-9
ISBN-10: 0-7607-9077-9

Printed and bound in the United States of America

1 3 5 7 9 10 8 6 4 2

The pages of this book contain 20% recycled fiber.

CONTENTS

INTRODUCTION
Americans have never quite known what to make of their bad guys. The glow of time and distance, folklore encrusted with myth, has given many of them the aura of fallen heroes.

A few of the bad guys profiled in this book were, in their time, recognized as no-good scum. Blackbeard plundering the Carolina coast. Simon Girty leading his Indians in mayhem across the Ohio frontier. The Harpe Brothers, the first serial killers of the nineteenth century, leaving a trail of blood across Kentucky.

No one celebrated these men or mourned their passing. In fact, their heads were more likely to be hung from tree branches or a ship's bowsprit as a warning to those who sought to imitate them.

The big change in the public's fascination with outlaws began in the decades following the Civil War. That was because of two simultaneous phenomena: the closing of the Western frontier and the rise of the Eastern mass media.

In the 1880s, when the country finally was secured from Atlantic to Pacific, the West became romanticized. The violent frontier that had defined the American experience for the entire life of the nation was now passing into history. It lingered on in the dusty cow towns of Kansas and Texas, the mining camps of Arizona and South Dakota, in the Indian Territories and the range wars of New Mexico.

Safe in the settled cities of the East and Midwest, Americans couldn't get enough of the Western frontier. It was thrilling now that it was vanishing. Buffalo Bill already was touring these cities with his Wild West shows, the sanitized show business version of the frontier. The final spasmodic, real acts of violence were regarded as part of the same grand pageant.

At the same time, a few journalistic entrepreneurs were discovering something wonderful. There was an untapped market for the printed word. With the rise of mass public education, America had become a literate country, and a stable working class in the cities was looking for new ways to be informed and entertained.

The Scripps family was the first to understand that a newspaper published in the afternoon, priced below the established rag, and filled with blood and thunder, crime, and sports could eclipse all known circulation records. Starting with the *Detroit News* in 1873, they built a national newspaper chain based on these principles. Soon their example was emulated across the country. William Randolph Hearst copied their basic ideas and brought this brand of newspapering to the big city with his *New York Journal*. Mass circulation magazines, such as *The Police Gazette*, aimed at the same audience, also grew in influence.

Personalities and events that once would have quickly passed into oblivion became magnified into major stories, told over and over again, with new angles and embellished details. The competition among these publications created legends.

In just six months, for example, between October 1881 and April 1882, the gunfight at the OK Corral and the violent deaths of Billy the Kid and Jesse James occurred. These were three of the most celebrated events in Western history, one right after the other. By no coincidence, they all happened at a time when the new media were most hungrily seeking new celebrity heroes.

So, Wyatt Earp's dubious past as a gambler and small-time thug was forgotten in the rush to glorify him. The far more vicious acts of Billy the Kid and the James Gang became, instead, the stuff of gallantry. Billy the Kid was no half-witted thug but a symbol of youth battling injustice. Jesse James was no cold-blooded killer but a Robin Hood, a defender of lost causes.

The criminal as celebrity was something new in our culture, and the effect has been long lasting. The stories of these first-heralded bad guys are so deeply embedded in the American mind that they have passed into folklore and myth.

The image of the criminal as hero was reinforced when the new medium of movies appeared and producers found that the most enduringly popular kind of film they could make was the Western. So the old legends were dusted off and trotted out before the cameras, to be remade over and over again.

The outlaw heroes were joined in the 1920s by the urban gangster. Prohibition was opposed by many Americans. In their eyes, an Al Capone was simply performing a public service. Besides, who got hurt? Only other gangsters. It was all a wonderful show, just like Buffalo Bill's, only now it was happening on the streets of Chicago.

When the Great Depression fastened upon the American heartland, America continued its love affair with outlaws. Now it was John Dillinger and Bonnie and Clyde who attained heroic status. After all, they only robbed banks. Everybody hated banks in the 1930s. The dramatization of their careers on the radio made them seem like ordinary folks who had some bad luck and were trying to make out as best they could.

Almost all of them got a new life when television arrived. Wild Bill Hickok rode again. Capone strode the streets of Chicago. Wyatt Earp brought the law to Dodge City. TV brought them all into our living rooms, and they remain there forever in reruns.

Some of the places associated with these bad guys have been attractions for more than a century. Pilgrimages have been made to the graves of Jesse James and Billy the Kid from the moment the two outlaws were lowered into them. Salem has never outgrown its witches. The gunfire still echoes at the OK Corral.

In more recent years, the fascination has grown. The house where Lizzie Borden's father and stepmother met their demise is now a bed and breakfast. Blackbeard's evil career is a powerful draw on remote Ocracoke Island off the North Carolina coast. In Skagway, Alaska, a summer pageant tells of the crooked, and often vicious, deeds of Soapy Smith. It seems that tourists like their history with just a touch of nastiness.

The apologists of these bad guys try to make a case that economic necessity, the rigors of war, and the hard realities of their times explain what they did. Upon closer examination, however, you will find that in every case the bad guys just found crime and duplicity much more fun than working. They made a simple, conscious decision to go bad and nasty.

I have also included in this book two of the most famous prisons in our history—Alcatraz and Yuma—and three notorious courts of law. There are also three women—Belle Starr, Lizzie Borden, and Bonnie Parker. No gender equity was required here. They earned their places among the bad guys with solid achievement.

Maybe, in the end, it is the sheer fascination with evil that makes these individuals so compelling. Quantrill's raid on Lawrence, Kansas. Dillinger's brief and murderous crime spree. Jay Gould ruining thousands of lives because of his own greed. The innocent evil and superstition surrounding the events of the Salem witchcraft trials. Benedict Arnold betraying everything he had fought for.

Bad guys provide such great stories.

GEORGE CANTOR, MAY 1999

Salem Witchcraft Trials

It began as an idle game for a group of young girls, a way of passing the dull winter hours with a harmless diversion. It ended with nineteen dead, neighbors sending friends to their doom, and a town that would forevermore carry the stigma of justice gone insane.

"God will give you blood to drink," Sarah Good warned her executioners from the scaffold. She was among the first to be put to death as a witch during Salem's infamous trials of 1692.

But her prophecy went unheeded and was, in fact, largely unrealized. Most of those directly responsible for the madness in Salem went

Courtesy Peabody Essex Museum, Salem, MA.

on, lives and reputations unscathed. If their consciences ever bothered them it didn't seem to be an especially severe twinge.

Posterity, however, did exact a price. Arthur Miller's famous play *The Crucible* made the trials into a parable of political persecution and condemned those who ran them as malicious fanatics.

Nathaniel Hawthorne, a descendant of one of the judges, borrowed Good's defiant cry and put it in the mouth of a man hanged as a wizard in his classic *The House of the Seven Gables*. Based on the trials, the novel's theme revolved around how past wrongs are visited upon future generations. Hawthorne, indeed, was so haunted by the actions of his ancestor, John Hathorne, that he added the "w" to his name to distance himself from the judge.

Even now, Salem residents ask whether the tourist trade associated with witchcraft and the madness of a few months hasn't come at the price of obliterating all other aspects of the town's long history. After three centuries, the trials still define Salem's past.

The foundation for witchcraft was laid when a new minister, Samuel Parris, was hired by the town in 1688. Salem residents had long argued over who should hold the position; three predecessors had been dismissed acrimoniously over the previous five years.

Early in 1692, Parris's young daughter, Betty, and some friends began to hold seances led by the minister's black slave, Tituba, who had come with the family from Barbados. Done as a lark, the meetings soon turned ominous when some of the girls began reporting strange visions.

This was a time in which the superstitious dread of the Middle Ages remained strong in the new colonies. It seemed to lurk in the dark forests that surrounded the coastal settlements. Moreover, the famous Boston minister, Cotton Mather, had recently published a book describing instances of witchcraft that he had seen personally, called *Memorable Providences Relating to Witchcraft and Possessions*.

The girls were surrounded by all this. It was part of their spiritual environment.

As the sessions with Tituba went on, the girls began exhibiting strange symptoms. They would crawl on all fours, bark like dogs, go into convulsions, and contort their bodies in strange shapes. In 1692 their behavior was a sure sign of witchcraft.

When Reverend Parris asked what was going on, the girls understandably were reluctant to tell the minister what they had been up to. So they blamed Tituba—she was a witch.

Tituba was quick on her feet. She saw at once the danger she was in and knew how to get out of it. She gave a graphic depiction of the devil loose in Salem, a tall man who could change himself into a dog. He demanded that she sign the book containing the names of those who had given up their souls to him, Tituba said, and then took her riding through the air.

Moreover, she was willing to name names, and that's what the elders of Salem wanted. They were willing to forgive those who had fallen in with the devil. Anyone can make a mistake, after all. If the witches only confessed and told who had enlisted them in the devil's work, Salem would soon get to the real instigators and the matter would be settled.

Tituba said she had seen others flying through the air and witnessed their signatures in the devil's book. They were, in fact, Sarah Good and Sarah Osborn. Both, as it happened, were elderly women, with no influence in the community.

Tituba's testimony and the ongoing behavior of the girls convinced Reverand Parris that there was a big problem. Villagers started remembering odd events from past years. A cow that suddenly sickened and died, a neighbor's muttered curse, a display of irreligious levity. Now it all fit. It had to be witchcraft.

Good and Osborn were arrested. So were tavern keeper Bridget Bishop and Good's four-year-old granddaughter, Dorcas. Someone recalled a disagreement with the town's previous minister, George Burroughs, who always had behaved a bit oddly and claimed to have knowledge of conversations out of his hearing. Constables were sent to his new pulpit, in what is now Maine, and brought him back in chains.

For the first three months, all the accused witches were simply thrown into jail without trial. No courts were operating because eight years previously James II had withdrawn the right of self-government to the North American colonies. But when he was dethroned by William of Orange, the Massachusetts charter was restored.

On May 14, 1692, Sir William Phips, the colony's first royal governor, landed in Boston with the charter of self-government, giving him the authority to convene courts. He wasted no time. When he heard what was going on in Salem, Phips convened a court of Oyer and Terminer (which considered criminal matters) and named a panel of eight judges.

Now the wheels of justice were ready to roll, and the first to be run over was Bishop. She was tried and convicted, and on June 10 she was hanged.

The critical testimony against her, and several others who followed her to the grave, was spectral. In other words, it was based on visions that only the accusers could see. Most of the accusers were the young women, who now numbered seven. They filled the court with screams, moans, animal noises, and hysterical outbursts.

Whether they realized that their prank had gone too far to be reversed, or whether they actually were gripped by a form of mass hysteria, is still open to conjecture. Even some of their victims were astonished by the performance, and the judges were absolutely convinced.

William Stoughton, the presiding judge, had no legal background, but he did have degrees in theology from Harvard and Oxford. In his mind, law was no match for religious conviction. It was his decision to allow spectral evidence, as well as to deny counsel to the accused and allow judges to interrogate witnesses. Judge Hathorne also accused defendants of lying if they tried to deny the charges.

One of the judges, Nathaniel Saltonstall, was so disgusted over violations of legal procedure that he resigned from the court after Bishop's execution. But his colleagues plunged ahead enthusiastically. Soon, more respectable members of the community were accused and the pace of trials picked up during the summer.

Rebecca Nurse, a woman noted for her piety, was found innocent, but Stoughton didn't like that verdict and persuaded the jury to change its mind. After praying for the souls of the judges, she was executed.

John Proctor, the central figure of Miller's play, challenged the court's legitimacy and honesty. He, too, was hanged, and his wife, Elizabeth, was spared only because she was pregnant. Giles Cory, an elderly farmer, refused to plead innocent or guilty, on the basis that if he denied the court's right to try him it could not confiscate his land after his death. He was crushed to death under heavy stones for his impertinence.

Reverend Burroughs's turn soon came, and he dumbfounded the crowd at his hanging by reciting the Lord's Prayer. Witches were not supposed to be able to pray, and many people began to protest his execution. To no avail. Judge Hathorne had been among the community leaders who had wanted Burroughs replaced as minister years before, and he wasn't about to back off now. His death, however, brought the first elements of doubt to the surface.

By autumn the executions were still going forward. But ministers throughout Massachusetts were contacting the court, expressing amazement that so many highly regarded people in one small area "should leap into the devil's lap at once."

Increase Mather, Cotton's father and the most respected clergy-man in the colony, issued a written statement, urging abrogation of spectral evidence. Since Satan created the specters, he argued, were you not taking the devil's own word in accepting them? "It is better that ten suspected witches should escape than one innocent person should be condemned," wrote Mather, albeit a bit too late.

Even Phips finally began to express reservations. When the accus-ers brought up the name of Phips's wife as a witch, everyone realized that things had gone too far. Fifty-two people awaiting trial or sentenc-ing were released by April, 1693, and the great witchcraft scare was over.

Stoughton, who had done so much to promote the trials, went on to replace Phips as governor, blamed his predecessor for interfering with a good job of witch removal, and was never called to account for his role in the deaths of the innocent.

Hathorne lived in Salem for another twenty-four years. Parris was forced to apologize, although he insisted it was all Stoughton's fault. He lost his job in Salem in 1697, but continued as a minister in Massachusetts until his death in 1720.

Of all the judges, only Samuel Sewall seemed to be afflicted with genuine remorse. While the diaries he kept during the course of the tri-als indicated no doubts, he became greatly troubled afterwards. In 1696, as a member of the Governor's Council, he proclaimed a public fast day and called on the government to repent its role in the perse-cution. Sewall personally observed the anniversary of the fast for the rest of his life and also was one of the first public figures in the colonies to argue for the abolition of slavery.

Later research indicates that there may have been more to the Salem outbreak than simple religious zealotry. Historians Paul Boyer and Stephen Nissenbaum, in their 1974 book, *The Geography of Witchcraft*, traced the cause of the trials to what may have been America's first dispute over urban sprawl.

Reconstructing a map of the area from old land titles, they drew a chart pinpointing where the accusers and their victims lived. A strik-ing pattern emerged. Those who were most eager to press the witch-craft charges generally resided in the town's more settled agricultural area while those engaged in commerce in the newer sections of the community were far more likely to be accused.

Boyer and Nissenbaum contend that the agrarian interests were using religious frenzy as a cover for reasserting economic control over the future of Salem. It was a fight they could not win and it came at a terrible cost.

According to local lore, a twenty-six-year-old woman stood up to speak at the Salem meeting house in 1706. She said that her name was Ann Putnam, and that she had been one of the children who had accused their neighbors of consorting with the devil fourteen years before. She begged forgiveness and admitted that it had all been a lie.

No one else was ever put to death for witchcraft in the United States.

THE SITES

The Witch House Jonathan Corwin was one of the examining magistrates in the witchcraft trials, a position he shared with Judge Hathorne. They were two of the most dedicated witch hunters and many of the victims were taken to Corwin's home for their first hearing.

The house, built in 1642, is one of the few surviving structures that played a role in the trials. Now known as the Witch House, it is a museum of the era, with an interior restored to its probable appearance of 1692.

It is located at 310 Essex St., just west of the downtown core. The house is open daily, 10 a.m. to 4:30 p.m., mid-March through November. Admission $8; children 6–14 $4. (978) 744-0180.

The Witch Museum A slightly more extensive museum of the witch hysteria is located at the northwestern edge of Salem Common. The Witch Museum features thirteen life-sized tableaux depicting scenes from the trials and executions, as well as an audiovisual presentation that goes on every thirty minutes.

The museum is at 19 1/2 Washington Square North. It is open daily, 10 a.m. to 5 p.m. Admission $7.50; children under fourteen $5. (978) 744-1692; www.salemwitchmuseum.com.

Witch Dungeon Museum The most graphic depiction of the Salem trials is put on at the Witch Dungeon Museum. Live actors portray a recreated scene from those events and although the "dungeon" is actually part of a nineteenth century church building it is still fairly gripping stuff.

The museum is located at 16 Lynde St., west of Washington St. and north of Essex St. Open daily, 10 a.m. to 5 p.m., April through November. Admission $6; children under fourteen $4. (978) 741-3570; www.witchdungeon.com.

The Nurse Homestead The home of Rebecca Nurse, the pious woman who prayed for her executioners before being hanged as a witch, stands in Danvers, 4 miles northwest of Salem. The seventeenth century salt-box is now a domestic museum of the era and overlooks the field in which she is buried.

The Nurse Homestead is at 149 Pine St. It is open 12 p.m. to 4:30 p.m., mid-June to Labor Day; weekends only through October. Admission $5; students $3. (978) 774-8799; www.rebeccanurse.org.

RELATED SITES

The House of the Seven Gables The home that inspired Nathaniel Hawthorne to write *The House of the Seven Gables* remains Salem's most popular attraction. Although not directly related to the witch trials, it stood while they were going on, having been built in 1668. In recent years, Hawthorne's birthplace and three other historic residences have been moved to the grounds. The oldest is the Retire Becket House, dating from 1655.

The House of the Seven Gables is located at 115 Derby St., near the waterfront and just east of Derby Wharf and the Salem Maritime National Historical Park. Open daily, 10 a.m. to 6 p.m., January through June; 10 a.m. to 7 p.m., July through October (open until 11 p.m. in October only). Closed first half of January. Admission $7; children under seventeen $4. (978) 744-0991; www.7gables.org.

ANNUAL EVENTS

Haunted Happenings Despite some qualms about its past, Salem capitalizes on its witchcraft days with a late October carnival called Haunted Happenings. There are costumed supernatural figures walking the streets, haunted houses, psychic readings, and seances, just like Tituba used to hold. It begins on the weekend preceding Halloween and continues through the holiday. For further information call (978) 744-3663 or visit www.hauntedhappenings.org.

BLACKBEARD

An air of romance clings to many of the pirates that figured in American history. Legends have built up over the years, turning them into gentlemen, loveable rogues, patriots. No danger of that happening to Edward Teach. He was every inch a villain. More than that, he seemed to enjoy it.

His goal seemed to be to conserve his weapons by frightening his victims to death. His beard itself was terrifying, an unruly black mass, which, according to one observer, was "like a frightful meteor and covered his whole face."

Braces of pistols hung at his belt. He favored a scarlet coat, under which he carried two swords. To complete the ensemble, he placed lighted wicks in his hair.

"This made him altogether such a figure that imagination cannot form an idea of a Fury from hell to look more frightful," wrote a contemporary observer, Captain Charles Johnson. Blackbeard was one of the great showmen of the high seas and also one of the nastiest.

Johnson, one of the few sympathetic chroniclers of Blackbeard's career, said that the pirate probably never killed anyone "who hadn't threatened him first." If that was the case, he was unusually touchy. Most historians seem to feel that he often killed just to leave no witnesses.

Painting by John Kachik

He was most likely born in Bristol, England, in the late seventeenth century, with the name of Teach, or possibly Thatch. By his late teens, he was in Jamaica working as a crewman on a merchant ship, perfectly positioned to take advantage of Queen Anne's War.

Queen Anne's War was one of a series of conflicts arising from competing claims to various European thrones that lasted nearly one hundred years. In Europe, it was known as the War of the Spanish Succession. Louis XIV sought to unify the French and Spanish dynasties, a move that was opposed by England, Austria, and Holland. Queen Anne's War began in 1701 and raged across Europe for thirteen years as well as in the American colonies of the nations involved.

With the war raging, it was as if the doors to the bank swung open for British sea captains. They were granted letters of marque, giving them the right to attack enemy merchant ships, and became known as privateers. In the war's final years, Teach joined the crew of one of the most successful of these captains, Benjamin Hornigold, who preyed mercilessly on Spanish and French shipping in the Caribbean.

Teach seemed to have a knack for the job, and when the war ended he saw no reason to switch careers. He and Hornigold switched their base to New Providence Island, in the Bahamas, and went after any vessel that came their way, no matter what flag she flew.

In 1717, they captured a large French merchant ship, the *Concorde*. It was outfitted with twenty-six guns, renamed the *Queen Anne's Revenge*, and taken by Blackbeard to command.

He celebrated in a rather unusual manner. While his men were drinking below deck, he locked the doors to the cabin and set fire to a number of brimstone bars. The crew began choking and pawed frantically at the door to get out. Teach kept it barred until the last possible moment and then allowed his suffocating crew to escape.

It was an indelible lesson about who was in charge on that ship. No wonder men who sailed under Blackbeard thought he was the Devil himself.

When Britain offered a general amnesty to all privateers in 1717, Hornigold decided to call it a career and retire. But Teach was just getting warmed up.

Within weeks, Teach was threatening the American mainland. British expeditions sent out to engage him were decimated. By the spring of 1718, he had four ships and three hundred men sailing under his command. He had become the most feared name in the American colonies.

In May, his armada appeared off the coast of Charleston, South Carolina, the richest port in the South. He blockaded the harbor and sent a messenger ashore with his demands, mostly involving food and medicine. If the goods were not forthcoming, the citizens of Charleston would receive the heads of a leading merchant and his son, who had been captured by Blackbeard on an outward bound vessel a few days before.

The debate in the city has a familiar ring. There were those who did not want to give in to terrorism, feeling it would only encourage the pirate to increase his demands and return again. But others felt the life of a prominent citizen was worth some food and medicine. In the end, Charleston gave in, and a much-relieved merchant, who reported the pirate "seemed very much intent on taking my head," was returned to shore.

Teach, meanwhile, moved his base to North Carolina. The hundreds of coves and inlets along the shoreline there provided an ideal hiding place for him. But he had an even greater advantage. Blackbeard cut a deal with Governor Charles Eden, who maintained his capital at the town of Bath—Eden would conveniently "look the other way" and in turn would share in part of the pirate's booty.

It was an open secret that much of the pirate's loot was stored in a barn owned by Eden's personal secretary, Tobias Knight. Blackbeard then moved into a house right across the creek from Eden's home, where he was often a guest.

Several of the governor's political enemies raided Knight's barn and found the looted evidence. When they tried to seize records from Knight, they were arrested and charged with breaking and entering.

"The governor can find men enough to arrest peaceable citizens," complained one of the raiders, "but none to arrest thieves and robbers."

Knight was acquitted, due more likely to weak evidence than his innocence. Eden was never tried but many historians are convinced he was very much involved with the pirate.

"As governors are but men," wrote Henry Brooke, who chronicled the history of American pirates, "and not infrequently by no means possessed of the most virtuous principles, the gold of Blackbeard rendered him comely in the governor's eyes."

The pirate captured eighteen ships during the seven months he commanded the *Queen Anne's Revenge*. But in June 1718, the big ship ran aground in Beaufort Inlet. Blackbeard abandoned her there after removing treasure and provisions. He also took the opportunity to maroon twenty-five of its crew on a sandbar to ensure a larger split for his remaining band.

Like any overburdened chief executive, Teach did not care for muttering in the ranks, and he felt the marooned men did not properly appreciate the sacrifices he was making for them.

Having murdered hundreds of strangers by gunfire, sword, and drowning, he did not hesitate to murder his own crew as well. "Such a day; rum all out," he wrote in his journal in 1718. "Our company somewhat sober. A damned confusion amongst us; rogues a-plotting. Great talk of separation. So I looked sharp for a prize."

And another entry in 1718 reported, "Such a day; took one with a great deal of liquor on board, so kept the company hot, damned hot. Then all things went well again."

A pirate king's life is not always a merry one.

There were also problems ashore. Teach had made a mockery of the Crown's amnesty offer, and yet his old pal, Governor Eden, decided to issue him a pardon. This gesture was too much for Alexander Spottswood, governor of Virginia and a far more incorruptible public official than Eden.

Blackbeard had inflicted great damage on Virginia shipping, retreating each time to safety in North Carolina. Spottswood instructed his finest seaman, Lieutenant Robert Maynard of the Royal Navy, to pursue Teach and not be overly scrupulous about the boundary line.

On November 22, 1718, Maynard found his man at Ocracoke Inlet, on North Carolina's Outer Banks. The ships maneuvered for position through the night. Although taken by surprise and, by some accounts, intoxicated, Blackbeard still managed to inflict heavy damage on Maynard's ship with a broadside cannon blast.

Maynard boarded the pirate's ship and engaged Teach in a hand-to-hand struggle. It ended when the pirate, with twenty-five gun and sword wounds, fell dead at Maynard's feet.

The lieutenant ordered the body decapitated, and he sailed back to Virginia with Blackbeard's head fastened to his bowsprit. Surviving members of his crew were hanged in Williamsburg. With the great colonial wars in a temporary lull and the economy of the British colonies improving, Blackbeard and the other privateers had been outpaced by history. His death ended the great era of piracy on the Atlantic seaboard.

On November 21, 1996, one day short of the 28th anniversary of

Blackbeard's death, underwater archeologists located the wreckage of the *Queen Anne's Revenge* in Beaufort Inlet.

THE SITES

North Carolina Maritime Museum The North Carolina Maritime Museum is located in Beaufort, one of two state towns that compete for the dubious honor of claiming Blackbeard as a local boy. Although the emphasis of this museum is primarily on the natural history of the Carolina coast, it also has an excellent display on Blackbeard and his ship, the *Queen Anne's Revenge*. The pirate scuttled the ship in 1718 in 20 feet of water off the port's inlet.

Artifacts found near the ship's wreckage in 1996 by an underwater recovery team working for the state of North Carolina are also on display here. They include a bell, blunderbuss barrel, cannon shot, and sounding weights. The ship was built in England as the *Concord* in 1710 and captured a year later during Queen Anne's War by the French. They Gallicized the ship to *Concorde* and outfitted her with twenty-six guns. The *Concorde* was involved in the African slave trade, between the continent's west coast and the Caribbean island of St. Vincent. Blackbeard captured it in 1717, expanded its armaments to forty guns and renamed it in honor of Queen Anne, under whose flag he once had sailed. It was scuttled after just seven months.

The museum is located at 315 Front St. and is open 9 a.m. to 5 p.m., Monday to Friday; Saturday opening at 10 a.m. and Sunday at 1 p.m. Free. (252) 728-7317. Best view of the inlet and recovery site is from Fort Macon State Park, east of the bridge to Atlantic Beach, off U.S. 70, west of Beaufort.

Hammock House The place most closely associated with the pirate in Beaufort is the Hammock House. It was built around 1700 in the Bahamian-style architecture favored by the early settlers, with an overhanging second-story porch. When Blackbeard occupied it, the house stood on a creek that led to Beaufort Inlet. But centuries of silting now have placed it 500 feet from open water. The house is believed to be the oldest in the town and has been used as an inn, a school, a residence for Union soldiers, and a residence. Of course, it is haunted, most unnervingly by one of Blackbeard's wives. He hanged her for being uncooperative in the yard, and it is said her screams can be heard when the wind blows just right. Information on tours and opening hours can be obtained through the offices of Beaufort Historical Association Welcome Center, (252) 728-5225.

Historic Bath The other town that also claims Blackbeard is Bath. Once the colonial capital of North Carolina, the pirate also lived here to be close to his good friend, Governor Charles Eden. Neither Blackbeard's nor Eden's home, which once stood adjacent to one another, remain. But just west of Bath from North Carolina 92, the turnoff on Archbell's Point Road leads to the site of Eden's house, which has an historic marker. There are also displays on Blackbeard's stay in the town at the visitor center of Historic Bath, on North Carolina 92. From April through October hours are Monday to Saturday, 9 a.m. to 5 p.m.; opening Sunday at 1 p.m.; closed Monday, rest of year. Free. (252) 923-3971.

Teach's Hole The area off Ocracoke where Blackbeard was defeated and killed is still known as Teach's Hole. It is located at the southern end of the island, off Springer's Point, near the town of Ocracoke. A local legend says that the island was named for Blackbeard, when on the morning of his fatal battle, eager for dawn, he hollered, "O crow cock." That sounds unlikely and most probably is. The likely derivation is an Algonquian word meaning curved, for the shape of the island. The Pyrate's Shoppe at Teach's Hole has exhibits on Blackbeard's career. Most of them are hokey, but there is also some solid historical information. The pirate souvenirs are great. Ocracoke, which is part of the Outer Banks National Seashore, can only be reached by plane or ferry. There is a free boat ride from Hatteras Island to Ocracoke's north end, and longer toll rides from Swan Quarter and Cedar Island, on the mainland, to the town of Ocracoke. Reservations are necessary for both mainland ferries and can be made by calling (252) 928-3841.

BENEDICT ARNOLD

In a corner of the battlefield at Saratoga, the fight that changed the course of the American Revolution, there is a strange monument.

It depicts a sculpted leg in a military boot. The inscription reads: "The most brilliant soldier of the Continental Army." No name appears on it anywhere.

The memorial honors Benedict Arnold, the general who led the assault on the Breymann Redoubt and sealed the victory for the colonial side. He had been wounded in the foot as the British position was stormed on October 7, 1777.

According to the National Park Service guidebook to the battlefield, if his wound had been fatal "posterity would have known few names brighter." Instead of a dead hero, however, Arnold became a live traitor.

Just three years after his gallantry at Saratoga, he attempted to betray the fortress at West Point to the British. It was an act that astonished the colonies and staggered Arnold's close friend, George Washington.

From one of the greatest heroes of the War for Independence, he became a despised memory in America and a figure of contempt in Britain, where he lived out his remaining years. His name has come to stand for, in Washington's words, "treason of the blackest dye."

How did he come to this? How did the man who was, perhaps, the most capable military leader in the American army seek to destroy the cause for which he had fought?

The probable causes include an ego that outstripped his enormous military talent, an inability to manage his finances, and a bad marriage to a woman who may have set up his disgrace for the sake of the spy who loved her.

Historians point out that Arnold is one of the few traitors who fought well for both sides

National Archives & Records Administration

in the same war. Arnold played critical roles for the colonies in the battles of Ticonderoga, Quebec, Lake Champlain, and Saratoga. After he changed sides, his raids on Richmond, Virginia, and New London, Connecticut, gave the British badly needed victories.

When the war began there was little indication of his military abilities. He was a thirty-four-year-old merchant in New Haven, with no other apparent talent than running an apothecary shop with occasional smuggling on the side. Almost every merchant in coastal towns smuggled in some items to avoid high British duties. But war seemed to call up some unknown reserves of decisiveness and leadership.

He saw immediately that Fort Ticonderoga, on the New York side of Lake Champlain, was a critical asset for the British. He went to Boston and persuaded the Massachusetts Committee of Safety to give him the rank of colonel and the authority to recruit four hundred men for an assault on Fort Ticonderoga, in May 1775.

Almost simultaneously, however, Ethan Allen was getting the same directive in Connecticut. The result was an early indication that Arnold could be troublesome. He found that Allen's Green Mountain Boys would pay no attention to his orders. So a fuming Arnold had to share command, which was especially galling when Allen received most of the credit for the successful attack.

To make matters worse, Arnold turned in a grossly inflated list of expenses and squirmed as every item was flyspecked by the Massachusetts authorities. The war was only one month old and already Arnold was unhappy over a lack of recognition and respect.

Nonetheless, he was given command of a force sent to attack Quebec that autumn. The strategy was for Arnold to move up the Kennebec River, through what is now Maine, and link up with the army of General Richard Montgomery, who would take Montreal before joining him. Capturing Quebec would detach the critical Canadian supply base from the British.

Through no fault of Arnold's, the plan was a misconceived mess. With almost total ignorance of the geography involved, American military planners had underestimated the distance to Quebec by one half. His army ran into delays, such as unexpected white water on the Kennebec and an early winter. By the time he reached Quebec, he had lost almost one-third of his one thousand men to illness, injury, and cold. Getting them through at all was an incredible feat of leadership.

The two American forces weren't able to link up until December 2, deep into the bitter Canadian winter. Enlistment terms of

Montgomery's men were coming to an end. He already had lost most of his Connecticut contingent because their service had expired, and the Massachusetts group would be the next to go.

There was no choice but to attack. Montgomery wanted to wait, however, until a heavy snowstorm covered his movements. It came on December 31. But the blizzard and ice floes, which were carried almost to the base of the city's walls by the St. Lawrence River, made rapid deployment next to impossible for the attackers. The well-entrenched British also had anticipated where the assault would come.

Montgomery was killed almost immediately, and Arnold took a bullet in the foot and had to be carried to the rear, unable to walk. The attack disintegrated with heavy American losses. Arnold managed to hold his position until spring and then had to retreat through Montreal. But his actions earned him a promotion to brigadier general, over the complaints of several officers who accused him of behaving in an overbearing manner.

Still limping from his wound, Arnold was quickly called upon to display another facet of his military genius. He created America's first naval fleet out of three captured ships and the wood of the northern forests in a desperate attempt to check a British sweep down Lake Champlain in the fall of 1776.

Supervising the construction himself, Arnold drove his soldiers and civilian workmen to finish the job before the British were ready to attack. Then he personally took command of the flotilla, manned mostly by amateurs who had never experienced a fight on water.

Arnold engaged the British under Sir Guy Carleton at Valcour Island, off the New York shore. The Americans suffered heavy losses, with eleven of their fifteen vessels sunk and more than one hundred casualties. But Carleton, not expecting this degree of resistance, turned back to Canada and abandoned the plans to invade. This retreat bought priceless time for the colonies, which were not yet ready to resist a concerted attack from the north.

The more dangerous invasion came one year later, in the summer of 1777. This thrust under General John Burgoyne was aimed at the Hudson Valley and intended to cut off New England from the other colonies.

When Burgoyne reached Bemis Heights, at Saratoga, in mid-September, he found the American forces entrenched and waiting for him. Again Arnold found himself in the thick of the fight. In the first phase of the battle, at Freeman's Farm, his counterattack stopped the

British advance and almost broke their lines. Only the arrival of Hessian reinforcements saved Burgoyne.

After a stalemate of two and a half weeks, the British general realized the anticipated relief army from the South wasn't coming. So he decided to risk everything in one more assault on the American lines.

Arnold, at this point, had been relieved of his duties. He had squabbled with General Horatio Gates, the American commander, who detested him. "A pompous little fellow," he called Arnold and did not even mention him in the official report on the battle at Freeman's Farm.

Even though Arnold wasn't wanted he refused to leave and when Burgoyne's attack began, once more he led the counterstroke. Those who witnessed it said he went into battle "with a sort of madness," and fired his troops, even though he was out of the chain of command, with the same sort of frenzy. This time they broke through the British defenses and scattered Burgoyne's army.

The victory at Saratoga persuaded France to enter the war on the American side, tipping the advantage to the colonies. Despite his tiff with Gates, Arnold, wounded for a second time, was promoted to major general.

He was by now too deeply embittered to care about any promotion. He was consumed by hatred of his fellow officers. He felt that Gates was typical of the mediocrities the Revolution had elevated to places of authority, political animals who won advancement by connections rather than talent. He couldn't let it go.

Publicly, Arnold was enormously popular. He was called the "Hannibal of the Revolution," and among the people was acclaimed second only to Washington. He had finally been given a rank commensurate with his abilities.

Still it wasn't enough. Arnold wanted more power, recognition, and especially wealth. In his heart he craved the very privilege and pomp that the war was opposing. He felt it was his due. When Washington decided to reward his friend by giving him the military command of Philadelphia, just after the British withdrawal in 1778, the stage was set for treason.

He was now thirty-seven years old, a widower, and walking with a pronounced limp because of his wounds. He described himself as "having become a cripple in the service of my country." Never a handsome man, his hard campaigning had aged him even more. But as a hero he was a prime catch for the belle of Philadelphia.

Peggy Shippen was then eighteen years old. Her father was a wealthy shipbuilder and, although suspected of harboring Loyalist sympathies, had carefully made friends on both sides. During the years of occupation, the Shippens frequently socialized with the witty, spirited young British officers. There were balls, theatrical performances, and dinners.

Among the most popular of these young men was Captain John Andre. He and Peggy became close friends. A sketch he made of her at one of these fetes is now exhibited at the Historical Society of Philadelphia. Were they lovers? There is no hard evidence, only suspicions.

When Arnold arrived in Philadelphia he was quickly smitten with the girl. He entertained lavishly on her behalf, far more than an officer's pay would allow. The old warrior began writing love letters that began with phrases such as, "Twenty times have I taken up my pen to write to you, and as often has my trembling hand refused to obey the dictates of my heart."

By September he was proposing marriage, and on April 8, 1779, the happy couple were joined at the Shippen home. Within weeks, Sir Henry Clinton, the only British commander in New York City, was receiving secret communications offering information on American forces for large sums of money. The communications were coded with a pre-arranged cipher, and there was no doubt by Clinton and his staff that they had come from Arnold and Peggy, who had encouraged his defection from the start.

Attached to Clinton's staff was Andre, who now was a major. A reply he sent to Peggy, known as the "millinery letter" because it discussed the purchase of some hats, actually contained coded instructions on terms of the agreement. All that was needed was an opportunity to put their plot in motion.

It came the following year. The newly fortified West Point, which controlled passage to the upper Hudson Valley, required a commander. A chain was stretched across the river here, blocking any boats from going through. Constructed by engineer Thaddeus Kosciusko, the chain was 1,700 feet across, with links two feet long and two and a quarter inches square. The British wanted the chain removed to clear the way for an invasion on the interior of New York, but they needed to take West Point to do it.

Arnold lobbied diligently for the West Point job, but Washington, thinking there was some mistake and that the post was beneath his abilities, offered him a field command instead. When his wife heard about the field command while at a dinner party she went into hysterics. The agreement had already been made that Arnold would turn over the fort to the British for a sum that would be the current equivalent of one million dollars.

Arnold told his old comrade that his leg wounds disqualified him for active service and Washington bought the explanation. On August 3, 1780, he was given the West Point assignment. Seven weeks later, Andre was carried up the Hudson from New York on a British reconnaissance ship, the *Vulture*, and came ashore near Haverstraw. He carried passes to get him through the American lines. They were signed by Arnold.

The two men met to discuss details of the betrayal and provide Andre with plans of the fort. Arnold then returned to West Point, and Andre went to reboard the British ship. But the ship had been discovered by an American shore patrol, and they had driven it off with cannon shots. Andre was stranded and would have to get back to the British lines on foot.

He crossed to the east bank of the Hudson and began working his way south. Andre got as far as Tarrytown, about 15 miles from his lines. This area was contested by both Loyalist and Patriot militia units. When Andre found himself surrounded by an armed patrol wearing Hessian coats, he assumed they were on his side. He was mistaken.

Not only were they Americans, they were also thieves. Believing they had captured a rich pigeon, they ordered him to remove his coat and boots. Out of the boot fell the plans for West Point, and the astonished militiamen realized they had captured more than they knew.

Washington had planned to dine with the Arnolds on September 24. He looked forward to it because he needed some cheering. The war was going badly in the south. Both Savannah and Charleston had fallen to the British, and the Carolinas were in severe danger. Things could hardly be worse. But they soon were.

The general arrived at West Point to find that Arnold was nowhere to be found, his wife was in bed and seemed to have gone mad, and reports of a captured spy were making their way up the river. It soon became clear that his cherished friend was a traitor and that the American cause had barely escaped a calamity.

"There are no terms that can describe the baseness of his heart," Washington wrote. He even supported a plan, which nearly succeeded, to kidnap Arnold in New York and return him to the Americans for hanging.

Andre was imprisoned in the town of Tappan. He was a personal favorite of Clinton's, and the British commander sent messages imploring Washington to spare his life. The young major had impressed the Americans with his charm and coolness during this dangerous situation. But he had been captured behind their lines in civilian clothes as a spy, and the populace was inflamed at Arnold's treachery.

Although Washington's instinct was to be merciful, it was politically impossible. On October 2, Andre was marched to the gallows. "You will all bear witness that I have met my fate as a brave man," he said. The American officers wept as he died.

A dispatch from Arnold arrived at Washington's headquarters within the hour promising retaliation if Andre were executed and threatening that "Your Excellency will be justly answerable for the torrent of blood that may be spilt in consequence."

Washington calmly allowed Peggy Shippen Arnold, still feigning insanity, to rejoin her family in Philadelphia. Later she would go to New York to be with her husband.

Arnold had fled to the British lines when his plans were discovered, and Clinton resented Arnold from the moment he arrived at his headquarters, holding him responsible for Andre's death. He was made a brigadier general of provincials but no British officers would serve with him. Although the war was turning against England, Clinton refused to allow him anywhere near the main flow of battle. Instead, he was sent to Richmond, where he burned some warehouses and plundered the city as a diversionary tactic.

Arnold's raid on New London, in September 1781, ended in one of the war's darkest episodes. When the American garrison fell after a fierce struggle at Fort Griswold, across the Thames River, in Groton, its commander, Lieutenant Colonel William Ledyard, offered his sword in token of surrender. In a moment of rage, a British officer, who has never been definitely identified, took the weapon and ran Ledyard through. This touched off a general slaughter of the American garrison, with eighty-four militiamen killed by rampaging British soldiers.

Clinton exonerated Arnold from the atrocity, explaining that he was nowhere near the fort at the time. He was busy burning New London to the ground. According to other accounts, however, he observed the course of the battle from a nearby rock outcropping.

Wherever he was, it happened on his watch and added to Arnold's already blackened reputation.

Two months later, the Arnolds sailed for England and never returned to America. He lived for another twenty years, mulling over old grievances. Despite the myth that he called for his old American uniform while on his deathbed, there is no evidence that he ever regretted anything except his lost chance at making a fortune.

He is buried in London, at the Church of St. Mary, Battersea. Peggy, who died three years later, rests beside him. The British papers barely noted his passing. In America, however, it was pointed out editorially that in all likelihood he had joined his consort "Beelzebub . . . the Devil." His great-grandson served as a major general in the British Army during World War I.

THE SITES

West Point The United States Military Academy wasn't established at West Point until 1802, which was twenty-two years after Arnold's plot to sell out the place. But there are some reminders of him on the academy grounds.

In the Old Cadet Chapel, near the Post Cemetery, are the shields, flags, and names of every general in the Revolutionary Army. At Arnold's place there is only a birth date and rank. Like the boot monument at Saratoga, his name never appears.

Follow the signs from the chapel to Fort Clinton. This was the Revolutionary era fortification, originally named Fort Arnold. (It was renamed for a New York political leader, not for the British general.) From this vantage point, you can understand the importance of West Point's position. Its guns commanded the entire sweep of the river. There is also a monument to Thaddeus Kosciusko. In Arnold's few weeks of command here he managed to pick a quarrel with the great engineer, irritating him so much that he requested a transfer out.

If you follow the walls of the fort to Trophy Point, you will find part of the great chain that Kosciusko stretched across the Hudson and a magnificent view of the valley.

The Cadet Chapel is open daily, 8:15 a.m. to 4:15 p.m. The grounds of the Academy usually are closed to visitors after 4:45 p.m. (845) 938-2638.

Andre's Landing Just south of Haverstraw, along U.S. 9W, is an overlook along the Hudson near the site of Andre's landing on the night of

September 21,1780. The *Vulture*, the ship that delivered him here, is anchored in the wide stretch of the river known as Haverstraw Bay. The actual landing site is a bit north of here, but it can be hard to find, as the commemorative rock is sometimes underwater.

The Treason House Near the village of Stony Point, further north on U.S. 9W, is the site of the Treason House, which belonged to Tory sympathizer Joshua Smith. This is where Arnold and Andre had their lone face-to-face meeting, at which Arnold turned over the plans to West Point. When the house was threatened with demolition in 1929, public opinion supported the move as a way to blot out the memory of treason. All that remains is an historic marker. It is right below the bluff from the New York State Rehabilitation Hospital, which formerly owned the house.

Andre's Brook/Patriot's Park The site of Andre's capture is near the brook that divides Tarrytown from Sleepy Hollow (formerly known as North Tarrytown) along U.S. 9. It is still called Andre's Brook. Patriot's Park contains a monument to the three militia members who arrested him here. The Captors Monument is topped by a statue of the unit's leader, John Paulding, wearing the Hessian coat that so confused Andre. There is no admission charge. There are more displays on Andre's capture and how the plot became unraveled at the Tarrytown Historical Society, on Grove St, off U.S. 9. It is open Tuesday, Wednesday, Thursday, and Saturday, 2 p.m. to 4 p.m. (914) 631-8374.

The DeWint House The story of Arnold's treason comes full circle in the town of Tappan, New York. Washington established his headquarters at the DeWint House during the summer of 1780, in this village on the New Jersey border. It was here that he gave Arnold the commission that put him in charge of West Point. Two months later, it was where he met with his staff to ponder the fate of Andre.

Many American officers, especially Alexander Hamilton, were insistent on devising an outcome that would spare Andre. They suggested a straight swap of the British prisoner for Arnold. Andre refused to consider it because he felt it was dishonorable. Washington was left with little choice but to approve the execution.

The only question was whether Andre would die a soldier's death by firing squad or be hanged as a spy. Washington, understanding the political impact of his decision, chose the rope. Once more he was bitterly opposed by many younger officers, but he held firm, although the shutters of the house remained closed tight on the day of the execution.

The DeWint House is located at Oak Tree Rd. and Livingston Ave., in Tappan, which lies just south of Exit 5 of the Palisades Parkway. The house, built in 1700, was purchased by the Free Masons of New York in 1931. It contains exhibits relating to the four occasions between 1780 and 1785, when Washington, who belonged to the Masons, lived there. It is open daily, 10 a.m. to 4 p.m. Donations. (845) 359-1359; www.dewinthouse.com.

Tappan Reformed Church Andre's trial was held in the Tappan Reformed Church, on King's Highway, Tappan's main street. It was here that a special board of inquiry, which included most of the generals on Washington's staff, came to the conclusion that Andre had been a spy. If he had admitted that he acted under Arnold's order, which the board very much wanted him to say, he could have escaped the verdict. But he refused to lie and was convicted. There is a plaque on the front of the church.

The Seventy-Six House One block away is the Seventy-Six House, which used to be Mablie's Tavern. It was here that Andre was imprisoned, and the room from which he was taken to his execution is separated from the present-day restaurant by a Dutch door. Much of the décor in the restaurant relates to Andre. Opening hours vary and it is best to call ahead, at (914) 359-5476. There is no charge for viewing Andre's room.

The prisoner was taken in a wagon up Main Street, and then along the Old Tappan Road. Near the crest of a hill just north of town is a street called Andre's Hill, which leads to the place of execution. It is now a residential area, and at the end of the street is a cul de sac surrounding a large inscribed stone. This is where Andre was hanged.

In 1821, his body was exhumed and placed on a ship bound for England. Andre's remains had been exchanged for those of General Richard Montgomery, who also, ironically, was associated with Arnold's career. He had been killed during their attack on Quebec City in 1775. Andre was reburied in Westminster Abbey.

Saratoga National Historical Park The monument to Arnold at Saratoga National Historical Park is near the Breymann Redoubt. Stop at the visitor center to pick up a self-guided driving map of the battlefield and to view exhibits and an audiovisual display about the struggle. The drive loops around the entire park, a distance of 9.5 miles.

The park is entered from U.S. 4, south of Schuylerville and 16 miles southeast of the Saratoga Springs resort. Open daily 9 a.m. to 5 p.m. Both the park and the museum are free. (518) 664-9821 ext.224; www.nps/gov/sara.

Skenesborough Museum Arnold's career as a shipbuilder is remembered in Whitehall. This is the site of the shipyard at which he assembled the American fleet for the battle of Valcour Island in 1776. The Skenesborough Museum is called after the original name of the town, as it was known when Arnold was there. When it was learned that Skene was a Loyalist, however, the town was redubbed Whitehall.

The Museum has exhibits on the shipyards and artifacts of the battle. It is located on New York 22, just north of U.S. 4, at the southern end of Lake Champlain. Open Monday to Saturday, 10 a.m. to 3 p.m., and Sunday, noon to 3 p.m., mid-June to mid-October. Admission $2; students fifty cents. (518) 499-0716.

Fort Griswold State Park The massacre of the garrison at Fort Griswold in 1781 is memorialized in a Connecticut state park at Groton. A monument at the crest of the hill, where the fort was situated, is 155 feet high, and the names of the victims are inscribed on an adjacent tablet. The Monument House has artifacts from the massacre and other displays relating to the Revolutionary era.

Ledyard is buried in a cemetery just outside the park boundary, and it was from this area that Arnold supposedly viewed the battle from a large rock.

Fort Griswold State Park is reached from Exit 87 of I-95, at Monument St. and Park Ave. It is open daily, dawn to dusk and is free. The Monument and Monument House are open daily, 10 a.m. to 5 p.m., Memorial Day to Labor Day; weekends only, 10 a.m. to 5 p.m., through Columbus Day. Both are free. (860) 449-6877.

JOHN BUTLER AND BUTLER'S RANGERS

As rumors of war reached upstate New York in 1775, Loyalist leaders gathered in the Lake Ontario town of Oswego. They were, for the most part, men of property and members of families who had lived in America for several generations, who were suspicious of those who trumpeted revolution.

They were particularly eager to preserve their alliance with the Iroquois. This powerful Indian confederacy traditionally allied itself with the British against France and was a barrier to colonial expansion westward. In the Quebec Act of 1774 (one of the Intolerable Acts that speeded the colonists toward revolt), Britain had virtually closed these lands to further settlement.

So the Iroquois had a vested interest in keeping the Tories in power. When Colonel Guy Johnson, superintendent of Indian Affairs, invited their leaders to Oswego "to feast on the flesh and drink the blood of a Bostonian," they answered the call.

The decision to use the Indians in guerilla warfare against American settlers would drench the New York and Pennsylvania frontier in blood and lead to a terrible retribution that, ultimately, would destroy the Iroquois. Captain John Butler, who attended the gathering at Oswego, would be the leading architect of that policy.

Butler was forty-seven years old and the second wealthiest man in the Mohawk Valley region, behind Colonel Johnson. He was born in Connecticut, the son of a British officer who had come to America in 1711 and then moved to the Mohawk Valley to accumulate land.

Butler grew up on this frontier, eager to expand his father's holdings. He served in the French and Indian War, and at its close he owned 26,600 acres in the neighborhood of Fonda, New York. His properties were valued at 13,000 pounds. There was no doubt which side he would back in the coming war.

With his eldest son, Walter, Butler was sent to Fort Niagara to manage the vital outpost and to maintain good relations with the Mohawk, Seneca, and Cayuga—the critical components of the Iroquois nation.

Their first major action didn't come until 1777. As part of the greater British strategy, which called for General John Burgoyne to invade New York from Quebec and sweep down the Hudson Valley, Butler's troops were to proceed east from Niagara and link up with the main force.

They were stopped, however, at Oriskany. This was one of the war's critical small engagements. It prevented Burgoyne from getting reinforcements and led to his defeat two months later at Saratoga. That, in turn, resulted in France entering the war on the side of the colonists.

The battle at Oriskany also prompted a change in British strategy from a more traditional strategy to the guerilla warfare used in the Western campaigns. Despite winning the battle, the colonists had suffered terrible losses at Oriskany, and Butler's troops were credited with inflicting much of that damage through guerilla tactics. Now a colonel, Butler was authorized to raise a Corps of Rangers to carry on a campaign of guerilla warfare in cooperation with the Indian allies.

Butler's men dressed in dark green uniforms trimmed in red, and the words "Butler's Rangers" were embossed on brass plates on their caps. By the summer of 1778, he had enlisted 200 men, Loyalists from upstate New York who were eager to fight for the Crown, for his Rangers. With an additional force of close to 1,000 Indians, Butler headed south along the Susquehanna River and into the unprotected and helpless Wyoming Valley of Pennsylvania.

The settlers in this area were aware of their danger and had pleaded with Congress to restore two companies of militia that they had raised locally. They were told, however, the troops were needed elsewhere and that they had better make preparations to fend for themselves.

Small outposts were quickly overrun by Butler, and on July 3 he reached Forty Fort. Settlers from the region had been pouring into this fortification for days, and its commanders were apprehensive about the effects of a long siege. So in a desperate move, although outnumbered three to one, they marched out to engage Butler's force at the town of Wyoming.

The colonists set up their left flank in a marsh and thought it was secure. But the Indians managed to get through the swampy terrain, turned the line, and attacked the colonial forces

Illustration by Scott Paterson/Fort George, Niagara Historical Sites from behind. The battle turned into a general slaughter, with survivors straggling back to Forty Fort.

Colonel Nathan Denison, one of the commanders of the lost battle, negotiated terms of capitulation with Butler. But when the Indians entered the fort, the Rangers were unable or unwilling to restrain them. In the battle and the massacre that followed, more than three hundred colonists, many of them women and children, were killed.

Atrocity stories swept across the colonies. The most vivid of them involved Queen Esther, leader of the Montour branch of the Seneca. Enraged by the death of her son in a previous engagement, she is said to have tied sixteen captured colonists to a large rock and then, while chanting a death song, dashed out each of their brains with a tomahawk.

Whether it is true or not the tale appears in every account of the battle, and Butler was blamed for it.

Four months later, the Rangers struck again. This time their target was the settlement of Cherry Valley, New York. Walter Butler led this foray along with the Mohawk chief, Joseph Brant.

Once more the colonists had been left underdefended and poorly led. Because snow already had fallen, the town was unprepared for the November 11 attack, although Colonel Ichabod Alden had been warned that it was a strong possibility. Officers, instead, were scattered in private houses.

Fog and rain shielded the approach of the Tory and Indian force. By the time Alden realized that there was danger, the enemy was already upon him. He was one of the first to fall, tomahawked as he ran from a house to the fort.

Cherry Valley had been founded in 1740 and was a fairly substantial settlement. It had a population of about three hundred people, spread out in a semicircular arrangement. The attackers fanned out through the town and systematically cut down all the men they found. Thirteen officers were killed in one house alone.

Defenders of Butler claim that his men had come upon soldiers who had been paroled on condition that they wouldn't take up arms again. Infuriated by this violation, they turned the Indians loose on the undefended civilian population. But even they concede that the events at Cherry Valley "blackened Butler's reputation."

The two Butler-led massacres stirred up demands for revenge throughout the colonies. George Washington heard them. He had always recognized the importance of the West in American ambitions and was aware of the opportunity these events gave him to destroy one of the most formidable barriers to expansion, the Iroquois.

He immediately began to plan a retaliatory campaign to carry the war into the Indian heartland. He ordered General John Sullivan to prepare an invasion of the Iroquois lands. "The immediate objects are the total destruction and devastation of the Indian settlements," he instructed Sullivan. "The country is not to be merely overrun but destroyed."

Sullivan's campaign of 1779 in western New York accomplished exactly what Washington desired. It was a scorched earth tactic, burning villages and crops and giving the Iroquois no way to continue to support themselves on their lands.

The colonials avenged themselves on Queen Esther by burning her "palace" on the Susquehanna. They then continued up the Chemung River. Just east of the present city of Elmira, the Butlers tried to make a stand.

They had mustered a force of 1,500 men, but Sullivan's army was bolstered by the addition of Iroquois fighters from the Oneida and Tuscarora tribes, who had turned against the other members of the Confederacy.

Butler had fortified a hilltop, but he was greatly outnumbered. Sullivan's artillery barrage shattered the nerve of the Indians, and despite the exhortations of the Rangers they broke and ran.

From that time on. Sullivan encountered no substantial opposition in his campaign to devastate the area. Forty villages were destroyed along with 160,000 bushels of corn. Only the fact that his supply lines were running thin prevented him from moving on Fort Niagara.

Sullivan's campaign sealed the outcome of the war in western New York. The Rangers were able to make another attack on Cherry Valley in 1780, burning the place to the ground. But the Iroquois were thrown into total dependence on the British for food and supplies, straining their already overburdened resources.

After the war, the Indians were forced to move to Upper Canada, what is now Ontario. Many of Brant's followers were granted lands along the Grand River and formed the basis of the present city of Brantford. Only a tiny portion of their ancestral lands in New York was retained.

By the mid-1780s, American settlers were thronging into the area. Many of them were veterans of Sullivan's campaign who could hardly wait to get back and farm the lands they had first seen as destroyers.

Butler's Rangers were transferred west to Detroit by the British command and participated in raids into Ohio, Kentucky, and western Virginia. The corps was mustered out in 1784, three years after Walter Butler had been killed in battle.

Although he had lost all his lands and become a figure of hatred in America, John Butler started life again in Upper Canada at the age of fifty-six. He became a prosperous landowner and leading political figure in the Niagara area.

The town he established, now known as Niagara-on-the-Lake, site of the popular George Bernard Shaw Festival, was the first capital of Upper Canada. Butler, excoriated on one side of the Niagara River, is considered a founding father of Ontario.

THE SITES

Wyoming, Pennsylvania Several memorials have been placed in the vicinity of the Wyoming, Pennsylvania, massacre. The site of the battle, where Butler's Rangers and the Iroquois overwhelmed the forces led by Colonel Nathan Denison, is at 4th Street and Wyoming Avenue. Nearby, at Wyoming and Schulde Lane, is a 60-foot-tall monument over the common grave of those slaughtered after the battle.

Queen Esther's Rock, where colonial prisoners were executed, is located at 8th and Susquehanna St. All memorials are open daily, dawn to dusk. Wyoming is located on U.S. 11; 10 miles north of the Wilkes-Barre exit of I-81, by way of Pennsylvania 309.

Cherry Valley Museum The Cherry Valley Museum, at 14 Main St., has exhibits on the massacre of 1778, including a topographical map that makes it easy to follow the course of the engagement. It is open daily, 10 a.m. to 5 p.m., Memorial Day to October 15. Admission $3; under 11, free. (607) 264-3303; www.cherryvalleymuseum.org.

Victims Monument/Alden Memorial A monument to the victims of the raid is located in the town cemetery, which occupies the site of Fort Alden. Turn left on Alden St. at the center of town and follow it past the Presbyterian church to reach the cemetery. The monument, with the names of the victims inscribed around the base, was dedicated in 1878 on the 100th anniversary of the raid.

The Alden Memorial is a few blocks beyond the cemetery on the right. It marks the place where the commanding officer, Ichabod Alden, was killed.

Newtown Battlefield Park Newtown Battlefield, where General John Sullivan scattered the resistance of Butler's Rangers and the Iroquois in 1779, is off New York 17, 5 miles east of Elmira. There is a monument to Sullivan and re-enactments of the battle are staged during the summer months. Call (607) 732-6067 for a schedule. The park is open daily, 10 a.m. to dusk, Memorial Day to Columbus Day.

The Mohawk Chapel Joseph Brant, the Mohawk chief who fought with the Butlers in New York, rests beside the oldest Protestant church in Ontario, near Brantford. The Mohawk Chapel was built in 1785 and is designated as Her Majesty's Royal Native Chapel, the only Indian church with a royal title. Brant's tomb is on the grounds.

The chapel is open Wednesday to Saturday, 10 a.m. to 6 p.m., and Sunday, 1 p.m. to 5 p.m., mid-May to mid-October. Donations. (519) 756-0240; www.mohawkchapel.ca. It is located on Mohawk St., 2 miles southwest of central Brantford, which is 24 miles west of Hamilton on Ontario 403.

Fort Niagara Fort Niagara was the base for Butler's Raiders during most of the Revolutionary War. It has been restored to its appearance of that era, although parts of it go back fifty years earlier when it was first fortified by the French.

Recognizing that this site, on a bluff commanding the outlet of the Niagara River to Lake Ontario, was a critical military position, the French instructed trader Louis Joincare to fortify it in 1726. He informed the Iroquois that he was building a trading post, but when he was done it somehow came out looking like a fort. Called "The Castle," it is the oldest example of a French military fort in the United States.

The three-story structure contains a barracks and a gun deck on the top floor. The British were so determined to hang on to the place that they refused to turn it over to the Americans until 1796 and then rushed back across the Canadian border to recapture it during the War of 1812.

The fort is open daily, 9 a.m. to 5:30 p.m. In July and August, it remains open until 7:30 p.m. It closes at 4:30 p.m., November to March. Admission $8.50; children under twelve, $5. (716) 745-7611; www.oldfortniagara.org. There are dress parades, drills, and battle re-enactments throughout the summer months. On clear days you can see the skyline of Toronto across the lake.

Fort Niagara is on New York 18F, in Youngstown, 7 miles north of the Lewiston Bridge to Canada.

SIMON GIRTY

According to legend, when American troops finally marched into Detroit on July 11, 1796, a full thirteen years after the British had promised to surrender the place, a middle-aged man with hatred gleaming in his eyes watched them arrive.

As they approached to within half a mile of where he sat, astride a black mare, the man shook his fist, and with a shouted curse spurred the horse into the swift current of the Detroit River.

On the far side of the river was Canada. Simon Girty, defiant to the end, emerged from the river and rode to his new home in the village of Amherstburg, a gift from the British for his years of faithful service.

The river is almost a mile wide in this area, and the current is extremely swift. It is hard to imagine a horseman making that crossing. But the story is meant to convey the depth of Girty's animosity toward the Americans he once had served. What the British regarded as "faithful service" made him a renegade and killer to colonial eyes.

His name was the most dreaded on the Western frontier of the Revolutionary War. In Ohio and Kentucky, children were frightened into obedience for years afterwards with the threat, "Simon Girty will come to get you."

Girty, however, has his defenders. They point out that nowhere was the Revolution more cruelly fought than in the West, and that Americans hardly had clean hands themselves. The slaughter of peaceful Christianized Delaware Indians at Gnadenhutten, Ohio, in 1782, is one of the blackest marks against the colonials in the entire conflict.

But Girty was regarded as especially repellent. He was a white man who chose to live among the Indians and adopt their methods of warfare. Even a fairly sympathetic biographer, Thomas Boyd, could write, "No famished tiger ever sought the blood of a victim with more unrelenting ferocity than Girty sought the blood of a white man."

When many of his descendants gathered at his grave in Amherstburg in 1955 for a memorial service they invited an historian from Detroit to address them, hoping to get a more dispassionate accounting of their ancestor's career.

They were told, instead, that "in a period of history marked with the slaughter of children and women, Girty's name is outstanding. Of the serious indictments in American history, the most serious are the names linked with his, renegade and traitor. His biography is more appalling than Benedict Arnold."

At this point, the speaker, M. M. Quaife, paused and asked the crowd if it wanted him to go on. They asked him to do so, enthusiastically, and at the end applauded the speech. If they had to be related to a villain, they felt it might as well be the worst of the bunch.

The best thing that can be said in justification of Girty's career is that he never had a very easy life. He grew up in western Pennsylvania and was captured by the Seneca during the French and Indian War. At fifteen years of age he was forced to watch as his stepfather was tortured to death by his captors.

Nonetheless, Girty lived with the Indians for three years and found himself drawn to their way of life. He learned several of their languages and customs and retained strong friendships among the frontier tribes. After his release in 1759, he made his way to Fort Pitt, where he grew to manhood.

This outpost where the Ohio River begins its long journey west was the focus of ambition for expansion-minded colonists. Those who had traveled any distance along this great river, including the young George Washington, brought back glowing reports of the land along its length. It was hunger for these lands that helped fuel Western enthusiasm for revolution, because British policy blocked the advance of settlement.

Girty made his living as an interpreter and trader at the fort, and when the Revolution finally came he joined the colonial side. But a great part of his sympathies remained with the Indians he had known in his youth. He felt that the only way of retaining their loyalty was to continue Britain's anti-expansion policy.

Ohio Historical Society

Although he worked to recruit settlers for the American army, the voicing of these sentiments made him an object of suspicion. While he had expected to be commissioned as a captain, he received only a lieutenant's rank. By late 1777 he was a deeply aggrieved man, and when an act of insubordination towards a superior officer landed him in the fort prison (he, apparently, slapped the face of a captain who had called him a liar), he made the decision to desert.

He slipped away from Fort Pitt, and when he learned that a price had been placed on his head he struck off for the one place where he thought his services would be most appreciated—Britain's western headquarters at Detroit.

He arrived there in 1778 and General Henry Hamilton, the British commander at the outpost, quickly put Girty's unique knowledge to use. Hamilton earned the nickname "the hair-buyer of Detroit," for his policy of paying a bounty for the scalps of American settlers. Girty became the chief instrument of that policy.

He was sent to live among the Shawnee and Wyandotte in Ohio and instructed to lead raids against American settlements. He played a part in the campaign against Fort Laurens on the Tuscarawas River and was present during the horrific massacre of civilians who had surrendered at Ruddle's Station on the Licking River in Kentucky.

Girty's biographer, Thomas Boyd, points out that Hamilton's feeling was "the Indians were raiding the border anyway, and they might as well be capably led."

It was during this time that Girty also was credited with the act that softens his otherwise harsh legacy. Kentucky frontiersman Simon Kenton had been captured by the Shawnees on the Indiana side of the Ohio River, opposite what is now Louisville. He was being prepared for torture and execution when Girty recognized him.

The two were old friends from Fort Pitt days; Girty admired him as a kindred spirit, a man who understood the price of survival in the wilderness. Girty, at some risk to his own standing with the Shawnee, decided to intervene and gave a tearful, impassioned plea to spare the life of his friend. Out of respect for Girty, the request was honored and Kenton was released.

But there were darker deeds to come. The worst of them followed the battle of Mingo Bottom, near Upper Sandusky, Ohio.

Colonel William Crawford had been placed in command of a company of Pennsylvania militia and sent into Ohio to subdue the Wyandotte. This was in the spring of 1782, half a year after the British surrender at Yorktown supposedly had decided the war. But in the West the conflict raged on as bitterly as ever, and Crawford's job was to diminish the threat of Indian raids.

But the invasion was no surprise to the Wyandotte. They had

watched Crawford's advance as soon as he entered their lands, and on June 7 they attacked. The two sides fought to a stalemate, and Crawford unwisely decided to hold his line as long as possible and attempt to retreat after dark.

But the Wyandotte, led by Girty, fell upon the rear of the retreating force and turned it into a panic-stricken rout. Crawford, separated from the main body, was captured.

Girty also knew Crawford from Fort Pitt but had no great regard for him. It also was known to the Indians that under his command the massacre at Gnadenhutten had taken place just three months before. Others had carried out the killing, but Crawford had been the senior officer. There was probably nothing Girty could have done to save him.

Crawford was stripped, beaten with sticks, and led to the stake. As Girty watched, burning wood was piled against him and his ears sliced off with a scalping knife. Crawford pleaded for Girty to shoot him and end the torture. According to eyewitness accounts, Girty simply turned his head with a harsh laugh. Crawford died as his body turned to charcoal. The story of his terrible death, and Girty's reaction to it, was retold with anger hundreds of times across the West.

By this time, the frontier war had developed a momentum of its own. It was as if the participants had lost all capacity for peace and fighting on was the only course they knew. Treaties were signed, but there could be no surrender for turncoats like Girty. All that awaited them was a court martial and a noose.

Meanwhile, Girty was still organizing raids into Kentucky and western Virginia throughout 1782 and was appalled when the prisoners he took back to Detroit were set free because the war had ended.

Girty took a break from combat at the age of forty-two. It was long enough, at least, to marry Catherine Malott. She was a woman with a background much like his, brought up by Indians after being taken from her white family, and she shared Girty's attitudes towards tribal claims to the western lands.

He tried to settle down as a farmer, but found that his war was not over. The new American government claimed the land north of the Ohio River, and a coalition of tribes united to resist them. The British were determined to hold on to Detroit and encouraged the Indians to keep the Americans at bay. Girty was the man sent to lead them.

Military expeditions sent from Cincinnati to smash the tribes were easily defeated. In 1791, Washington sent his personal friend, General

Arthur St. Clair, to take charge of the western army and thrash the tribal alliance. The campaign turned into a complete disaster.

The inept, aging St. Clair lost his army near the headwaters of the Wabash River, in western Ohio. As he was laid up with an inopportune attack of the gout, two-thirds of his force was either killed or wounded. It was one of the worst military defeats ever suffered by American troops.

Girty, at the head of the Wyandotte, and the Miami leader Little Turtle led the assault. Girty was implicated in the deliberate slaughter of wounded soldiers in the battle's aftermath, including Maj. Gen. Richard Butler.

For a time it appeared that the Indians would move south and threaten Cincinnati.

But the Indian alliance could not hold, and the Americans were not to be denied these lands. Finally, in 1794, a properly organized army, with the battle-tested General "Mad" Anthony Wayne at its head, began its deliberate advance into the tribal heartland.

Initial defeats disheartened the Indian leaders, and when the critical engagement came at Fallen Timbers on the Maumee River, their force was scattered and numerically inferior. Girty raged in frustration but could not organize his followers in time to enter the fight. The defeat opened the way to Detroit, and less than two years later Girty left the outpost with his final curse at the Americans.

He lived on at Amherstburg for another twenty-two years and died in his bed of pneumonia in 1818. American raiders had approached to within a mile of his farm during the opening months of the War of 1812, and it is interesting to guess what his fate might have teen if they had captured the old man.

There were also reports that Girty had been killed at the Battle of the Thames during the War of 1812, where the Indian leader Tecumseh fell. But he would have been seventy-three years old then, and even Girty had his physical limits. It was just wishful thinking on the part of Americans in the West, who could never rest easy until Girty was in his grave.

THE SITES

Fort Recovery State Memorial The place where General St. Clair's army was destroyed in 1791 was renamed Fort Recovery by Wayne when he camped there three years later at the start of his victorious campaign against the tribal alliance. At a place associated with defeat he won an initial victory, which was regarded as an especially bad omen by the Indians. They quickly lost enthusiasm for the campaign against him, much to Girty's disgust.

A memorial shaft to St. Clair's men (the general escaped and made it back safely to Cincinnati) rises in a square near the middle of town, about 300 feet from where the defeated army was slaughtered. Names of the officers who died there are inscribed on the base.

Two blocks away is a reconstruction of two fortified blockhouses as they appeared during Wayne's campaign. An adjacent museum displays artifacts of the Indian wars of the 1790s.

Fort Recovery State Memorial is located 55 miles southeast of Fort Wayne, Indiana, by way of U.S. 33 and Ohio 49. The museum is open daily, 12:00 p.m. to 5 p.m., June through August; weekends only, 12:00 p.m. to 5 p.m., May and September. Admission is $3. (419) 375-4649.

Fort Laurens State Memorial Fort Laurens was the only American fort established in Ohio during the Revolutionary War. Intended as a colonial foothold on the Tuscarawas River, it turned out to be a tactical error.

The fort came under pressure from Girty and his Indian allies almost from the moment it was built, in the late autumn of 1778. It could not be supplied. Those who left its walls were picked off by sharpshooters and raiding parties. At one point, its defenders were reduced to boiling deerskins in order to eat.

To make matters worse, Girty held a personal grudge against its commander, Colonel John Gibson, from his days at Fort Pitt. He made it his mission to keep things as miserable as possible for Gibson's forces.

The place was finally abandoned in August 1779, and the colonial units retreated into Pennsylvania.

Fort Laurens State Memorial is located just off the Bolivar exit of I-77, 13 miles south of Canton. The outline of the blockhouse can be seen on the grounds, and there is also a memorial to an unknown colonial soldier whose remains were found here. A museum has exhibits on the Revolutionary War in this area.

The grounds are open daily, 9:30 a.m. to dusk, April through October. The museum hours are Wednesday to Saturday, 9:30 a.m. to 5 p.m.; Sunday, 12:00 p.m. to 5 p.m., Memorial Day to Labor Day. Saturday and Sunday only, Labor Day through October. Admission to museum, $4; under 12 $3. (800) 283-8914.

Crawford Memorials The town of Upper Sandusky was built on the site of the Wyandotte village that Colonel Crawford was sent to destroy in 1782. The battle in which he was defeated was fought about 3 miles north of the town. There is a memorial to Crawford along Ohio 199, between Upper Sandusky and Carey, north from U.S. 23. Another state memorial, where Crawford was tortured to death before Girty's eyes, is nearby but is located on private property and is presently inaccessible to the public.

Girty's Island Girty established a trading post on an island in the Maumee River to meet with Little Turtle and other Indian allies during the campaigns of the 1790s. Gifts from the British command in Detroit were handed out here and military strategy against the Americans was planned. The site is visible from Ohio 424, a scenic drive along the river, just west of Napoleon, Ohio. It is still called Girty's Island.

AARON BURR

The Vice President of the United States took the floor of the U.S. Senate chamber on March 2, 1805, to make his final address in Congress. "This house is a sanctuary," he said, "a citadel of law, of order, and of liberty. It is here—it is here in this exalted refuge, here if anywhere, will resistance be made to the storms of political frenzy and the silent arts of corruption. If the Constitution be destined ever to perish by the sacrilegious hands of the demagogue or the usurper, which God avert, its expiring agonies will be witnessed on this floor."

Many senators were in tears as he walked out of the chamber. It would have been hard to imagine that at that very moment Aaron Burr was under indictment for murder in New York and New Jersey and was already involved in machinations to take New Orleans out of the Union, conquer Mexico, and install himself as an emperor.

A bit more than two and a half years later, he would be on trial for his life in Richmond, Virginia, charged with treason.

Burr remains one of the strangest figures in all of American history. A brilliant man who could not contain his ambitions, he came within a whisper of realizing his dream of defeating Thomas Jefferson for the Presidency in the election of 1800.

Instead, he has become

Library of Congress

known as the killer of his equally brilliant rival, Alexander Hamilton, and a conniver who made two serious attempts to split apart his own country.

Burr was a grandson of the Puritan minister Jonathan Edwards and a prodigy who graduated from the future Princeton University as a teenager. Joining the Continental Army when the Revolution began, he served with gallantly at the unsuccessful siege of Quebec, pulling the mortally wounded General Richard Montgomery out of the line of fire.

He became an aide to George Washington at about the same time as Hamilton. But while Washington trusted Hamilton to the point of regarding him as a son, he quickly cooled to Burr. There are reports that Burr was one of the leading gripers at Valley Forge and that Washington once caught him reading confidential dispatches.

Both Hamilton and Burr were rather small men, quick-witted, and attractive to women. But Hamilton was constantly trying to overcome the stigma of an illegitimate birth and lack of social position. He did not laugh at himself easily. Burr, however, had no such concerns. He eschewed wearing the still fashionable powdered wig even though his own forehead was unfashionably high. Burr's sense of humor also turned more to the sardonic.

While maintaining an outward show of cordiality, the two men developed into bitter rivals for the duration of their careers. They became established after the war as lawyers in New York City, an especially good career plan because most of the attorneys had been Tories and their licenses to practice were revoked.

Hamilton was a political theorist who fought mightily for adoption of the Constitution and a strong central government. He was also a man of aristocratic leanings, retaining strong sympathies towards Britain, and with no greater political ambition than to serve as an insider.

Burr, on the other hand, remained uninvolved in the battle over the Constitution. He became a Federalist for a time, but after the French Revolution he detected that a strong tide was building in America for the rights of the common man. He became active in the opposition party, which evolved into the Democratic-Republicans; not that he had any great love for the common man, but it seemed a promising pathway to power.

The towering figure in the new party was Jefferson. Burr had a fundamental disagreement with him. While Jefferson had a mystic faith in the wisdom and moral superiority of small farmers, Burr suspected that the real fulcrum of power would be in the cities. To that end, he organized the first urban political machine in America in New York. It would eventually grow into Tammany Hall and practically rule the nation's largest city for more than 150 years.

While Jefferson and Burr had their disagreements, they both detested Hamilton. Had anyone laid odds in 1790 on who eventually would wind up in a duel, Jefferson vs. Hamilton would have been the runaway favorite. They clashed over the rule of the federal government, the interests of merchants versus farmers, sectionalism—almost every major issue. They didn't care for one another personally, either.

But it was Burr who saw that Hamilton was the man who stood in the way of his ambition. The first clash came in 1791. Hamilton had married into the wealthy and politically influential Schuyler family, and his father-in-law, Philip, was the U.S. Senator from New York. Burr, the state's attorney general, saw an opportunity. He allied himself with the state's other political leader, Governor George Clinton, and defeated Schuyler in the legislature, where senators were then elected.

Hamilton remembered the political loss, and when Burr came up for re-election in 1797, he dropped everything to defeat him. It was a nasty campaign, and for the first time the men realized that they truly hated each other. Hamilton regarded Burr as a rank opportunist, believing in nothing but attaining power. In a letter to his father-in-law, Philip Schuyler, Hamilton wrote, "I feel it a religious duty to oppose his career."

Shortly after the campaign, international tensions increased, and America began to fear the possibility of an invasion by France. President John Adams felt the need to create a permanent army, and on the advice of the retired Washington named Hamilton as major general to organize it.

Adams wanted Burr as a brigadier, but was forced to back down when both Washington and Hamilton vigorously opposed him. Adams was furious and described Hamilton privately in his journal as "the most restless, impatient, artful, indefatigable and unprincipled intriguer in the United States."

Unfortunately, the same description could have been written of Burr, whose hatred for Hamilton now knew no bounds. But there was more to come. In the election of 1800, both Jefferson and Burr finished with the same number of electoral votes. It had been understood that Burr was to be Vice President, but when the election was thrown into the House of Representatives this "restless, impatient" intriguer saw his chance.

The House split between the candidates on a North-South basis. Some historians insist that Burr married off his daughter to a South Carolina planter at this time in hopes of breaking through the logjam. As ballot after ballot ended in a tie and the country teetered towards a Constitutional crisis, Hamilton finally persuaded enough Federalists to leave their ballots blank to swing the election to Jefferson.

He may have hated Jefferson but he could not trust Burr.

The Vice Presidency had no appeal to Burr, especially since Jefferson froze him out of his inner council. So while still holding that office he decided to run for Governor of New York and try again for the gold ring in 1808.

By now Burr was deeply embittered. There were persistent rumors that he intended to use New York as a power base to take that state and New England out of the Union in protest of the growing political dominance of the South—which would control the White House for the next twenty years.

Hamilton believed Burr was fully capable of splitting the Union to further his own ambitions. Although the Federalists were now a dying political force, he worked assiduously and privately to use their remaining influence to defeat Burr's ambitions. None of his accusations ever reached print and thus could not be publicly denied. Hamilton held no elective office that Burr could attack. He was beyond his reach and a relentless enemy.

Then, in June 1804, in the midst of the campaign, a letter surfaced that Hamilton had written to John Rutledge of South Carolina during the presidential balloting three years before. Hamilton called Burr a voluptuary, insolvent, a corrupt lawyer, an opponent of federalism, unprincipled, and "ambitious as Cataline." To those schooled in classical history, the name of Cataline, the symbol of sinister intrigue in ancient Rome, was the essence of back-stabbing.

When the note was passed on to Burr, he sent a letter to Hamilton demanding an apology or a denial of this "despicable opinion." The letter was actually the first step in a well-established code of dueling. He had given Hamilton a way out by offering him a chance at a denial. Instead, Hamilton waffled.

In an exchange of letters that grew in ferocity of tone, Burr repeatedly demanded retractions and Hamilton refused, saying that his statements "would not have been found to exceed the limits justifiable among political opponents."

Hamilton must have known where this was going. What remains astonishing is that his own son, Philip, had been killed in a duel over a trivial political disagreement in 1801. He had stood in agony over his son's deathbed. Moreover, Burr was known as an excellent marksman who had fought an inconclusive duel in 1799 with Hamilton's brother-in-law.

When the date for their confrontation was set up, Hamilton's curious choice of weapons was the very pistols that had been used in both of these previous duels.

In the two weeks that elapsed before the duel, Burr practiced daily with firearms, while Hamilton composed letters indicating that he would not fire a shot to do harm "and thus giving Colonel Burr a[n] . . . opportunity to pause and to reflect." He also stated that he disapproved of dueling, which was then still a fairly common means of settling disputes, political and otherwise.

But Burr never received the letters, and at dawn on July 11, 1804, as the two men were rowed across the Hudson River to the bluffs overlooking Weehawken, New Jersey, he fully intended to fire at his adversary with deadly intent. They stood on the very ground at which Philip Hamilton had received his fatal wound.

Each man was accompanied by a second. With Hamilton was an old friend, Major Nathaniel Pendleton, and Burr brought along a young lawyer and political protégé, William P. Van Ness.

The agreed upon distance was ten paces. The two men loaded their pistols and at Pendleton's call of "Present" they were to fire. Beyond this, the three surviving witnesses to the scene could not agree. Van Ness said that Hamilton shot first and deliberately aimed high into the branches above Burr's head. Pendleton insisted that Hamilton fired as a reflex action after Burr's shot hit his stomach.

Burr, in his sardonic manner, stated that when Hamilton "stood up to fire, he caught my eye and quailed under it. He looked like a convicted felon." He said that Hamilton had fired first and he heard the ball whistle in the branches above his head. Unrepentant and convinced that he had done nothing wrong, he added that Hamilton's last written statement, in which he opposed dueling, "read like the confessions of a penitent monk."

"I am a dead man," Hamilton gasped. "This is a mortal wound." He then lost consciousness and his seconds thought he was dead. But he came to on the boat ride back to New York and lingered into a second day before dying in his bed with his family at his side.

Burr felt that he had done nothing wrong and had simply followed accepted practice. He had no idea that his political career had ended on the field at Weehawken.

A few days after Hamilton's death, his letters about the upcoming duel were published. In a matter of days Burr was deserted by all his political allies, including the Tammany organization he had founded. A coroner's jury returned a finding of murder. Hamilton's military funeral raised passions even higher.

Before the duel, one might have found advocates for either party who agreed the other had acted maliciously. Afterwards, Burr had no friends. Hamilton became a venerated figure in history, winding up on the face of the ten dollar bill. Burr's path led to oblivion.

He fled back to Washington, D.C., where his position protected him from arrest. Jefferson greeted him with some sympathy, even though he had already decided that he wanted him out of the government.

So in 1805, with no other prospects, Burr turned west, hatching the scheme that would only add to his evil reputation. The idea of establishing an American empire in Mexico was appealing to a lot of people. Andrew Jackson listened to him with interest and even considered raising troops in Tennessee to help him with the plan.

Burr eventually charmed an eccentric Irish aristocrat, Harman Blennerhassett, who lived on an Ohio River island near what is now Parkersburg, West Virginia. A romantic who had moved to the wilderness from England in 1798 with his young bride (who was also his niece, one of the main reasons they had to leave England), he was intrigued by Burr's plans. But Blennerhassett had more money than sense—in a very short time he would have neither.

Burr also enlisted an old chum from his Revolutionary days, General James Wilkinson, commander of the Army of the West. This was a bad choice. Wilkinson was not a man to rely on. He had all of Burr's unscrupulous ambition and very little of his intellect.

Wilkinson had married well, left the Army, and moved to Kentucky to engage in land speculation in the 1780s. He became involved with the Spanish authorities in New Orleans and entered their employ in a scheme to detach Kentucky from the Union. That didn't work out and Wilkinson had to be bailed out of bankruptcy by Burr in 1790.

He rejoined the military and, with Hamilton removed from the scene, had become its highest ranking officer. In 1805 he was also appointed governor of newly acquired Louisiana.

Burr met with him that year and outlined his plans. They sounded good to Wilkinson, but as he became more deeply involved he came to understand the scheme had no chance at all of working. New Orleans would not revolt, and the military task before the conspirators was impossible.

So he turned whistle-blower and warned the authorities in New Orleans that mischief was afoot. Burr, meanwhile, proceeded down the Ohio and Mississippi rivers with a flotilla of flatboats to Natchez, never dreaming that he had been exposed. But when he landed there he found that Jefferson had ordered his arrest and Wilkinson had raised the ante by offering a bounty on Burr, alive or dead.

Burr knew that with all the incriminating evidence he had on Wilkinson, the preferred choice was dead. So he made a run for it, getting as far as the present state of Alabama before being captured and charged with treason.

Since Blennerhassett Island, which then fell within the borders of Virginia, was chosen as the scene of his crime, the trial took place at the Capitol in Richmond. It was presided over by the Chief Justice of the U.S. Supreme Court, John Marshall.

Burr's acute legal mind saw the way out of this mess. Wilkinson had the evidence that would convict him, but Burr also possessed the goods on Wilkinson, and he let the general know that. Jefferson was eager for a conviction, but Chief Justice Marshall bore no great love for the President, and, in the end, his critical ruling favored Burr.

The government contended that the assembling of an armed force was enough to establish guilt. Marshall stated that was not sufficient, that an overt act must be proved. Providing the proof was in Wilkinson's hands, and he was not about to lose his own skin to get Burr. So the case ended in acquittal, although most of the principals involved were convinced of Burr's guilt.

With Blennerhassett and a host of other creditors trailing him, Burr managed to make his way to New York and catch a boat for England. He ran up more debts there, was forced to move to Sweden and then to France, where he advanced a plan to reconquer Canada and Louisiana. The French sent him home.

He returned in 1812 and for the next twenty-four years lived on as a notorious figure, making a living at the law. At the age of seventy-seven, he married Madame Jumel, whom he had been linked with years before when she was known as New York's most attractive harlot. She was now a respectable and wealthy widow. After a year of marriage, however, she threw him out, charging adultery.

Burr died in 1836 on Staten Island after a series of strokes; he was eighty. He had been pointed out on the streets of New York as "the wickedest man alive" and had lost his beloved daughter in a storm at sea. But his life had really ended thirty-two years before, when he fired the fatal shot at Hamilton. The same bullet killed them both.

The Sites

Blennerhassett Island and Museum Harman and Margaret Blennerhassett thought they had created a new Eden on their island in the Ohio River. Instead, it turned out to be their gateway to purgatory.

The wealthy couple arrived at Marietta, Ohio, looking for a new home in the American West. The island a few miles downstream appeared to be the answer. They moved onto the island in 1798 and built the most elaborate home ever seen in this part of the Ohio Valley.

Constructed in the Palladian Style, then at the height of its popularity in the cultivated circles of Britain, the Blennerhassetts entertained visitors, conducted natural science experiments, and rejoiced in this almost perfect world they had made. But when Burr arrived in 1805, they succumbed to his plans for a southwestern empire and advanced $50,000 to further the scheme.

When word leaked out, Blennerhassett had to flee just ahead of the militia, who had been ordered to seize the island. The mansion was looted of its furnishings, the rest of the property was confiscated by creditors, and in 1811 the home accidentally caught fire and burned to the ground.

Blennerhassett was imprisoned briefly, but no proof of a crime was ever put forth and he was released. But he could never regain his fortune. A Mississippi plantation failed, an appointment in Canada fell through, and his loan to Burr was uncollectable. They were forced to return to England to live on the charity of Blennerhassett's sister.

They later moved to the Channel Island of Guernsey. He died there in poverty in 1831 and Margaret, having moved to New York, passed away eleven years later. One of their children disappeared in the West, another died in a poorhouse in New York City.

The island was an amusement park and picnic ground for much of the nineteenth century. After archeologists uncovered its original foundations in 1973, the mansion was reconstructed on its original site and furnished with some original pieces and others consistent with its time.

Blennerhassett Island is now a West Virginia historical state park and is reached by stern-wheeler from Point Park in downtown Parkersburg. The boat operates Tuesday to Sunday, 10 a.m. to 5:30 p.m., May through Labor Day; 11 a.m. to 5 p.m., in April; Thursday to Saturday, 10 a.m. to 4:30 p.m., and Sunday, 12:00 p.m. to 4:30 p.m., Labor Day through October. The boat fare is $6, with tours of the mansion an additional $3.

The Blennerhassett Museum, containing exhibits on the island's history and part of the original mansion's entrance steps, is located at 2nd and Juliana St., in Parkersburg. It is open Tuesday to Sunday, 9:30 a.m. to 6 p.m., May to Labor Day; 11 a.m. to 5 p.m., in April; Tuesday to Saturday, 9:30 a.m. to 5 p.m., and Sunday, 11 a.m. to 5 p.m., Labor Day through October; opening at 1 p.m. on Sunday, in November. Saturday, 11 a.m. to 5 p.m., and Sunday, 1 p.m. to 5 p.m., December through March. Admission to the museum is $2. (304) 420-4800; www.blennerhassettislandstatepark.com.

The Capitol The Virginia Capitol Building, in Richmond, still contains the site of Burr's trial for treason. It was held in the Old Hall of the House of Delegates, which is where the state assembly met from the time the Capitol was finished in 1788 until 1906. It is the same hall in which the Confederate Congress met from 1862 until the end of the Civil War.

The Capitol is located on Capitol Square, off 9th St., in the heart of Richmond. It is open daily, 9 a.m. to 5 p.m., April through November; Sunday hours from 1 p.m. to 5 p.m., rest of year. Free. (804) 698-1788; www.virginiacapitol.gov.

Hamilton Park The place where Burr and Hamilton fought their fatal duel sits amid the industrial tangle of New Jersey's Hudson River shore, just north of the entrance to the Lincoln Tunnel. Follow County Road 505, Hudson Blvd. E., which runs on the ridge of land between the base of the Palisades and the railroad tracks along the river.

The former dueling ground is now a park, with an historic marker near the road. Nearby is a bronze bust of Hamilton. The park is open daily, dawn to dusk.

Jumel Mansion The Jumel Mansion is one of the oldest residences on Manhattan Island and was the home of Burr during his brief marriage to Madame Jumel. The house was built around 1765 by Loyalist Roger Morris, who abandoned it and fled to England at the start of the Revolution. Washington used it as his headquarters just before the Battle of Harlem Heights, in September 1776, in which the Continental Army was driven out of New York. Afterwards, it was used by the British as one of their military headquarters.

Merchant Stephen Jumel took the Georgian house over after the war and it was his widow whom Burr married in 1833. He lived here for about a year until he got tossed out for adultery.

The mansion is now a museum of Revolutionary era New York City. It is located just east of St. Nicholas Ave., north of 160th St. It is open 10 a.m. to 4 p.m., Wednesday to Sunday. Admission $4; students with ID, $3. (212) 923-8008; www.morrisjumel.org.

JEAN LAFITTE

There is a temptation to think of Jean Lafitte more as a patriot than a pirate. His romantic legacy pervades Louisiana folklore. His treasure is said to be hidden in a dozen different places, and his ghost walks one of the great Mississippi River plantation houses.

There is a U.S. historical park named for him. He even received an official pardon from President James Madison and later a commendation from President Andrew Jackson. But he was still a pirate. He directed his men to put innocent people to death, and although most of those people sailed under the Spanish flag they died just the same.

Moreover, the product Lafitte traded in most often was black slaves. At a time when it was illegal to import slaves, Louisiana plantation owners knew they would have a ready supply from the obliging pirate leader.

But because of his decision to defend New Orleans against invading British forces in January 1815, he has been portrayed over the years as a swashbuckling rogue. The image of Yul Brynner, saber in hand, fighting for America in the 1950s adventure classic *The Buccaneer* is the one that stays in the mind.

Lafitte was definitely a part of the historic Battle of New Orleans (fought a few days after the close of the War of 1812), but the saber bit is pure invention. The rest of Lafitte's life, however, is shrouded in mystery, legend, and blood. Lord Byron had it right when he wrote of him in his 1814 poem "The Corsair": "He left a corsair's name to other times, / Linked one virtue to a thousand crimes."

His birth date is usually given as 1780, although no one is sure of that. In some versions of his biography, his birthplace is given as Bordeaux, where he was supposedly the son of a well-to-do family engaged in maritime trade. Other stories suggest that he began life in the French colony of Haiti.

Around 1806, he made his first appearance in Louisiana. By that time, smuggling was a way of life in the bayou country at the mouth of the Mississippi. The area was already known as Barataria, a word derived from *barateur*, the French word for "deceptive." It was applied to the smuggled goods that found their way into the homes of New Orleans' wealthiest families, who loved a bargain and didn't much care how it was obtained.

High tariffs under Spanish and French rule had entrenched the practice hi Louisiana life. So when the territory came under American authority with the Louisiana Purchase of 1803, smuggling came along with the deal.

Governor William C. C. Claiborne was determined to stamp it out, declaring that a normal economic life was impossible as long as these goods were imported without regulation. For the most part he was mocked and ignored.

At one point, Claiborne put a $500 price on Lafitte's head, so exasperated was he by the pirate's large-scale defiance of the law. Lafitte responded by printing a parody of the handbill and placing a $1,500 price on the governor's head.

National Archives & Records Administration

Lafitte and his brother, Pierre, operated a blacksmith shop on Bourbon Street, in the French Quarter. But this was merely a cover for their illegal activities. It was an open secret in New Orleans that the shop was actually a slave market.

The traffic in African slaves had been technically illegal in Louisiana since 1805. But demand remained high, and Lafitte was ready to fill it with the human cargo plundered from slavers on the Spanish Main.

At this point in his career, he was the organizer of this slave trade. The actual high seas piracy was left to his able captains, Dominique You and Rey ne'Beluche. But Lafitte traveled freely between New Orleans and the base of his pirate fleet, in the heart of Barataria.

This was a pirate fantasy out of Captain Hook's wildest dreams— warehouses bulging with stolen goods, ships, slaves, bordellos, rollicking sea dogs. A fort protected it from attack, while food and provisions came in from the compliant residents of Barataria, who made their living from the trade.

By 1811, the operation was so enormous that Lafitte moved there full-time. He oversaw widening of the waterways to accommodate the steady stream of barges that traveled to New Orleans. He arranged to sail under the flag of the rebel colony of Cartagena to give a cover of legality to his attacks on Spanish merchant vessels.

According to some accounts, he kept order by personally executing mutinous crew members, publicly and at close range. When Pierre Lafitte was arrested by Claiborne in New Orleans and charged with piracy, there was no jury in Louisiana that would convict him.

But as the War of 1812 wore on, public opinion changed. The economy soured, and some of the banks blamed the smugglers. A slave rebellion was traced back to a purchase made from the Lafittes. Pierre was arrested again, and this time it was taken seriously.

In the midst of these troubles, on September 5, 1814, a British ship arrived off Lafitte's headquarters. An invasion fleet was gathering in Jamaica, and emissaries of the Royal Navy wanted to know if Lafitte would assist them. He was offered a captain's commission and a bribe of $30,000 (actually a piddling amount compared to the booty he was pulling in).

Lafitte said he needed time to think this over and requested a plan of the invasion so he could study it. He then forwarded the documents to Claiborne and volunteered his men to help defend the city.

Claiborne, rather than expressing gratitude, feared that Lafitte would betray the rear gateway to New Orleans. So on September 16, he ordered an attack on his base.

Lafitte refused to fire on the American flag. His stronghold was taken, stripped of its contraband, and burned to the ground. Most of the pirates escaped, but their base was left in ruins.

Nonetheless, Lafitte repeated his offer in a secret meeting with General Andrew Jackson. The commanding general was deeply concerned about defending the city against British troops who had fought Napoleon with the Duke of Wellington. This time, he accepted, and Pierre Lafitte mysteriously "escaped" from prison a few days later.

The rout of the British at Chalmette on January 8, 1815, is the stuff of American folk legend and song. Thanks to Lafitte, the element of surprise was gone. While neither of the brothers was on the actual battlefield, their able captains, You and ne'Beluche, manned batteries number three and four.

The British commander, Sir Edward Pakenham, was killed in a frontal assault on the well-entrenched American lines. About seven hundred crack British troops died in the carnage, while the total death count of Americans was thirteen.

Jackson was generous in his praise for the pirates, and President Madison swept away all charges against the Lafittes.

In his letter of pardon Madison wrote: "Offenders who have refused to become the associates of the enemy in war, upon the most seducing terms of invitation, and who have sided to repel his hostile invasion of the territory of the United States can no longer be considered an object of punishment, but as objects of genuine forgiveness."

For a while, Lafitte basked in the admiration of the city he had helped save. But he had no intention of giving up his old life. While a few of his former crew settled down in Barataria, most of them accompanied their leader across the Gulf of Mexico to a new home, on Galveston Island, Texas.

Within two years, he was back in business at the island, which he called Campeachy. His Maison Rouge, part residence and part fortress, was the base for a pirate fleet that preyed on Spanish shipping across the Caribbean. By some estimates, Lafitte's men captured up to three hundred vessels. But preoccupied with war in Europe and revolution in Mexico and South America, Spain did not have the manpower to oppose him.

Galveston was then situated in an area that was not clearly American or Mexican. As long as Lafitte left American shipping undisturbed, the U.S. authorities looked the other way.

But in 1819, like an aging chief executive, he began to lose control of this demanding business. One of his ships disobeyed orders and fired at a U.S. cutter. Lafitte, with grim humor, had the captain hanged "for piracy." The following year his base was nearly destroyed by a hurricane.

In desperate need of supplies, Lafitte sanctioned the seizure of an American schooner. That was a fatal error. A U.S. Navy force under Lieutenant Lawrence Kearney soon arrived at Campeachy. Lafitte was told that Galveston was now considered American soil, and he was ordered off. In May 1821, he burned the last few buildings and sailed off into the mists of legend.

It is believed that with a small portion of his force he tried to establish himself on the island of Mujeres, off the coast of Yucatan. But he was now in his forties, his energy flagging, a leader of a dwindling crew that no longer inspired fear.

Most history texts give the date of his death as 1826, although there is no evidence where that occurred or where he was buried. Or, more to the point, where the immense fortune he looted is buried.

In Barataria, they know. They say Lafitte is buried there, next to Napoleon and John Paul Jones, both of whom he had secretly brought to Louisiana. They say the treasure is there, too, hidden in the cypress swamps and sawgrass, waiting for the fortune hunter with enough luck and wit to find it.

They guarantee, too, that his great days as a patriot more than balance his years as a slave trader and pirate. But that is history's call.

THE SITES

Jean Lafitte National Historical Park and Preserve Established in 1978 by Congress, Jean Lafitte National Historical Park and Preserve has three distinct units. One is a wetlands preserve that seeks to keep much of Barataria as it was when Lafitte made his base there in the early nineteenth century. It extends along the west bank of the Mississippi River, southwest of the city, and is reached by Louisiana 45, from Gretna. There are guided boat tours through the swampy area, which gives visitors some idea why Lafitte was so hard to find. This unit of the park is open daily, 9 a.m. to 5 p.m. Free admission. (504) 589-2133; www.nps.gov/jela.

Jean Lafitte and Lafitte Village Just south of the park, on Louisiana 45, are the villages of Jean Lafitte and Lafitte. (How many buccaneers have not one but two towns named after them?) At Lafitte is the probable site of the pirate encampment. It is now a fishing port and recreational boating center. Just north of the town, as the road crosses Bayou des Oies (Bayou of the Geese) is the cemetery where, according to an old local tradition, Lafitte is buried along with Bonaparte and John Paul Jones. The Invalides in Paris and the U.S. Naval Academy in Annapolis, Maryland, have opposing views on where the latter two rest. But since no one really knows Lafitte's burial place, no one can argue that he's not buried here.

Chalmette Battlefield The second unit of the Jean Lafitte Historical Park encompasses Chalmette Battlefield. This is located just east of New Orleans, along Louisiana 46. A self-guiding tour loops around the area and leads to the critical points of the battle, including the location of the pirate batteries. There is also a visitor center with audiovisual displays on the battle. The unit is open daily, 9 a.m. to 5 p.m. Free admission.

French Quarter Stops The park's third unit lies within the French Quarter. Several sites in this historic district have associations with Lafitte, although the park is meant to include the entire Vieux Carre. Walking tours of the Quarter begin at the visitor center near the French Market, at 916 N. Peters St. The usual starting time is 10:30 a.m., but it's best to call in advance, at (504) 589-2133. The visitor center is open daily, 9 a.m. to 5 p.m. Free admission.

The Lafitte Brothers blacksmith shop is located at 941 Bourbon St., near St. Philip St. But don't let the guide try to tell you that the cast iron grills that decorate so many balconies in the Quarter were made here. The shop was never anything but a cover for the smuggling and slave-trading operations.

Many places in the Quarter claim to be the spot where Lafitte and Jackson met secretly to plan the defense of the city. The best claim to the distinction is probably held by Maspero's Coffee Exchange, at 440 Chartres St., at St. Louis St. Built in 1788, it was a favorite rendezvous for leading politicians and one of Jackson's hangouts.

Destrehan Plantation Destrehan Plantation is located in a town named for Creole planter Jean Noel Destrehan and was part of his vast holdings. He built the great house in 1788. The area has been surrounded by oil refineries since 1914, and for a time the plantation was used as a recreation hall for employees. But it has been restored to its Greek Revival luster and is once more a showplace. It is also haunted. Lafitte was a frequent guest here and tales have been told for generations that he left his treasure somewhere on the premises. Those who attest to seeing his ghost say that it points mournfully at the great hearth on the ground floor and disappears. That would seem to be a clue, but nothing has ever turned up. The plantation is located 25 miles west of New Orleans, off I-310. Destrehan is open daily, 9 a.m. to 4 p.m. Admission $10. (877) 453-2095; www.destrehanplantation.org.

St. Louis Cemetery No. 2 St. Louis Cemetery No. 2 in New Orleans contains the tomb of Dominique You, who was Lafitte's most trusted captain, a skilled gunner who knocked out the British artillery at the Battle of New Orleans. The cemetery is at St. Louis St. and Claiborne, just west of the French Quarter. (The cemeteries of New Orleans have been the sites of some well-publicized crimes in recent years. It is best to visit by day and in a group.)

Galveston Island Not much remains, beyond a few historic markers, of Lafitte's stay in Galveston. The town's historic museum has no displays. "This is a man whose entire life was pursued outside the law," says a docent there. "He didn't leave a paper trail, so it's hard to find anything to exhibit." Nevertheless, there is a film. At the Great Storm Theater, a movie about Lafitte's life on Galveston is shown daily on the hour and half hour, from 11 a.m. to 6 p.m. Admission $5; $4 students. (409) 763-8808.

ANNUAL EVENT

Contraband Days Contraband Days are held the first two weekends in May in Lake Charles, another Louisiana city that lays claim to the legend of Lafitte. It, too, believes that part of his swag is buried here. The town's founder was Carlos Salia, a man of Spanish ancestry from New Orleans. When he moved here in 1805 he changed his name to Charles Sallier, and the French version is what stuck to the town. He was a friend of Lafitte and gave the pirate refuge when he was being pursued. According to legend, Lafitte removed his treasure from his ship, buried it, and then sank his schooner with a cannon shot. There was a sunken schooner here for many years, and it was believed to have belonged to Lafitte. This is a city-wide celebration with dancing, races, arm-wrestling competitions, food booths, and tributes to the spirit of Lafitte.

THE HARPE BROTHERS

Many of the bad guys described in this book have left legends encrusted with explanations or apologies. They weren't driven to crime by greed or evil. It was because of economic desperation or war or misplaced ambition or a terrible misunderstanding.

No one tries to make that argument for the Harpe Brothers. They were bad to the bone. Everyone knew they were no good and the world was clearly a better place when they left it. From their base on the Ohio River, and later on the Natchez Trace, they preyed mercilessly on westward-bound pioneers and merchants, murdering for their own delight.

They were killers who were even shunned by other outlaws, who regarded them as somewhat abnormal. That was a wise policy, because they would not have hesitated to kill a fellow criminal if some profit could be gained from it. The Harpes seem to have been dredged up from some of the darkest places in America's nightmares.

Their names were Micajah and Wiley—but they have become known through the years as Big Harpe and Little Harpe. (More recent genealogical research indicates that their names may well have been William and Joshua and that they might have been cousins.)

As brothers go they are not nearly as well known as the Youngers, the Jameses, or the Daltons. But in their time they were fully as feared and possibly even more unsavory.

They came from somewhere in the southeast; some historians say

National Archives & Records Administration

Virginia and others North Carolina. Three women traveled with them, all claiming to be their wives. Big Harpe, apparently, had two wives.

They first appeared in Kentucky in 1799. Like thousands of other pioneers, they made their way through the Cumberland Gap and headed west on Boone's Trace. At an inn near the Rock Castle River (U.S. 150 now retraces the route of Boone's Wilderness Road) they met a traveler named Langford.

Langford was traveling alone, which was unusual in this dangerous area. Moreover, he was carrying a sizable amount of money, and the Harpes made note of it when Langford generously bought them breakfast.

Langford apparently decided to continue his journey with the Harpes. This was the last and worst decision he ever made. His body was found a few days later in a gully near the Rock Castle, covered with brush and leaves and hidden behind a log.

The Harpes were apprehended and charged with the crime. But they broke out of the jail at Danville and quickly made their way to the most lucrative hunting grounds in the state.

The Ohio River was then the great highway to the West. Settlers heading for newly opened lands in western Kentucky, southern Illinois, and Indiana passed through continually. The deadliest obstacle they encountered were river pirates, and the most dangerous stretch of the journey, infested with bandits, was the area around Cave-in Rock.

This deep crevice in the northern riverbank is now an Illinois state park. But in the first years of the nineteenth century it was perfectly situated for piracy.

Its 80-foot-wide entrance commands a clear view of the river in both directions and yet is concealed from westward-bound travelers. The unsuspecting flatboats would approach almost to the entrance of the cave before its occupants realized the danger they were in.

By the time the Harpes arrived in the area, the pirates had been organized under the leadership of Samuel Mason, who allegedly had once been an officer in the colonial army. He arrived there in 1797, and his agenda seemed to be in perfect accord with that of the Harpes. By 1800, they were connected with his band.

Soon the figures of this Mutt and Jeff pirate pair had become objects of terror along the Ohio. The Harpes were restless, however, and chafed at being submitted to another man's leadership. Within a year they transferred their base of operations a bit east, to Henderson County, Kentucky.

This part of the state, between the mouths of the Green and Cumberland Rivers, was a wild, unsettled area. It was still a place of backwoodsmen and isolated families who lived miles away from their closest neighbors. To predators like the Harpes, they were all fair game.

"It seems incredible that such atrocities could have been often repeated in a country famed for the hardihood and gallantry of its people," wrote Judge James Hall in his book *Letters from the West*. "But the vigilance of the Harpes ensured impunity. The spoils of their dreadful warfare furnished them with the means of violence and of escape. Mounted on fine horses they plunged into the forest, eluded pursuit by frequently changing their course, and appeared, unexpectedly, to perpetrate new enormities, at points distant from where they were supposed to lurk."

The misdeeds of the Harpes became known across western Kentucky when their culminating act of viciousness occurred at the home of Moses Stigall.

It was the custom in those times for travelers to seek shelter with pioneer families. Judge Hall insists that the Stigalls had previously sheltered the Harpes and had escaped unharmed. The Stigalls felt they had reached a mutual agreement with the Harpes that if they continued to offer them lodging they would not be harmed. When they arrived this time, Mrs. Stigall was alone in the house with her infant child and a local schoolteacher, William Love, who was also spending the night.

Mrs. Stigall perhaps expected what Love's fate might be in that company, but felt she had no choice but to let the Harpes stay. When Stigall arrived home the following day, he found the bodies of Love, his wife, and his son in the burned-out ruin of his cabin. The Harpes had decided to leave no witnesses to the crime.

Stigall rode to his home of his neighbor, Captain John Leeper, and they quickly raised a pursuit. The Harpes had not anticipated being followed so closely and were taken by surprise at their campsite. But they were able to run to their horses and rode off in separate directions.

In their haste, however, they had taken the wrong horses. Big Harpe climbed on the smaller of the two animals, the one his brother had been riding. The weaker horse could not support the larger man's frame, and Leeper was able to get within shooting distance. Harpe went down, and the horse rolled on top of him.

Trapped beneath the animal, Harpe was helpless. Leeper waited until Stigall caught up to him, and then, after a brief discussion, it was agreed that the newly made widower should do the honors. He killed

Big Harpe with a single shot, and Leeper cut off his head, which was placed in the branches of a nearby tree and left there until it rotted. For years afterwards, the nearby road was called Harpes Head.

Little Harpe made his escape, however, and in 1803 he rejoined Mason, the pirate leader. Mason had decided that the pirate game wasn't what it used to be, however, and that there were easier pickings available on the Natchez Trace.

Flatboatmen would make the trip down the Mississippi River to Natchez in those days, unload their cargo onto larger craft for the rest of the journey to New Orleans, and then return home overland on the Trace, which had been cut through to Nashville, Tennessee.

Mason figured that it was foolish to attack the boats on the river because the crews hadn't been paid yet. It was much smarter to spring the trap on the Trace and relieve them of their earnings.

This was so effective that soon the authorities in Natchez put a price on Mason's head. That appealed to Little Harpe. So in cahoots with a third member of the band, James Mays, he managed to kill Mason and brought his head back to Natchez in a large sack.

It was a simple plan, except that Harpe hadn't counted on his fame preceding him. He was recognized in Natchez and had to make a run for it. He and Mays got as far as Old Greenville, 26 miles away, where they were captured and hanged.

Like his brother, Little Harpe was decapitated and his head placed on a pole as a lesson to others.

The three wives of the two brothers were placed on trial in Kentucky but were acquitted of any complicity in the various crimes.

"These horrid events will sound like fiction to your ears," wrote Judge Hall in summation, "when told as having happened in the United States, so foreign are they from the generosity of the American character."

THE SITES

Cave-in Rock Park Cave-in Rock was cleared of its last pirates in the 1820s and since then has become a recreation area along the Ohio River. It became an Illinois state park in 1929 and has been expanded to 200 acres, including the bluffs atop the cave itself.

A system of trails leads along the riverbank, into the cave, and into the surrounding hills. There is also a lodge and restaurant in the park, as well as campsites and a trout pond. The cave was featured as a backdrop in the movie *How the West Was Won*, which depicted the activities of the river pirates who gathered here.

The park is off the main roads and is connected to Kentucky across the river by an all-year ferry service. From the Illinois side, it is 59 miles southeast of I-57 from the Marion exit on Illinois 15 and Illinois 1. For information and reservations call (618) 289-4325.

Harpes Head Road The site of Big Harpe's demise is marked on U.S. 41, 2 miles north of Dixon, Kentucky, and 50 miles south of Henderson. The crossroad at the site was known for many years as Harpes Head Road.

Old Greenville Old Greenville lies along the Natchez Trace Parkway, between Washington and Fayette, Mississippi. The place was abandoned long ago, but markers point out its location. Little Harpe's head was placed on a pole at the northern end of the town, while the head of James Mays was mounted similarly at the southern end.

Natchez Trace You can get an idea of what the Natchez of those days looked like by visiting the Under-the-Hill district of the old river town, along Silver St. It was the hangout of pirates and thieves, filled with taverns and bordellos during Natchez's boom days in the early nineteenth century. Flatboats lined up fourteen deep along the riverfront in a row 2 miles long. Now an entertainment area featuring a riverboat casino, several of the restaurants and shops facing the river were built into caves where stolen loot was stashed away.

WILLIAM CLARKE QUANTRILL

When the cannons roared at Fort Sumter in April, 1861, the Civil War officially began. But to those who lived on the Kansas-Missouri border, war already had been raging for six long, bloody years. The declaration just formalized the slaughter.

With a savagery almost without parallel in American history, abolitionists and pro-slavery forces raided back and forth across the border to pillage, kidnap, burn, and kill. The campaign unleashed all the fury and hatred of a European religious or ethnic war, with neighbors rushing to kill each other.

In Kansas were the Jayhawkers, organized in Fort Scott by Captain James Montgomery. He likened the actions of his group to a vicious bird who seizes small animals and shakes them to death. Just 20 miles to the east, in the town of Nevada, Missouri, was the headquarters of the Bushwhackers, who retaliated in kind.

The athletic teams at Kansas University still proudly bear the name of Jayhawks. But Bush-whacker has passed into the language defined as a sneak who shoots from ambush. That isn't a measure of relative culpability, but merely of which side won the war.

Out of this dangerously chaotic situation emerged William Clarke Quantrill. In the breakdown of law and social structure, he found the perfect setting for a career as a guerilla leader. He directed what has been described as the greatest single atrocity of the war—the raid on Lawrence, Kansas.

The situation on this border was brought on by passage in Congress of the Kansas-Nebraska Act of 1854. As with many disastrous pieces of legislation, it was drawn up with the very best of intentions. Instead of designating the two new territories as slave or free based upon a line of latitude on the map, democracy would enter the process. Residents would vote on whether to allow slavery or not.

It replaced the Missouri Compromise, which had kept the lid on this issue for thirty-four years. The Compromise had admitted one free state to the Union for each slave state to maintain a balance. It was hoped now that Kansas would vote for slavery and Nebraska would become a free state. But abolitionists decided that this was their big chance and began organizing bands of settlers to move into Kansas and carry the election.

When residents of Missouri, a slave state, saw what was afoot, they sent in their own colonies. Soon the two were electing separate state legislatures and officials. After that the killing began.

By the time Quantrill entered the border area, in 1857, as a man of about twenty, the pattern of violence was well established. He seemed to be an opportunist, quite willing to play both sides. He even declared himself in sympathy with the anti-slavery party and taught school in the abolitionist center of Lawrence.

But while he participated in a few raids into Missouri to free slaves, he was also in contact with pro-slavery groups and frequently transported stolen horses from Kansas to that side of the border. He played this double game for three years. Then, in late 1860, with events rapidly moving towards war and the Free Staters in control of Kansas, he made his commitment.

While accompanying a group of Jayhawkers on a raid upon the home of a wealthy Missouri planter, Quantrill suddenly ducked inside the house. A volley of rifle fire came from within and all the raiders were either killed or wounded. Quantrill, who had organized the ambush, had emphatically joined the cause of slavery.

He explained later that he did it because Jayhawkers had killed his older brother. Since he had no older brother, that seems unlikely. A more likely reason was that the divorced daughter of the planter secretly had become his mistress. Quantrill had made his choice for the oldest of reasons.

State Historical Society of Missouri, Columbia

When war broke out a few months later, he organized a group of a dozen men to stage raids into Kansas. He said that they were meant as a reply to Jayhawker raids led by Jim Lane, who was also a U.S. Senator. But even other Confederate officers wanted little to do with Quantrill. One said of him, "He deemed the life of a man less than that of a sheep-killing dog."

Lane was no picnic himself. The governor of Kansas, Charles Robinson, albeit Lane's political rival, described him as "a blood-thirsty maniac clothed with authority from Washington." Union General H. W. Halleck wrote in July 1861 that "the conduct of the forces under Lane has done more for the enemy in Missouri than could have been accomplished by 20,000 of his own army. I receive almost daily complaints of outrages committed by these men in the name of the United States."

Quantrill and his men fought at the Battle of Independence in August 1862 and acquitted themselves so well that he was offered the rank of captain in the regular Confederate Army. But he had other ideas.

The Union command in Missouri had declared him an outlaw, to be shot on sight. Quantrill took this as a challenge. Instead of fighting by the rules of conventional warfare, he would retaliate against the enemy, whether military or civilian, wherever he could.

He raided deep into Kansas and then vanished back into Missouri, sheltered by farmers who were deeply hostile to the Union cause.

His group had become guerillas. By the summer of 1863 he commanded a formidable group of fighters. While they considered themselves Confederate irregulars, they managed to keep most of the plunder they carried off.

On August 18, his column of 448 men slipped across the Kansas border. Riding with him as his chief aide was Bill Anderson, driven half-mad by the death of his sister in the collapse of a building where she was being held prisoner by Union forces. Anderson was said to carry the scalps of Union soldiers around his belt. Also in that force were Cole Younger and Frank James—names that would soon figure prominently in the postwar history of violence in this area.

Their objective was Lawrence, hometown of the hated Jim Lane. Quantrill intended to burn it to the ground and kill Lane in the process.

Lawrence had figured prominently in the border wars. Settled by the Massachusetts Emigrant Aid Society, it was a vigorous supporter of the Free State movement. It had been sacked by pro-slavery forces, led by Sheriff Samuel J. Jones, in 1856. But the town quickly recovered and was now a prosperous community of three thousand inhabitants.

There was no advance warning of Quantrill's arrival on the morning of August 21. The men swooped into the sleeping town from the east. The first to die was Reverend S. S. Snyder, gunned down as he sat in his farmyard milking a cow.

Unarmed U.S. Army recruits were shot where they stood at their camp south of downtown. The raiders rode on into the heart of the city, surrounding their main objective, the Eldridge Hotel. A white sheet was quickly hung from the building's window and its occupants were allowed to surrender unharmed. Then the horror began.

The hotel was set afire and as occupants of other buildings came into the street they were shot down. Storekeepers and their clerks, German immigrants who had no idea what was happening, unarmed passers-by-all were killed without a chance of defending themselves. The raiders broke into saloons and quickly downed whatever drink was available, then rode into the town's residential area.

Their objective was Lane, but he had been given warning and ran off to hide in a nearby cornfield. Other homeowners were dragged outside, sometimes out of the arms of their wives and children, and shot to death on the street. The raiders were inflamed, and every man and boy they saw had become their target.

At one hotel, they lined up the male residents and methodically executed them. According to one eyewitness account, two wounded men were thrown into the flames of a burning building. The mayor was murdered and so was the publisher of the local paper.

No women or small children were hurt. But no mercy was given to anyone else.

Many towns were burned in the course of this war. But in almost every case there was some military or economic advantage to be gained. The massacre in Lawrence went on beyond the point of reason. It turned into a four-hour orgy of plunder and revenge, a personal vendetta against civilians who were not part of the war.

When at last the signal to leave was given, between 150 and 180 dead lay in the streets of Lawrence. Several of the bodies, immigrants and blacks, were never identified. Only one raider was killed, shot with an arrow by an Indian resident of the town.

Lawrence was left a smoking ruin, its business district wiped out. Quantrill easily eluded a pursuing Union force and triumphantly led his column back to safety in Missouri. But his actions had blackened his name forever, in both the North and South.

Confederate officials were sickened when reports of the carnage reached Richmond. They knew that retaliation would be forthcoming. They only had to wait two days before the infamous Order Number 11 was issued in Missouri by the Federal military authority.

Lane, burning for revenge, had virtually dictated it to the commanding general. Under its terms, almost every county along the Missouri side of the border was depopulated. Families who could not prove their loyalty to the Union beyond question or refused to sign an Oath of Allegiance were forced to abandon their homes, carrying only what they could haul away in their arms.

Farms were burned, livestock confiscated. Even Union supporters were forced off their land. The Order was the culminating act of bitterness in the border wars, one that resulted in hatreds that lasted for generations after the Civil War ended.

Lane's intent was to strip Quantrill of his base of support, leaving him nowhere to hide. In that regard it worked. But the very savagery of the attack on Lawrence had alienated many of Quantrill's former supporters in the Confederacy, who felt it violated every rule of warfare.

Quantrill retreated south, but he wasn't finished with Kansas yet. At Baxter Springs, on the Oklahoma border, his men, wearing captured Federal uniforms, surprised a detachment of Union troops. According to General James G. Blunt, who managed to escape with a handful of men, wounded prisoners, including the brigade band and clerks, were shot to death.

The raiders moved on to Texas, where any pretense of being a guerilla force was abandoned. Quantrill broke off all contact with the Confederate command. He raided, instead, towns that were securely Southern in their sympathies. He could not control Anderson, and within months the band had split into rival factions.

By the early months of 1864, his band had dwindled to about twenty men. He decided to move his operations to Kentucky. Frank James stayed with him, although his younger brother, Jesse, who was just sixteen years old, decided to remain in Missouri.

Even after the formal Confederate surrender in April, 1865, Quantrill fought on. He understood that there could be no surrender for him. All that awaited him was a rope. So without a cause, without a war, he continued to engage in banditry and call it resistance.

On May 10, 1865, the tiny remnant of his band rested at a farm near Bloomfield, Kentucky. They were surprised there by a Federal cavalry unit employing the same sort of ruthless guerilla tactics Quantrill had used in Kansas. As Quantrill's men scattered to save themselves, their leader went down with a bullet in the spine.

He was taken to a hospital in Louisville, lingered on paralyzed for almost a month, and died on June 6. He was twenty-seven years old. He left his mistress of the time $2,000 in gold, which she used to open a bordello in St. Louis. His mother disinterred his body twenty-two years later and sold his bones for souvenirs.

Some writers tried to idealize Quantrill as a daring, unconventional, and gallant fighter for the lost cause. There was no denying his daring and imagination as a leader. But as for gallantry, the dead civilians left piled on the streets of Lawrence will have to speak to that.

THE SITES

Watkins Community Museum of History The best place to get an overview on the Lawrence raid is at the Watkins Community Museum of History. It is located downtown, at 1047 Massachusetts St., in what was once the community's foremost bank building. There is an exhibit area devoted to the raid, with displays on the events that led up to it and a case of artifacts from that day.

The museum is open Tuesday to Saturday, 10 a.m. to 4 p.m.; Sunday, 1:30 p.m. to 4 p.m. Donations accepted. (785) 841-4109; www.watkinsmuseum.org.

Lawrence Memorials Memorials and monuments relating to the raid are scattered throughout Lawrence. On New Hampshire St., between 10th and 11th, is the memorial to the seventeen U.S. Army recruits who were slaughtered where they stood. The site of the old Eldridge Hotel, replaced by another hotel of the same name, is at 701 Massachusetts. Just down the block, at 729-31 Massachusetts, is the House Building, the only structure in the downtown area to survive the raid.

Another marker has been placed at the site of the Griswold House, on the south side of 7th St., between Illinois and Mississippi. Four prominent Lawrence residents were executed there. Jim Lane's house stood near the northwest corner of 8th and Mississippi, and the cornfield in which he escaped was directly in back of the home.

Oak Hill Cemetery Oak Hill Cemetery is east of downtown by way of 15th St., north on Elmwood St., and then east on Oak Hill Ave. There is a monument to the victims of the raid, most of whom are buried here, in Section One.

The Bushwhacker Museum The Bushwhacker Museum, in Nevada, Missouri, tells the story of the border wars from the perspective of the Southern side. There are several displays on the Bushwhacker leaders, many of whom were based in this town, which was burned down by Union forces in 1865.

The museum moved into expanded new quarters in the spring of 1999, at 212 W. Walnut St., on the northeastern edge of the Courthouse Square. It is open Monday to Saturday, 10 a.m. to 4 p.m. Admission $3. (417) 667-9602; www.bushwhacker.org.

JOHN BROWN

To say that he is among the most controversial figures in American history is an understatement. There are some who will be outraged to see John Brown listed in a book about bad guys. There are also those who are convinced he was a nut case, no less of a danger than the abortion clinic bombers and political terrorists of our own times—people who don't care whom they kill in the name of a righteous cause.

In times as passionate and dangerous as the late 1850s, in the years preceding the Civil War, Brown was as incendiary a figure as there was in America.

In her journal, Louisa May Alcott referred to him as "St. John the Just," and abolitionist orator Wendell Phillips said that he carried "letters of marque from God Almighty" in a speech at the Cooper Union in New York. Henry David Thoreau wrote in a letter that Brown was "a primitive idealist of rugged mold, a stern moralist who set justice above the law."

But the most influential Abolitionist publication, *The Liberator*, called his raid on Harpers Ferry "a misguided, wild and apparently insane, though disinterested and well-intentioned effort."

Said Abraham Lincoln at the time of Brown's hanging: "Old John Brown has been executed for treason against a state. We cannot object, even though he agreed with us in thinking slavery wrong. That cannot excuse violence, bloodshed, and treason."

In Stephen Vincent Benet's epic poem "John Brown's Body" one of his characters says: "I didn't say he was wrong. I said they had the right to hang the man, / but they'll hang slavery with him."

Since the day of his hanging, December 2, 1859, the debate has raged. His anti-slavery accomplishments in Kansas and Virginia were scant and drenched in blood. But as much as any single figure, he knew what was in store.

"No political action will ever abolish the system of slavery," he told an alarmed Frederick Douglass at their first meeting in 1846. "It will have to go out in blood. Those men who hold slaves have even forfeited their right to live."

There was a strain of insanity that has been traced in his mother's family, and at his trial Brown's lawyers tried to use that as a defense, although they were shouted down by Brown himself. One of his biographers, Oswald Garrison Villard, wrote: "John Brown escaped the family taint. He lived too long and too intimately with many men to have been able to mislead them always."

Brown spent the early years of his life, which began in 1800, in Connecticut and Ohio. His career was marked by repeated failures in business and a long string of lawsuits resulting from them. He was nominally a wool merchant, but his calling was ending slavery.

An avid reader of the Bible, he came to believe that he was chosen by God, like a figure from the Old Testament, to erase the stain of slavery from America. He also fathered twenty children, much like his role models from Genesis.

When his wool business went bankrupt, a sympathetic patron gave him some land in upstate New York to use as a haven for escaped slaves.

National Archives & Records Administration

But Kansas was where the action was. Five of Brown's sons, well-schooled in their father's hatred of slavery, had made their way there for the fight to make Kansas a free state. In 1855, Brown left the New York farm to head west to join them and begin the journey that would end on a gallows in Charles Town, Virginia.

He was then in middle age, but still a vigorous man, and he plunged avidly into the carnage that characterized the Kansas-Missouri border wars.

He settled in Osawatomie, one of the strongholds of abolitionist Kansas. Brown's brother-in-law, Reverend Samuel Adair, was active in the Underground Railroad there and gave the newcomer a warm welcome. But Brown was soon to make things even warmer.

Until his arrival, the Free Staters had been on the defensive, under attack from the slavery forces from Missouri. Several of them had been gunned down in 1855, and when residents of Lawrence attempted to arrest one of the accused killers the following year, the town was sacked by pro-slavery forces.

Brown decided that it was time to send the slave owners what he regarded as a message from the Lord. On May 24, 1856, he led his sons and a few other followers to nearby Pottawatomie Creek and an isolated settlement of pro-slavery families. He dragged five defenseless men from their homes and hacked them to death mercilessly with sabers.

Even in "bleeding Kansas" this was regarded as too much. Brown had to go into hiding, while denying that he had been involved in the slaughter. Later that summer, the slavery forces retaliated by attacking Osawatomie. Although his force was greatly outnumbered, Brown reportedly fought with courage in an unsuccessful defense of the town. One of his sons, Frederick, was killed in the engagement.

The valiant defeat made Brown's reputation among influential abolitionists in the East. From then on he was known as Osawatomie Brown and received a steady flow of financial support. He was intimately involved with the leaders of the Jayhawkers, anti-slavery men who raided Missouri to burn out slaveholders.

In December 1858, he led a raid into Vernon County, Missouri, and liberated several slaves, carrying them back into Kansas. The story caused a sensation in the Northern states, and Brown emerged heroically as a man of action. That suited him perfectly, because he had far bigger things in mind.

Things had calmed down in Kansas with the Free State Party firmly in control. Brown was now looking to the national scene, a chance to strike a blow right at the Southern heartland and lead a great insurrection of slaves.

An arsenal had been established at Harpers Ferry by order of Congress in 1796. Because of its site, at the confluence of the Potomac and Shenandoah Rivers, it had abundant water power and soon became one of the most important communities in the northern part of the state.

By the 1830s, it was connected to the rest of the country by railroad and canal. It was here, at the head of the great Shenandoah Valley, one of the South's greatest agricultural areas, in Brown's mind a symbol of slavery, that he chose to strike. He had discussed the outlines of his plan with abolitionists for two years, but most of them recoiled from a direct assault on an installation of the U.S. government. That would not deter a true believer like Brown. He answered to a higher authority than anyone in Washington, D.C., and he also had what he described as a "well-matured plan."

In the summer of 1859, a small, secretive group of men began gathering in the Maryland hills across the Potomac from Harpers Ferry.

Their leader called himself Isaac Smith. By early autumn their number had grown to twenty-two, and their supply of arms slowly increased. Then on the night of October 16, they struck.

After rounding up several prominent local residents, including George Washington's great-grandnephew, Colonel Lewis Washington, as hostages, they crossed the river and captured the arsenal. Smith was, of course, John Brown, and his "well-matured plan" began to unravel almost immediately.

The first person killed was a free black man, the baggage master of the railroad station. The westbound Baltimore and Ohio train, carrying ammunition Brown had counted on, was stopped by its conductor, who had been warned that the arsenal had fallen. He then proceeded to the next station and telegraphed an alarm.

No slaves rallied to Brown. As the hours went by, the men inside the arsenal began to realize that they were all alone. There would be no insurrection. Some historians believe Brown never really thought there would be; that the entire operation was undertaken as an act of sacrifice and martyrdom, although he never let his cohorts in on that little secret.

By noon of the following day, militia units from the surrounding country poured into the little town and laid siege to the arsenal. Brown and his group retreated into the arsenal's engine house but came under intense fire.

When a force of U.S. Marines, under the leadership of Colonel Robert E. Lee and Lieutenant J. E. B. Stuart, arrived at nightfall, the issue had been settled. Fifteen of the raiders, including two of Brown's sons, were either dead or wounded.

When he still refused to surrender, a dozen Marines crashed through the engine house doors. Brown was beaten to the ground with the butt end of a sword as he attempted to reload his gun. Although Brown claimed the Marines had fired their weapons as they stormed the building, subsequent testimony revealed that they had been ordered to charge only with fixed bayonets. One Marine, in fact, had been killed by gunfire from Brown's force.

Most of the Northern press was convinced the raid was, in the words of the *New York Tribune*, "the act of a madman." But Southerners felt it indicated the true depth of sectional antagonism in the North and that Brown's attack was a real step towards disunion.

Within a week, Brown was on trial for treason in nearby Charles Town. For most of it, he lay on a cot placed on the courtroom floor. He said that the head wounds he received during his capture had incapacitated him.

At other times, however, he roared defiance. "If you seek my blood," he said in an opening statement, "you can have it at any moment, without this mockery of a trial. I am ready for my fate."

In his closing statement, the prosecutor accused Brown of organizing a rebellion and planning to establish a new government within Virginia, "a real thing and not a debating society." The jury took less than two hours to delivery a verdict of guilty, a conclusion that was obvious from the start. On November 2, just seventeen days after Brown seized the arsenal, he was sentenced to hang.

Asked if he had anything to say, Brown made a brief, powerful address. He was obviously speaking to an audience beyond the walls of the courtroom. He said that his only plan was to free a number of slaves and take them to Canada. "Had I acted in behalf of the rich, the powerful, the intelligent, the so-called great . . . it would have been all right and every man in this court would have deemed it an act of reward rather than punishment.

"Now if it is deemed necessary that I should forfeit my life for the furtherance of the ends of justice, and mingle my blood further with the blood of my children and with the blood of millions in this slave country whose rights are disregarded by wicked, cruel, and unjust enactments, I submit: So let it be done."

Brown was executed on December 2, 1859. Many in the North exulted as he was marched to the gallows, realizing that his martyrdom had stirred passions in support of the abolitionist cause as few events had in the past. Even in the South it was understood that the moral landscape had been altered by Brown's actions.

Historian Bruce Catton summed up its meaning in his book *The Coming Fury*. "John Brown was a brutal murderer if there ever was one," he wrote. "And yet to many thousands he had become a martyr, made a martyr by the character of the thing he attacked. Unbalanced to the verge of outright madness, he had touched a profound moral issue, an issue that ran so deep that he took on a strange and moving dignity when he stood upon the scaffold."

The legend that he had stopped to kiss a black infant as he walked down the steps of the jail to the gallows wagon was a journalist's invention, although a poem by John Greenleaf Whittier was written on the theme shortly after his death.

He did, however, hand a note to one of his guards, which read: "I,

John Brown, am now quite certain that the crimes of this guilty land will never be purged away but with blood. I had as I now think vainly flattered myself that without very much bloodshed it might be done."

"This is a beautiful country," he said, as he looked out at the Blue Ridge Mountains from the scaffold. "I never had the pleasure of seeing it before."

Among those who came out to see Brown die were the young actor John Wilkes Booth and, in a unit from Virginia Military Institute, Major Thomas J. Jackson, soon to be known as "Stonewall." Brown's body was taken to his former farm in New York for burial.

Nineteen months later, as troops from the 12th Massachusetts Regiment marched through Boston bound for war, they improvised a song to an old military tune. Their new words went: "John Brown's body lies a'moldering in the grave . . . but his soul goes marching on."

THE SITES

Harpers Ferry The arsenal at Harpers Ferry was destroyed by retreating Federal troops in April 1861 to prevent its machinery from falling into the hands of Stonewall Jackson's occupying army. The town changed hands repeatedly during the early years of the Civil War, before being secured by Union forces following the Battle of Gettysburg. It then became part of the newly formed state of West Virginia.

But with the town in ruins, most residents of Harpers Ferry never returned after the war, and it dwindled down to a village of a few hundred souls. It has been a National Historical Park since 1963.

The engine house where Brown and his group made their stand remains on Old Arsenal Square. It was dismantled and shipped to the Chicago Columbian Exposition of 1893 as an attraction, then was returned. It stood on the top of the bluff for many years but now has been moved nearer to its original location. A monument to Brown, erected by the Baltimore and Ohio Railroad in 1895, marks the site of the engine house at the time of the siege.

An excellent visitor center offers exhibits and interpretive programs, including walking tours to many points of interest around the town associated with Brown, black history, and the Civil War.

Harpers Ferry is located 65 miles west of Washington, D.C., by way of I-270 and U.S. 340. The park is open daily, 8 a.m. to 5 p.m. Admission is $5 per vehicle. (304) 535-6222; www.nps.gov/hafe.

John Brown Wax Museum Outside the boundary of the historical park in the town of Harpers Ferry is the John Brown Wax Museum, depicting the life of the liberator in various tableaux. It is open daily, 9 a.m. to 5 p.m., mid-March through mid-December. Admission $6; children 6–12, $4. (304) 535-6342; www.johnbrownwaxmuseum.com.

Charles Town Charles Town, where Brown was tried and hanged, is 6 miles south of Harpers Ferry, on U.S. 340. The Courthouse, built in 1836, sits on land donated to the town by its namesake, Colonel Charles Washington, younger brother of the first President.

The room in which Brown was tried has been restored to its appearance of 1859. The courthouse is located at the corner of George and Washington Sts. and is open daily, 9 a.m. to 5 p.m. Free admission. (304) 728-3240.

The Jefferson County Museum, in the basement of the Charles Town Library, has displays relating to the trial and also some Brown memorabilia. Its location is 200 E. Washington St., and it is open 10 a.m. to 4 p.m., Monday to Saturday, April to November. Free admission. (304) 728-8628.

An historic marker commemorates the site of Brown's execution, on S. Samuel St., between McCurdy St. and Beckwith Alley. It is one block north and four blocks east of the Courthouse.

John Brown Park John Brown Park is just west of the business district of Osawatomie, Kansas, on Main at 10th St. The park is situated on the battlefield where Brown's force tried unsuccessfully to defend the town from pro-slavery troops avenging the massacre at Pottawatomie Creek in 1856.

A life-sized statue of Brown was dedicated here in 1955. It bears the inscription: "He fought. He lost. But in losing won." Kansas Governor Alf Landon, who ran for president the following year, eulogized Brown at the dedication by saying: "Our institutions can best be safeguarded by recalling the courage that made them possible."

Atop the highest ridge in the park is the cabin built by Brown's brother-in-law, Reverend Samuel Adair. Brown stayed there often during his time in Osawatomie. The log house is enclosed by a granite portico, which was dedicated by Theodore Roosevelt, in 1910. It is open 1 p.m. to 5 p.m., Wednesday through Sunday. Donations accepted.

Osawatomie is located 26 miles south of the Olathe exit of I-35 by way of U.S. 169.

Kansas State House The most famous artist's rendition of Brown is John Steuart Curry's depiction of him as a flaming-eyed, white-bearded figure of wrath, trailed by a pillar of fire, straight out of the Old Testament. It is part of a series of murals on Kansas history in the State House, Topeka. The Capitol building, at Jackson and Harrison Sts., is open Monday to Friday, 8 a.m. to 5 p.m. Free admission. (785) 296-3966.

Brown's Grave The grave in which Brown's body molders is located near the resort town of Lake Placid, in New York's Adirondack Mountains area. The burial place and Brown's restored farmhouse are reached by a landscaped walkway. The site is 2 miles south of town, off New York 73. The grounds are open all year. The house is open 10 a.m. to 5 p.m., Wednesday to Saturday; opening at 1 p.m., Sunday; Memorial Day to late October. Free admission. (518) 523-3900.

ANNUAL EVENT

John Brown Jamboree Osawatomie remembers Brown's sojourn there with the John Brown Jamboree. There are parades, crafts shows, carnival attractions, and an antique car show. It is held the weekend following the third Thursday in June.

JOHN WILKES BOOTH

He had been disappointed in almost everything in his life. Professionally, John Wilkes Booth was regarded as no match for his late father, Junius Brutus Booth, Sr., and was a far less accomplished actor than his celebrated brother, Edwin. He never received critical acclaim in the nation's largest cities and had to be content with starring roles on the Richmond stage before the Civil War.

While his dark good looks and deep-set eyes made him popular with the ladies, his profession and his politics made him an unsuitable match for the one woman he loved. Lucy Hale was the daughter of New Hampshire's abolitionist senator John P. Hale. The two were secretly engaged, but marriage seemed out of the question. He had looked on in anguish and rage as the Southern cause, in which he believed wholeheartedly, was crushed.

Although his name was known and he made the then princely sum of $20,000 a year, he bristled with grievances.

In April 1865, John Wilkes Booth was a man willing to attempt anything to set his frustrations right and achieve the fame he felt he deserved. He became, instead, the most despised man of his era, the killer of a president who approached sainthood in popular esteem.

The assassination of Abraham Lincoln may be the most painstakingly examined incident in all of American history. For generations scholars have pored over every scrap of evidence, trying to sift fact from legend. How extensive was the plot to kill the President? Were there conspirators who were never found?

More than 130 years later, the family of Dr. Samuel Mudd, who set Booth's broken ankle on his escape from Washington, are still trying to convince the government that their forebear was an innocent man, convicted wrongfully.

The details of Booth's final act are known to everyone with the slightest interest in American history. On April 14, 1865, just five days after the surrender of General Robert E. Lee's army at Appomattox, and with Washington still rejoicing at the end of the terrible war, Booth made his way to the President's box at Ford's Theatre. In the midst of a performance of the comedy *Our American Cousin*, he murdered Lincoln with a single shot to the back of the head from a Derringer pistol.

Booth was twenty-six years old. His last stage role had been five months earlier, as Mark Antony in a production of *Julius Caesar*, in

New York. It had been the first and last time he appeared with his two brothers, Edwin and Junius Brutus, Jr.

But he had been busy since then, rehearsing what he saw as his greatest role. He plotted first the kidnapping and then the murder of the President he had grown to hate.

"What a glorious opportunity there is for a man to immortalize himself by killing Lincoln," he had said. "Our country owed all her troubles to him and God simply made me the instrument of His punishment," he had written in his diary.

Booth was born in Belair, Maryland, just a few miles south of the Mason-Dixon Line. But he

National Archives & Records Administration

identified totally with the South, partly because it was where he had enjoyed his greatest fame and partly because he believed in the superiority of the white race.

He had joined a Richmond military unit in 1859 but only because, he told friends, he wanted to witness the hanging of John Brown. He did and then resigned, taking a pass on combat in the Civil War. He explained later he had promised his mother that he would not join the Confederate Army.

There was some speculation that he had engaged in smuggling medical supplies to the South. But for the most part, he spent the war in the company of beautiful women, one of whom slashed him across the face with a knife when she learned that her affections had been betrayed. Pictures of five women, including Miss Hale, were found on Booth's body after his death.

In the autumn of 1864, just before his New York engagement, he traveled to Montreal and met with a group of Southerners. They devised a plot to kidnap the President, carrying him off to Richmond and holding him hostage to obtain an armistice.

Booth returned to Washington, and with an indeterminate number of conspirators—seven were put on trial after the assassination and four were hanged—began to devise a scheme. But one attempt after another was foiled. Either the President's plans were changed at the last minute or Booth's group could not get close enough to their man.

On one occasion, they managed to surround the President's carriage on the streets of the Capital, only to find that he wasn't inside.

When Richmond fell to the Union army, Booth changed the plan. The President had to die.

He arrived at Ford's Theatre to pick up some mail on the morning of April 14 and learned that Lincoln would attend that evening's performance. Observers said later that he turned pale and seemed to be sick.

Booth quickly hired a horse to be waiting for him that evening at the stage door. He returned to the theater and jammed open the door leading to the Presidential box, then drilled a peephole directly behind the chair where Lincoln would sit.

Finally, he met with his fellow conspirators to go over plans to kill Vice President Andrew Johnson and Secretary of State William Seward that would eventually prove unsuccessful.

He went back to the theater at 9:30 p.m., paced around the back of the house, went next door to a saloon for a quick brandy, and began to climb the stairs towards the box at 10:15 p.m. He showed his calling card stating his name and occupation to get past the police guard, who had moved into a dress circle seat to watch the play instead of stationing himself at the door to the box.

Unobserved, Booth opened the door to Lincoln's box, walked quickly to the President and fired one bullet into his brain. One of the play's biggest laugh lines had just been spoken by Harry Hawk. "Don't know the manners of good society, eh? Well, I guess I know enough to turn you inside out, old gal—you sockdologizing old man trap."

The theater was filled with laughter. Aside from those sitting beside the stricken President, no one seemed to hear the shot.

Smoke from the pistol curled upwards as the women in the box began to scream. Major Reed Rathbone, sitting behind and to the side of Lincoln, leaped up to grapple with Booth, who slashed him with a knife. Booth then leaped from the box, which sat 12 feet above the stage, but caught his foot in a piece of bunting and fell heavily to the ground, breaking a bone in his ankle.

"*Sic semper tyrannis*," he hollered, brandishing his knife as Mrs. Lincoln screamed hysterically. Only as he limped to the wings did the theater recover from its shock. Men ran towards the Presidential box and in pursuit of Booth. He slashed at the orchestra leader as he tried to restrain him, then grabbed the reins of his waiting horse, mounted it, and galloped off through the streets of Washington.

Booth crossed the Anacostia River, talked his way past an Army sentry (although, incredibly, giving the soldier his name), and made for the inn owned by Mary Surratt. He gathered supplies that had been stored there and was joined by David Herold, another of the plotters.

Moving steadily south, they reached the town of Waldorf, Maryland, at 4 a.m., and went to the home of Dr. Mudd. Here is where the conspiracy stories intersect. There is a good deal of evidence to suggest that Booth and Mudd had met before and that the doctor may have been brought into some of the early kidnapping plans.

Mudd's defenders insist even if that were true, the doctor had no way of knowing that Lincoln had been murdered and, moreover, he did not recognize the actor because of his "facial hair."

When Mudd learned the truth the following morning, he ordered Booth and Herold to leave his house. They moved on through swampland and made contact with a Confederate agent, Thomas A. Jones. He advised them to stay concealed in the thicket, so they remained hidden there for six days.

By this time, all other suspected plotters were in custody and the entire country had been roused in a furious manhunt for the assassin. The fugitives crossed the Potomac and entered Virginia on April 22. Booth had expected a hero's welcome there, but instead he found frightened people who wanted nothing to do with him.

Dr. Richard Stuart, suspicious of the unkempt pair, would not allow them in his house or give them food, but said they could rest in his barn. Booth sent him a sarcastic note and a $5 bill "for what we did get." Stuart threw the papers into the fire, but his son-in-law pulled them out. The sarcastic tone of Booth's note, indicating that he had received no help from Stuart, was all that saved Stuart from arrest when he was charged with being part of the conspiracy.

On April 24, Booth and Herold came to the farm of Richard Garrett, across the Rappahannock River, near the town of Port Royal. They posed as Confederate veterans trying to make their way home, and the Garretts sympathetically put them up.

Two days later, just before dawn, units of the 16th New York Cavalry arrived at the Garrett farm. Seeing the two men in the barn, they surrounded the structure and demanded identification. Herold ran out with his hands up, but Booth continued to shout defiantly at the soldiers.

"Well, my brave boys," he called, "prepare me a stretcher and place another stain on our glorious banner."

Someone at the back of the barn set some straw on fire, and in a matter of minutes the entire building was ablaze. Booth could be seen leaning on a crutch with a carbine rifle in his hand. There was a shot, fired by Sergeant Boston Corbett, and Booth crumpled, paralyzed with a wound at the top of the spine.

There had been strict orders that Booth was to be taken alive, but Corbett testified he saw him raise his rifle towards one of the officers. No one else noticed such a threatening move, however, and in an act eerily similar to that of Jack Ruby in 1963, Corbett killed the one man who knew all the details of the assassination plot.

Corbett was a severely disordered individual. He was a religious zealot and had castrated himself in order to resist temptation more effectively. After shooting Booth, he was given a job as sergeant-of-arms for the Kansas Legislature. He lost the assignment, however, when he fired several shots into a session of that body.

He was committed to an asylum, escaped, and vanished. But he had done his harm to history.

Booth was carried to the Garrett front porch. He told the soldiers that the Garretts had no idea of his identity and apologized for the destruction of their barn.

He clung to life for about a day but was beyond medical help. Finally, he murmured, "Useless! Useless!" He summoned the commanding officer and said: "Tell my mother I died for my country. I did what I thought was best." A few moments later he was dead.

His body was returned to Washington by gunboat and buried under the floor of the federal prison there. On July 7, Herold, Mrs. Surratt, and two others were hanged at the same penitentiary. At his family's request, Booth's remains were reinterred in the family plot in Baltimore in 1869.

Edwin Booth was overwhelmed at the enormity of his brother's crime. He retired from the stage but was forced to come back to pay off debts in 1866. The audience jeered his opening night in *Hamlet*, but the actor's repeated statements of contrition eventually won back the public.

He reimbursed the Garretts for the loss of their barn. But his theater failed, his wife went insane, and several of his siblings were also afflicted with financial distress and acute depression. Edwin Booth died in 1893 a shattered man, "looking forward to death as the great-est boon the Almighty has given us."

At the hour of his funeral in New York, the upper three floors of Ford's Theatre collapsed, killing twenty people.

Ten years later, a man named John St. Helen poisoned himself in Enid, Oklahoma. Before his death, he told several people that he was actually John Wilkes Booth. He had escaped the burning barn, he claimed, and had wandered through Texas and Oklahoma for the last thirty-eight years.

His body was mummified and was a carnival attraction at small-town circuses until the 1970s. Six physicians who examined the corpse stated in affidavits that it bore wounds consistent with those sustained by Booth after the assassination and with other of his known injuries.

Convinced by amateur historians that the body in the family plot wasn't Booth's, several of his descendants petitioned a Baltimore court to exhume it and conduct tests. Cemetery records, however, indicated that to avoid desecration Booth's body had been removed to another part of the cemetery shortly after burial. Its exact location had been lost.

The court ruled in 1995 that whoever is buried in Booth's grave would rest in peace. The request for exhumation was denied, and the final answer to the riddle of Booth's death declared unknowable.

THE SITES

Ford's Theatre Ford's was a relatively new addition to Washington's theatrical life when Lincoln was assassinated there. John T. Ford, sens-ing an opportunity, bought the former First Baptist Church building in the early days of the Civil War and turned its interior into a theater. Ford's instincts were right. The capital was crowded with soldiers seeking entertainment, and his theater was filled on many nights. Booking the popular actress Laura Keane in April 1865 was a master stroke. It was one of Ford's most popular attractions.

After Lincoln's death, the theater operated under the shadow of tragedy. Ford was arrested for suspicion of complicity, but was soon released. The theater, however, was confiscated by the government, which plastered over the auditorium and used it as a warehouse. Eventually, Ford was paid $100,000 for the property.

For years, the building was abandoned, although a museum of Lincoln memorabilia was brought there from Illinois in the 1930s. Shortly after the centennial of Lincoln's death, however, restoration of the theater's interior to its appearance of the 1860s was begun. Now operated by the National Park Service it is once again an active theater, with a full schedule of performances and galas through the year. An excellent museum of the assassination, displaying many original artifacts from that night, including the pistol used by Booth, occupies its basement level.

Ford's Theatre is located at 511 10th St. NW. The interior is open daily, 9 a.m. to 5 p.m., except when performances are scheduled. Call in advance for times at (202) 426-6924; www.fordtheatre.org.

The Museum opens the same hours and is not affected by the performance schedule. Both the Theatre and the Museum are free.

The Surratt House The Surratts were once the most prominent family in Clinton, Maryland. In the 1860s, the place was called Surrattsville and the Surratt Tavern, built in 1852, was a noted stopping place for travelers in Maryland's Tidewater area. It was also known as a safe house for Confederate agents. This was Booth's first stop after fleeing Washington, and it was here that he picked up previously stashed supplies.

Innkeeper Mary Surratt was arrested and charged with being his accomplice. Although the debate still goes on over her degree of involvement, she became the first woman hanged by the federal government in July 1865. The tavern and house have been restored and are now a museum of that era, with costumed guides explaining its involvement with Booth.

The Surratt House is located at 9118 Brandywine Rd. It is south from the I-95 Beltway on Maryland 5, into Clinton on Maryland 223, and then left on Brandywine Rd. It is open Thursday and Friday, 11 a.m. to 3 p.m., and weekends, 12 p.m. to 4 p.m., except for the last two weeks in December. Admission is $3. (301) 868-1121; www.surratt.org.

Dr. Samuel A. Mudd House and Museum The story of Dr. Samuel Mudd is even more controversial than that of Surratt. He was thirty-one years old when he was arrested after setting Booth's broken ankle in his house at Waldorf, Maryland. Tried by a military court in Washington, Mudd escaped execution but was sentenced to life imprisonment on an island in the Dry Tortugas, off Florida.

During an outbreak of yellow fever, Mudd performed heroically to save lives. A movie about his work there, *Prisoner of Shark Island*, was made in the 1930s and directed by John Ford—coincidentally, the name of the man who owned Ford's Theatre. Mudd was pardoned by

President Andrew Johnson during his last weeks in office in 1869. But he was a broken and bitter man. He went to his grave asserting his innocence in 1883, "the victim of a nation's rage," said his wife.

His descendants have fought ever since for a full exoneration. They contend that a military court had no authority to try him as a civilian. That was also the argument used by Dr. Mudd's attorney in 1865. It failed then, and it has not moved the U.S. Army yet, being turned down by the Board of Correction of Military Records in 1998. Complicating the procedure is the contention of other researchers that Mudd had indeed known Booth previously and also gave his pursuers confusing directions.

The Dr. Samuel A. Mudd House and Museum is just east of the intersection of Maryland 5 and 228, about 18 miles south of I-95. It is furnished with family belongings. The house is open on Wednesday, Saturday and Sunday 11 a.m. to 4 p.m., early April to Thanksgiving weekend. Admission is $3. (301) 274-4232.

The Garrett Farm The Garrett Farm no longer exists, but a Virginia historical marker points out the site of Booth's death. It is located on U.S. 301, 3 miles south of Port Royal. The crumbling farmhouse stood here until the late 1930s, but only a suggestion of its location remains.

RELATED SITES

Fort Jefferson Work began on Fort Jefferson in 1846, and after thirty years, although still unfinished, it was abandoned as obsolete. It was here, on Garden Key, in Florida's Dry Tortugas, that Dr. Mudd was imprisoned for four years, until his pardon in 1869. The island was occupied by federal troops during the Civil War and then became a prison for deserters and the Lincoln conspirators. It was prone to outbreaks of yellow fever and was also hit by a hurricane in 1874, which were major considerations in its abandonment. Located in the Gulf of Mexico, off Key West, the island is accessible by private boat or chartered plane. It is open all year. Information is available through Everglades National Park, at (305) 242-7700; www.nps.gov/ever.

William Petersen House After he was shot, Lincoln was carried across the street from Ford's Theatre to the William Petersen House. There he was pronounced dead the following morning. The home, at 516 10th St. NW, has been restored to its appearance of that time and is administered by the National Park Service as part of the Ford's Theatre Site. Open daily, 9 a.m. to 5 p.m. Free admission. (202) 426-6924.

Henry Ford Museum The chair in which Lincoln was sitting at Ford's Theatre is now part of the displays at the Henry Ford Museum in Dearborn, Michigan. A vast collection of Americana, the museum acquired the chair at auction in 1929. It still is marked by the blood stains from the dying President's head wound. The chair underwent restoration to protect the upholstery in 1998, but the stained area was not touched. The Museum is located at the Village Rd. exit of Michigan 39, about 8 miles west of downtown Detroit. Open daily, 9:30 a.m. to 5 p.m. Admission to the Ford Museum is $14. The ticket is also good for the adjoining Greenfield Village during the winter months. Otherwise, that part of the complex requires a separate admission. (313) 271-1620; www.hfmgv.org.

BELLE STARR

The camera doesn't lie. Well, not much, at least. So if that's the case, reports about Belle Starr's fatal attraction to men on the wild Oklahoma frontier must be somewhat exaggerated. The wildest looking thing in the old photographs is Belle herself. The kindest description of her, even allowing for changes in standards of beauty and the toll of sun and wind, is frumpy.

The most famous picture of Belle, standing beside a gentleman friend, an outlaw with the evocative name of Blue Duck, shows a woman as plain as an Oklahoma haystack. Thin-lipped and hawk-nosed, she appears old before her time, with a face accustomed to hard use; more grandmotherly than ravishing even in a silk dress, feathered hat, and earrings.

She was thirty-seven years old when the photograph was taken.

It may also be an overstatement to describe her as a bandit queen, which is how she is most frequently pigeonholed. She certainly ran with some of the more infamous lawbreakers of the time. Cole Younger probably sired her daughter. Jesse James was an old pal. She married into the Starr family, the most notorious bunch of thugs in the Cherokee Nation.

But Belle herself, while possibly participating in some horse-stealing and maybe being present while an elderly couple was being tortured to get at their savings, was no worse than she had to be.

Myra Belle actually was born into rather genteel circumstances. Her father traced his lineage back to the distinguished Shirley family of Tidewater

American Stock/Archive Photos

Virginia. She grew up in Carthage, Missouri, and, as her biographers note with delight, attended a school for young ladies. Exactly what sort of school that may have been on the Missouri frontier of the early 1860s is not quite clear, but the Shirleys were one of the fashionable families of the area.

That childhood idyll ended, however, with the start of the Civil War. The family sympathized with the South and Carthage was bitterly contested territory. Her older brother rode with Quantrill's Raiders and was killed in 1865. Some accounts describe Belle as a spy during these years, but since she was just fifteen years old when her family left the area that sounds improbable.

The Shirleys departed for Texas to get out of the war zone, settling outside of Dallas in sharply reduced circumstances. By the spring of 1866, however, the family had rebuilt its fortunes and was farming 800 acres.

But back in Missouri the war never really ended. Former friends from respectable families had taken in bitterness to the outlaw life. When in need of a place to hide out for a while, they called upon the Shirleys and were welcomed. One of these travelers, fresh from the holdup of the Clay County Savings and Loan, in Liberty, Missouri, was Cole Younger.

He knew the family through their mutual association with Quantrill and during his stay in Texas he got to know eighteen-year-old Belle even better. A few months after his departure, she gave birth to a girl named Pearl.

There are those who insist that the relationship with Younger was innocent, the timing of her pregnancy mere coincidence or misrepresented by scandal-mongering biographers. Nonetheless, the arrival of Pearl is irrefutable, and Belle chose to give her the last name of Younger, which would seem to indicate an attachment stronger than a handshake.

In later years, moreover, when Belle settled in Okla-homa, the name she gave to her place on the Canadian River was Younger's Bend.

Still, in 1867, Younger moved on, there had been no marriage and she had a child to raise. So when another friend from the old neighborhood in Missouri, Jim Reed, turned up in Texas, Belle was inclined to surrender her charms to him.

This was the beginning of a string of liaisons that led one historian, Paul I. Wellman, to characterize Belle as a sort of Typhoid Mary, "a carrier of outlawry." One affair merged seamlessly with another and each of her new lovers seemed to be connected somehow with her former one, either through being related or having murdered him.

Always, however, Belle was in control, choosing each paramour with an independence rare in a woman of those times.

She may actually have married Reed, although the evidence is, at best, inconclusive. She did have a son by him in 1869, and called him Ed after her dead brother.

Reed was a wild sort, a man with a gift for choosing precisely the sort of companions who would get him deeper into trouble. He rode with the James Gang and became involved in an endless string of illicit activities in Texas and California.

Belle testified during a civil lawsuit years later that she had been with Reed in 1873 when he and two buddies obtained $30,000 from an aged chief of the Creek Nation. They accomplished this by stringing up the man and his wife seven times and nearly strangling them until he revealed where he was hiding the money (which he, in turn, had stolen from the tribal treasury).

Reed was eventually killed for reward money by a deputy sheriff, whom he thought, mistakenly as it turned out, was a friend. That event left Belle without funds and resulted in her marriage in 1880 to Sam Starr, whose last name she took.

The Starrs had been involved in an intra-tribal feud with another Cherokee family, the Rosses, for almost 50 years. The leader of the clan, Tom Starr, actually signed a peace treaty between himself and the entire Cherokee Nation, so feared was he in Oklahoma. But the vendetta still smoldered in the following generation and it, eventually, would cost Sam his life.

In the meantime, though, he and Belle settled down on Cherokee land at Younger's Bend, happily running a rustling operation and giving refuge to the odd outlaw who came their way. The Starrs were each sentenced to a year in prison in 1882 for stealing horses by Isaac Parker, the feared "hanging judge" of Fort Smith, Arkansas.

That was a fairly lenient sentence by Parker's standards and there is some indication that Belle somehow charmed the old boy. It was the only jail time she ever served and she spent it making cane-bottomed chairs in the Detroit House of Correction, regarded as a model reformatory.

Reform, however, was not in Belle's game plan. After Starr was gunned down in 1886 by a member of the Ross clan (who met his end in the same battle), Belle took up with a long succession of outlaw lovers. Most notable among them were Jack Spaniard, Jim French, Jim July, and the aforementioned Blue Duck.

Life was good and the occasional sale of other people's livestock brought in a decent amount of money. She was known for riding into Fort Smith, wearing six-guns and sitting in for a few hours with the boys at a poker game. Belle always rode side saddle. She felt any other position was not ladylike.

But there were unfortunate family problems. Her daughter, Pearl, had become pregnant and Belle was highly offended by this, perhaps forgetting the circumstances of Pearl's own birth. She sent her daughter off to Arkansas to give birth and then refused to allow her granddaughter into her home.

Her son, Ed Reed, was also a handful. He had been involved in stealing horses and Belle had disciplined him with a whip. There are also reports that the mother-son relationship had taken a much darker turn.

Reporters found their way to Younger's Bend to interview the Bandit Queen for the eastern press. "I regard myself as a woman who has seen much of life," she told one of them, obviously recalling the lessons in modesty she had learned back at school in Carthage.

New settlers also were moving in on the land. Belle entered into a rental agreement with a newcomer, Edgar Watson, and there were problems with the terms of the deal. Several nasty confrontations had taken place and she was insisting that Watson move out.

On February 3, 1889, on the way home from an overnight stay with friends, Belle was gunned down on the road to Younger's Bend. She had been blown from her horse by a shotgun blast to the back, and then finished off by another shot to the face at point blank range.

No one was ever convicted of the killing. Watson was arrested and arraigned before Judge Parker but had to be released for lack of evidence. He, eventually, was killed by a posse in Florida.

There are those who believe the killer was her son, Ed. In several documents relating to Belle their incestuous relationship is attested to by neighbors and members of the Cherokee Indian police. The road on which the shooting took place gave no chance for concealment and Belle would have ridden right past her killer before he shot her. It isn't likely that she would have turned her back on Watson. But she may have done so if the gunman were her son.

He, too, was never tried, and was killed seven years later in a saloon brawl in Wagoner, Oklahoma.

Pearl Younger found a burial place for her mother on a ridge above the Canadian River, near Younger's Bend. She had a bell, a star and an image of Belle's favorite horse carved on the stone, along with the following inscription: "Shed not for her the bitter tear, Nor give the heart to vain regret. Tis but the casket that lies here; The gem that fills it sparkles yet."

Then Pearl decided to go to work as a prostitute.

THE SITES

The Shirley family home, at Carthage, Missouri, is preserved as part of an historical village setting called Red Oak II. Local artist Lowell Davis purchased several buildings in his boyhood home, the village of Red Oak, which had been abandoned.

He assembled them in a community-like setting, recalling the town he had grown up in during the 1930s. Among the other structures he moved to the area was Belle Starr's girlhood residence. It is a substantial frame house, one that a leading citizen would have been proud to own in the Carthage of the 1860s. It now contains a small museum describing her life.

Red Oak is located east of U.S. 71, from Carthage, on Missouri 96. Turn north at County Road 120 (watch closely because the sign to Red Oak II is hard to spot) and follow it another 2 miles to the turnoff.

The village is open only occasionally and it is best to call in advance. Posted hours are daily, 10 a.m. to 5 p.m., March through Christmas Eve, but it is best to call in advance at (417) 358-9018. Free.

The area around what was once Younger's Bend, Oklahoma, has become prime recreation land after an extensive dam building program on the Canadian River. Belle Starr's grave site, near her former ranch, is south of Porum, about 12 miles from I-40 on Oklahoma 2.

The original burial site was bought at a tax sale in 1940. Through the years, weather and tourists had damaged the stone so severely, even though it was located on an unmarked and unpaved side road, that only two separated pieces were left. A duplicate of the original was made and moved to the present site.

HENRY PLUMMER

On a bitterly cold January day in 1864 a group of angry, determined men walked through the snowy streets of the mining town of Bannack, Montana, to arrest Sheriff Henry Plummer and two of his deputies.

In a matter of moments the deputies had been lynched. "You men know me better than this," protested the thirty-one-year-old sheriff.

He was ignored, another rope was produced, and despite his pleas for a trial or, at least, a few moments to pray, Plummer was hanged on gallows that he had built for the bandit gang terrorizing the area.

In the opinion of the vigilantes who performed the executions, Plummer himself was the mastermind behind the recent holdups and killings, the organizer of a secret band of outlaws who hid behind the authority of the sheriff.

In six weeks, the vigilantes strung up twenty-two men. The hangings stopped the crime wave, but for the next three years the vigilance committees went on to function as the effective law in Montana's mining country, with no one held responsible for their actions.

Eventually, the miners warned that they would retaliate unless the vigilantes disbanded. When the territorial governor issued an order for them to cease operations in 1867, the cycle of violence ended.

The hanging of Henry Plummer remains the most notorious incident in Montana's frontier history. Most accounts of the affair agree with the original take on his guilt. He was, indeed, running a highly organized gang of cutthroats who had engulfed the towns of Bannack and Virginia City in a wave of lawlessness.

A few revisionist historians argue, however, that Plummer actually was hanged because he was trying to protect innocent men from the power-mad vigilantes. If that was the case, Plummer had to be one of the most unlucky men in the history of American law enforcement, because misfortune and mayhem dogged his every move.

He was born in Maine and moved to California as a teenager to get in on the Gold Rush. In 1851, Plummer appeared in Nevada City, where he ran a bakery and gambled at the Hotel Parie. He, apparently, did well in this booming community in the heart of the Mother Lode country. He was elected marshal within five years, but in an unsuccessful attempt at capturing an accused killer, he gunned down the sheriff, instead.

This caused some talk, although it never progressed much farther than allegations. Plummer, in fact, became the Democratic Party candidate for a state assembly seat, but was defeated. Still, his career in

Virginia City, Montana. National Archives & Records Administration

California politics seemed bright. Then he became involved in the unfortunate Vedder affair.

Plummer rented a house in Nevada City in 1860 to a gambler named John Vedder and his wife, Lucy. Vedder was a nasty piece of work, a bully and wife-beater who flew into jealous rages whenever anyone paid attention to Lucy. Plummer, for whatever reasons, became quite concerned over Mrs. Vedder's well-being.

He tried to arrange a divorce through a local attorney and scheduled special police guards to protect her. On an evening when her husband planned to take a stagecoach out of town, he thoughtfully arranged to stand guard duty himself. When Vedder changed his mind and arrived home at 2 a.m., he was vexed to find Plummer there.

There was an exchange of gunfire, and Vedder got the worst of it. Lucy ran into the street screaming that the marshal had shot her husband, a rather peculiar reaction from one who was supposedly being protected. Apparently, a jury thought so, too. Plummer was convicted of second-degree murder and sentenced to ten years in San Quentin Prison.

He was taken seriously ill, however, and his sentence was commuted by the governor after six months as an act of mercy. But the incident ended his political aspirations in California.

Upon recovering his health, he decided to try his luck in the new gold fields of the Idaho Territory. While in Orofino, Plummer got himself in another scrape, this time with a saloonkeeper, and shot the man dead. He fled town two steps ahead of a lynch mob, amid accusations that he had organized several holdups of miners in the area.

Plummer decided to cross the Bitterroots into what is now

Montana (but was then still part of the Idaho Territory), arriving in Bannack in January 1863. But he could not shake the past. A man named Jack Cleveland soon turned up in Bannack. He claimed to be tailing Plummer and to have information of his doings in California.

There are two versions of the events that followed. According to contemporary accounts, Plummer shot Cleveland to shut him up. Plummer's apologists insist that this yet again was simply a matter of self-defense and that Cleveland had first drawn a pistol on him.

By May, Plummer had been elected sheriff of the entire mining district. From all accounts, he was a highly personable man, "flamboyantly courageous," and one who seemed to inspire confidence. But things soon began to go terribly wrong.

A string of robberies took place on the road from Bannack to Virginia City, and all of them seemed to happen when large shipments of gold were being moved out or when wealthy passengers were traveling. Most historians trace this crime wave to Plummer's organizational abilities.

Virginia Rowe Towle, a Montana historian, credited him with being the greatest "genius of American crime until the Prohibition era and it is doubtful if any of the racket kings topped him." His gang was blamed for the deaths of anywhere from one hundred to three hundred men. They called themselves the Innocents and identified one another by a special knot in their ties.

As sheriff, Plummer knew about gold shipments and could tip off his cohorts. He also gave scarves to miners carrying large sums of money as a bon voyage gift. That enabled his men to identify them readily.

The revisionists, such as R. E. Mather and Michael Umphrey, insist, however, that the total number of robberies was four and only one man was shot. But the real reason Plummer was disliked was that he was "too tolerant" in the face of growing impatience with the robberies.

Late in 1863, a man named George Ives, known to be friendly with Plummer, was arrested and charged with an especially brutal slaying of a miner. He was placed on trial in Virginia City and hanged on December 21. Before his death Ives apparently implicated others, and the first vigilance committees were formed to act upon what had been learned.

On January 4, 1864, the vigilantes overtook two members of the Innocents, Red Yeager and George Brown. Yeager, in an effort to save himself, gave up Plummer's name. Six days later, they came for the sheriff.

Even after Plummer's death, the lynchings went on, capped by five at one time in Virginia City before a crowd of several thousand. Chief executioner for the vigilantes was John X. Beidler. When asked if he hadn't felt for the fellows that he had hanged as he put the rope around their necks, Beidler replied: "Yes, I felt for the left ear." For his efforts he later became a deputy marshal.

It has to be recognized that many of the newspaper accounts of these events were written by men who were either sympathetic to the vigilance committees or intimidated by them. The vigilantes operated ruthlessly and with a high degree of secrecy. There are just enough questions about their methods to give credence to the accusation that Plummer was actually killed for opposing them.

Still, with a trail of so many dead men in his past, one has to wonder if Plummer was quite the innocent his defenders claim. It seems more likely that desperate times required desperate measures in Montana.

The Sites

Bannack State Park Bannack is now preserved as a state historical park. The town, which reached a peak population of about 3,000, grew up around a gold strike on Grasshopper Creek in July 1862. Four months after Plummer was hanged it became capital of the newly-created Montana Territory. But within a year the gold gave out and the state government moved to Virginia City.

Bannack slowly deteriorated, its buildings falling into ruins. But the remnants of the first territorial capital, hotel, and jail have been stabilized and still stand along the main street. A few miners' cabins are also in the area. Displays at the state park visitor center explain the town's development and recapitulate the story of Plummer and his fate.

The town is located on a paved road running south from Montana 278, 21 miles west of I-15 from Dillon. The park is open daily, dawn to dusk. Visitor center hours are 10 a.m. to 6 p.m., Memorial Day to Labor Day. $3 per vehicle. (406) 834-3413; www.bannack.org.

Virginia City There are several reminders of Plummer and the vigilantes in the Alder Gulch area, surrounding Virginia City. This was the second and larger gold strike in Montana, and the community soon eclipsed the older settlement at Bannack. At its peak, Virginia City had 10,000 inhabitants.

This settlement, by the way, should not be confused with the roughly contemporary mining camp at Virginia City, Nevada. Many of the miners in both places were Confederate sympathizers during the Civil War years. In Montana, they wanted to name the town Varina, to honor the wife of Jefferson Davis. But a local judge would have none of that and declared it to be Virginia City—even though that also spoke of the South and touched off a good deal of confusion with its Nevada namesake.

This Virginia City was in its turn replaced as Montana's capital in 1876 by the newer mining camp at Helena. As with Bannack, the process of decay went on until local preservationists managed to begin restoration efforts in the 1940s. Virginia City is now one of the largest and best-preserved old-time mining camps in the West. It is located 60 miles south of I-90, by way of U.S. 287 and Montana 287.

Several old buildings have been restored and contain historical exhibits. The best of these museums is the Thompson-Hickman Memorial, at 218 E. Wallace St., a structure donated to the town by a local resident who made good in New York City. It is open daily, 10 a.m. to 5 p.m., mid-May to mid-September. Donations accepted. (406) 843-5346.

Nevada City Just west of Virginia City is Nevada City, one of the smaller Alder Gulch mining towns. It is now run as a museum of the era, with several buildings from around the territory moved to the location. The place where George Ives was hanged, the first of the vigilante actions in late 1863, is marked. The museum is open from 10 a.m. to 7 p.m., mid-May to mid-September. Admission $5. (406) 843-5377.

Laurin and Robber's Roost North from Nevada City on Montana 287 is the town of Laurin and the spot of the Yeager-Brown lynchings, which led the vigilantes to Plummer in Bannack. Three miles past Laurin is the traditional site of Robber's Roost, a stagecoach station which was identified as the main base for the Plummer Gang.

ANNUAL EVENTS

Bannack Days Bannack celebrates its past with Bannack Days on the third weekend of July. It is an Old West festival with crafts, food, entertainment, wagon rides, and races. (406) 834-3413.

WILD BILL HICKOK

At the close of its most terrible wars, America has looked for heroes. Following the two world conflicts of the twentieth century, the media obliged by providing them in sports. But at the close of the Civil War, the country turned, instead, to the West.

On this frontier, where all sorts of new possibilities and hopes were taking shape, Wild Bill Hickok stepped out of the pages of a magazine to become the symbol of a new breed, the gunfighter. Or, in the language of the time, a shootist.

The February 1867 edition of *Harper's Magazine* contained startling information about this Western superstar. He could draw faster than any man alive. He dressed dashingly in buckskin. His piercing blue eyes revealed a formidable intelligence. He stood for truth and justice.

The figure that emerged in this article captured the imagination of the entire country. He was the prototype for the images of Wyatt Earp and Billy the Kid, who would soon follow him; for the Lone Ranger and the Hollywood cowboys who would keep the myth alive long after the frontier had faded into memory.

American Stock/Archive Photos

The author of the *Harper's* article, George Ward Nichols, created an American legend. But Nichols, like many journalists of the time, was not terribly interested in facts.

The truth was that Hickok was an obscure Army scout and hunter who had grown up in a frontier culture that accepted embellishment of stories as perfectly natural. So when he sat down with Nichols he had some whoppers to tell, and Nichols was more than willing to go along. While not altogether a bad guy, Hickok was far short of a hero and left some serious unanswered questions in his past.

Moreover, his name wasn't even Bill. He was born James Butler

Hickok, son of a deacon in the Presbyterian Church in Illinois. He drifted West at the age of twenty and somehow managed to get the tag of "Wild Bill" on his wanderings. His enemies claimed it was because of a protruding upper lip that led some to call him (out of his hearing) "Duck Bill." But thanks to the efforts of Nichols it may be the most commonly bestowed nickname in American history.

Hickok had many tales to tell. But the one that fascinated Nichols most was the incident at the Rock Creek Station in Nebraska, when he single-handedly routed the notorious McCanles Gang.

Hickok was twenty-three at the time and working for the Overland Stage Company. In the *Harper's* piece he described the McCanleses as "'desperadoes, horse thieves, murderers, regular cut-throats, who were the terror of everybody on the border.

" 'The ruffians came rushing in at both doors. I never aimed more deliberate in my life. One, two, three, four—and four men fell dead . . . Then I got ugly and I remember that I got hold of a knife, and then it was all cloudy like, and I was wild, and I struck savage blows, following the devils up from one side to the other of the room and into corners, striking and slashing until I knew that every one was dead.' "

But there seemed to be a slight discrepancy between that tale and the account of others who were familiar with the fight. According to their version, published some sixty years later, the McCanles family owned the station and was in the process of selling it to Overland Stage.

After showing up to collect payments several times and being stiffed, an outraged David McCanles decided to have it out with Overland and its employees, including Hickok. Wild Bill opened fire through the front door with a rifle as McCanles approached the house, killing him instantly.

Two others accompanying McCanles were also slain, one by being bashed over the head with a hoe and another with a load of buckshot as he was fighting off a dog. Hickok had a hand in neither of those killings. Only a twelve-year-old boy escaped alive.

Historians differ about the veracity of either story. Clarence Paine notes that this happened in the tension-filled summer of 1861, the McCanles family came from the South, and Hickok had an Abolitionist background. He feels that may have something to do with the outburst of violence. Still, it is evident that it didn't quite happen the way it was written in *Harper's*.

Nonetheless, the story of the fearsome Rock Creek Station fight made Hickok's name. In time it would also kill him.

When Hickok met his biographer he was hanging on without much purpose in Springfield, Missouri, where he had settled after serving with the Union Army in the Missouri campaign. All at once, he was in demand. General George A. Custer hired him as a scout and later praised him lavishly in his book *My Life on the Plains.*

He later claimed credit for cleaning up the town of Hays, Kansas, as sheriff. But since he only served three months in 1869 and then was defeated at the next election, that may be a bit of a stretch, too. After his term of office expired, he hung around Hays long enough to shoot three men, including two soldiers from nearby Fort Hays, before moving on.

Still, the legend fueled by the original magazine article continued to grow. He claimed to have killed one hundred men, not counting Indians.

"I never think much about it," he told one reporter. "The killing of a bad man shouldn't trouble one any more than killing a rat or an ugly cat or a vicious dog."

Once, he said, he shot two men running at him from opposite directions. It was generally believed that Wild Bill Hickok was the fastest gun in the West.

At least, Abilene believed it. One of the wildest of Kansas cow towns, Abilene hired Hickok as marshal on the basis of his reputation. The pay was $150 a month plus one-fourth of the fines he collected.

His predecessor, Tom Smith, actually had pacified the place, but he expired in late 1870 from the combined effects of a rifle blast to the chest and an ax blow to his head. With 600,000 head of cattle from Texas due to pass through town in 1871, Mayor Joseph McCoy decided a man of Hickok's unique talents was needed.

Wild Bill had an unusual theory about effective law enforcement. He hung out in the gambling rooms of the Alamo Saloon and kept the peace through his reputation. He also cut quite an imposing figure, standing well over six feet tall (at a time when few men reached that height) and favoring Prince Albert coats, checkered pants, and a silk vest.

There are stories, largely unsubstantiated, that he faced down such fearsome shootists as John Wesley Hardin and Ben Thompson. From the records on hand, however, it seems that most of his energy went towards collecting fines from Abilene's red light district and saloons.

One documented confrontation did take place with Phil Coe, Thompson's partner in the ownership of a local bar. After a wild night of revelry, the two men met in front of the Alamo on October 5.

According to some reports there was bad blood between them because of a woman. Others say Coe was simply being loud and unruly.

Hickok dropped him with two bullets in the chest. Unfortunately, he then heard a sound behind him, whirled and fired again. The shot took the life of his deputy, Mike Williams, who was running to assist him.

Six weeks later, Hickok was fired, and from then on his life went on a downward spiral. There are those who say he was distraught over shooting Williams. Some offer evidence that he began secretly to suffer from vision problems that would bother him the rest of his life. He understood that he would have to enter another line of work.

For a time, he tried touring with Wild West shows, first with Colonel Sidney Barrett and then in 1873 with Buffalo Bill's famous troupe. But the frontiersman was embarrassed by the job. Telling old stories to gullible writers was one thing. Acting them out in a New York City arena was another.

He returned to the West, moving to Wyoming, but found that he had outlived his legend. He was arrested for assault in Evanston and then thrown out of Cheyenne on a vagrancy charge. He was a weary man of thirty-eight, with no place left to go and a reputation too deadly for his own good.

Then he met Agnes Lake. They had known each other briefly in Abilene when she owned a circus. She had gone on to tour the country with the show in which she starred as both a tightrope walker and lion tamer. The friendship was rekindled, and she and Hickok were married in Cheyenne on March 5, 1876.

The problem of making a living remained, however. But Wild Bill had the answer. The Black Hills gold strike had just come in, and the town of Deadwood was the biggest boomtown in America. If he went up there, Hickok reasoned, his well-honed gambling skills, combined with a little prospecting on the side, would give him the stake to settle down happily with Agnes.

He left for Deadwood in June. He would never see his bride again.

His arrival in the mining town alarmed many of its less reputable citizens. His reputation had preceded him and they were convinced he was coming in to bring the law, which was the last thing they wanted. They were afraid, however, of confronting him directly.

On the afternoon of August 2, 1876, Hickok entered Saloon Number 10 in Deadwood and sat down in a poker game. According to one report, Jack McCall, a local hanger-on and alcoholic, sat in on the game briefly and exchanged words with Hickok when he short-changed the gunman on the gold dust he had thrown into the pot.

Others insist McCall was never in the game but entered the bar unseen by Hickok and took up a position behind him. Hickok never knew what hit him. McCall's bullet went through the back of his head and Hickok slumped dead across the table, holding the two pairs that have come down through legend as the "dead man's hand," aces and eights.

McCall ran from the bar but was tracked down and arrested. A miner's court, called by the men who wanted Hickok removed, put McCall on trial and voted for acquittal.

McCall testified that Hickok had shot his brother in Kansas and he was only seeking retribution. In his own addled mind, he may have sought to take on the gunman's glory by murdering him, a thought that most likely was encouraged by the element who wanted Hickok dead.

One month later, McCall was rearrested by a federal marshal in Wyoming and taken to Yankton, capital of the Dakota Territory. His attorney argued that trying him again for Hickok's killing was double jeopardy. But the prosecutor argued that the Deadwood court had no legal standing. This time McCall was convicted and hanged at Yankton in March 1877.

In a letter dated August 1 and produced later by Hickok's friend, riverboat captain Jack Crawford, the gunman had written his wife: "If such should be we never meet again, while firing my last shot, I will gently breathe the name of . . . Agnes, and with wishes even for my enemies I will make the plunge and try to swim to the other shore."

Although the story had been debunked many times, it should be mentioned that there was never a romance between Hickok and Martha Jane Canary, who has come down through history as Calamity Jane. Although feminist historians have done their best to try and turn her into a figure worthy of emulation, contemporary accounts in Deadwood depict her as a bit of a slob, a heavy drinker who became delusional in later life. Any romance with Hickok existed only in her own head.

Nonetheless, to honor its longtime local character, Deadwood buried her next to Hickok. It was August 1, 1903, one day short of the twenty-seventh anniversary of Wild Bill's death.

THE SITES

Deadwood's Main Street Deadwood's Main Street has come full circle in the years since Hickok's death. It remained at the center of a rich mining area until the first decade of the twentieth century. As the population slowly dwindled from 25,000 to 2,000, the gaming houses remained as the last vestige of the town's past. When they were closed down in a fit of postwar morality in 1946, it seemed the air went out of Deadwood. That is, at least until the hit HBO show *Deadwood* rekindled interest in the town.

But in 1993 legalized gambling returned and transformed the town. Although far more sedate than it was in Wild Bill's day it is again a place where the economy is based on chips and slots. Virtually every place of business along Main Street is now a casino. This includes Old Time Saloon Number 10, at 657 Main, the site of Hickok's murder. It now has displays on the fatal incident, with markers indicating where the principals involved were located on that August afternoon. The saloon is open daily, twenty-four hours. Admission is free.

Adams Memorial Museum More formal displays about Deadwood's gaudiest era can be found at the Adams Memorial Museum, at Deadwood and Sherman Sts. It has exhibits on Hickok as well as many other Black Hills figures, including Custer, Teddy Roosevelt, Preacher Smith (Deadwood's only minister, who was shot to death eighteen days after Hickok), and Calamity Jane. It is open Monday to Saturday, 9 a.m. to 6 p.m., Sundays, noon to 5 p.m., May to September; Monday to Saturday, 10 a.m. to 4 p.m., rest of year. Donations accepted. (605) 578-1714.

Mt. Moriah Cemetery Deadwood has one of the West's more colorful Boot Hills. The official name is Mt. Moriah Cemetery and it is reached by way of Sherman Street from the center of town. There are monuments to Hickok and the other leading figures of Deadwood's past, including Seth Bullock, the U.S. marshal who fought with Roosevelt in the Rough Riders during the Spanish-American War. The cemetery is open daily, 7 a.m. to 8 p.m., May-September; 9 a.m. to 5 p.m., rest of year. Admission $1. (605) 722-0837.

Rock Street Station Rock Street Station, site of Hickok's controversial shootout with the McCanleses, has been preserved as a Nebraska historical park. The station was situated on a branch of the Oregon Trail and Pony Express, so it was a natural selection for the Overland Stage route. Visitors can still see the deep wagon ruts left by hundreds of westward-bound pioneers. Living history exhibits show what life at a frontier stagecoach station was like, with a working blacksmith and a covered wagon ride. There is a slide presentation on the McCanles incident, too. The station is 4 miles east of Fairbury, on a paved county road, off U.S. 136. The grounds are open daily. The visitor center museum opens daily, 9 a.m. to 5 p.m., Memorial Day to Labor Day; Saturday, 9 a.m. to 5 p.m., and Sunday, 1 p.m. to 5 p.m., April, May, September, and October. Admission $2.50 per vehicle. (402) 729-5777.

Abilene Abilene remembers its frontier past at the Dickinson County Heritage Center and Museum. There is a small exhibit on Hickok's lively year as marshal. It is located at 412 S. Campbell St. Open Monday to Saturday, 10 a.m. to 6 p.m.; Sunday, 1 p.m. to 5 p.m., April-October. Admission $2.50. (915) 263-2681. There is also a "re-creation" of Texas St. across from the town's biggest attraction, the Dwight D. Eisenhower Center. But there really isn't much to offer there. Spend your time learning about Ike, instead.

Hays Hays features Wild Bill's likeness on its home page on the Web. Aside from that, not much of Hickok remains there. You may want to look in at the Ellis County Historical Society Museum if you're passing through. It is located at 100 W. 7th St. Open Tuesday to Friday, 10 a.m. to 5 p.m. Admission $3. (785) 628-2624; www.elliscountyhistoricalmuseum.org.

ANNUAL EVENTS

Days of '76 Deadwood's Days of '76 is one of the oldest and most popular of Western festivals. It first was celebrated in 1923 and has been held continuously ever since on the first weekend of August. The party is built around the legend of Hickok, and it includes covered wagon parades, costumed recreations of notable events, cookouts, music, and a rodeo. (800) 345-1876; www.daysof76.com.

The Trial of Jack McCall The Trial of Jack McCall goes on throughout the summer at Deadwood's Old Towne Hall, on Lee St. It is a re-enactment of the miner's court that acquitted McCall of Hickok's murder and is one of the best-attended Western pageants. It usually runs from Memorial Day through the last weekend in August.

JAY GOULD

He may not have been the most rapacious of the Gilded Age's robber barons. He was an acutely shy man, who twisted his legs nervously when seated and forced to converse. He enjoyed art, good music, and growing orchids. Everyone who met him came away admiring his intellect.

Yet Jay Gould's financial manipulations ruined thousands of lives, brought scandal to a President of the United States, and filled the coffers of the country's most corrupt political machine. He dared to take on Commodore Vanderbilt and beat him at his own money game. He was the first target of Teddy Roosevelt's political career and indirectly helped found one of the country's great newspaper dynasties.

"A settled conviction that money was the only thing in life worth having must have become established in . . . Jay's mind as soon as he was able to understand that the lack of it was the cause of the deprivations he had to endure (as a child)," wrote Robert Fuller, in his biography of Gould's fellow swindler, Jim Fisk.

Gould and Fisk combined to bring on one of the worst financial crises in the history of Wall Street: the attempt to corner gold on Black Friday, 1869.

In the end, he even double-crossed Fisk, selling out when he got advance word that the U.S. government was about to break their hold on the metal by releasing some of its supply. Afterwards, Gould piously explained that he never had any intention of cornering the market but was just trying to keep prices up for the benefit of America's Western farmers. He also, incidentally, made $11 million on the transaction.

The wife of a fellow financier said he had "the eyes of a snake." They were deep and black, and observers said they seemed to look right through you. He was of slight build, abstemious, close-mouthed—with none of the more florid characteristics of the other big shooters of his time. But in an era when capitalism ran amok and took no prisoners he may have been the most ruthless, most formidable adversary of them all.

He was born poor in 1836, on a family farm near the town of Roxbury, in New York's Catskills. But the Goulds were from old New England stock, and it was impressed on him from boyhood that hard work, thrift, and dedication were needed to make one's way in the world. The lessons took with a vengeance.

By the time he was twenty-three, Gould was on Wall Street in his own firm. But not until he first teamed with Fisk to take on the mighty Vanderbilt in 1867 did he make his mark. Fisk was the opposite of Gould; bluff, hearty, likable. He was called Jubilee Jim and he lived large. While he didn't have Gould's passion for detail, he was an organizational genius and was able to connect with the right people.

The two decided to go after the Erie Railroad. Vanderbilt had just acquired the New York Central and needed the Erie to give him access to Chicago. That would make him the most powerful rail tycoon in America, if not the world.

The Commodore seemed to have the inside track. He had been on its Board of Directors and had also paid off Boss William Marcy Tweed, head of the Tammany Hall political machine, with a $19,000 bribe to make sure the right rulings were made in court and the state legislature.

But he was not playing with children. Gould and Fisk upped the ante for Tweed's services to a block of Erie stock, seats on the board, and $1.5 million for "legal" services. At those prices, Tweed did not stay bought, and the advantage quickly shifted to Gould.

The two men converted the railroad's bonds into a new $10 million issue of stock, driving the cost of acquiring the Erie beyond even what Vanderbilt could afford. A very sore loser, the Commodore located a judge he could buy and obtained a restraining order to stop Gould and Fisk from taking control of the railroad's assets.

They got around this by racing to the Hudson River and hiring a boat to take them to New Jersey, beyond the reach of Vanderbilt's order. They set up

Courtesy Lyndhurst, Tarrytown, NY

company offices there and the Erie was all theirs to plunder; which they quickly proceeded to do.

But the Erie was just a warm-up. Gould was ready for the main event.

He was now a very rich man. But always in the back of his mind was the specter of the poverty from which he had escaped. Those who knew him felt he never could enjoy his wealth. It was never enough. While his partner, Fisk, with his walrus mustache and a chorus girl on each arm, loved the notoriety, Gould would just as soon have stayed in the shadows and made millions in obscurity. Everything else was subordinated to making money.

Along with that materialistic attitude, however, came a total indifference to those who might be hurt by his actions. The Erie Railroad scheme had wounded not only Vanderbilt but a host of small investors. Black Friday would be much, much worse.

Flush with his profits from the railroad, Gould bought up some smaller lines as well as the ferry service from New York City to New Jersey. In the course of these deals he became friendly with Abel Rathbone Corbin, the brother-in-law of President Ulysses S. Grant.

Gould juggled dozens of schemes in his head simultaneously and this chance friendship with Corbin put one of the balls higher than the rest. The United States was not on the gold standard in 1869 and the metal was scarce. Gould knew that only about $15 million was in circulation, although the U.S. Treasury held $95 million of gold in its reserves.

If Gould were able to corner the available gold, which was doable, he would bid its price up before new supplies could be imported from the European markets. The only hitch was finding out how the federal government would respond to such a move. If it released the reserves, the price would fall. With Corbin as his contact he hoped to penetrate the Grant administration and find out.

In March of 1869 gold was selling at $130 an ounce, the lowest point in three years, and Gould began to buy. Fisk was soon in on the game, along with a handful of other speculators who followed Gould's lead. They weren't quite sure what he was up to, but whatever Gould bought was good enough for them.

His cover story was that he wanted the price of gold to rise so farmers would ship their grain East aboard his Erie Railroad for export abroad. Daniel Butterfield, a Grant appointee to head the New York subtreasury, joined the scheme. Butterfield managed to persuade Grant to travel to Boston on a steamship owned by Fisk, who liked to wear an admiral's uniform when he went aboard.

Gould tried to pump the President on what his reaction would be to gold's price rising—all in the interest of helping the farmers, of course. Grant said little, but finally he told Gould: "Well, it seems to me that there's a good deal of fiction in all this talk about prosperity. The bubble may as well be pricked one way as another."

That didn't sound like good news to Gould. Nonetheless, he convinced Corbin to write an opinion piece for the *New York Times* that supported higher gold prices and made it seem as if it came from the President. On September 2, Gould placed orders for $5 million in gold through forty different brokers.

These transactions were handled in the Gold Room, an exchange set up exclusively for this commodity. A fountain of Cupid stood in its main room, at the corner of Broad Street and Exchange Place, in New York, a block from the Stock Exchange.

By September 22, the price had climbed to $144, and the government's apparent inaction, bolstered by the newspaper articles, fueled other buyers. Two days later, on a Friday, gold crashed through the ceiling. The climb knocked the props out of the paper money that was in circulation, and those who had been selling short, expecting a downturn, were ruined.

Fisk walked into the Gold Room and shouted that gold was bound for $200 and he'd bet $50,000 it would get there. Crowds began gathering outside the doors and armed deputies had to be called to protect the speculators inside. By 11:30 a.m. the price reached $160 and there was panic across the floor.

With Gould and Fisk buying constantly they had orders in for all the gold that was available, and no sellers. They had succeeded in cornering gold. "I'm not in this thing as a philanthropist," said Fisk scornfully, as the price passed $162.

Those numbers meant ruin to financial houses and small businesses across the country. All assets had to be disposed of by those who had predicted a bear market and were forced to cover their mounting losses on gold. In the Gold Room itself there was pandemonium. No one knew where this ride was going, and men who had come to Wall Street that morning as solid businessmen had turned into frightened rabbits. A few of them dived into the pool at Cupid's feet in an attempt to cool off.

Shortly after noon, with gold at $162½, Grant decided to act. He released $4 million in gold reserves. Butterfield got the word and immediately notified Gould what would happen. Gould immediately turned around and started to sell. He neglected to notify his old pal, Fisk, however, who still was buying at $162.

The government's action broke Gould's corner, but the damage had been done. His manipulations led directly to the financial depression of the early 1870s. Investments were wiped out, fortunes lost. The

Stock Exchange had to shut down. "The spectacle was one such as Dante might have seen in the Inferno," wrote a financial reporter. A few speculators went mad and one killed himself.

"I regret very much this depression in financial circles," clucked Gould, "but I predicted it long ago. I was in no way instrumental in producing the panic."

Gould's corner of the gold market will have to go down as one of the whoppers of the nineteenth century. Never in American history would so many suffer from the actions of one man.

Fisk managed to wiggle out of his contracts on gold and ruefully told friends that he had been sure Grant was in on the deal. The public thought so, too. Black Friday was one of a series of scandals that tarnished Grant with the reputation as one of the least competent U.S. Presidents.

Gould was just thirty-three years old on Black Friday, and his reputation as a dark wizard was secure. Eventually, he controlled the New York Republican Party, four railroad lines, Western Union, and New York City's entire elevated railroad system (and did his best to block construction of the city's subway to protect his interests).

He was also one of the founders of the Metropolitan Opera Company. One of his incidental possessions was the *New York World*. He sold it in 1883 to Joseph Pulitzer, who remade the face of American journalism and turned the publication into the best-written newspaper of its era, a voice for the sort of progressive Republican Party that Gould detested.

Teddy Roosevelt, who had been looked on as an eccentric rich boy when he was elected to the New York legislature, made his reputation by attacking Gould for grabbing control of the Manhattan Railway by deliberately driving down its stock. He accused the former State Attorney General and a justice of the New York Supreme Court of colluding with Gould on the illegal deal. Moreover, he attacked Gould by name on the floor of the legislature, a breach of decorum that absolutely staggered members of that august body who were in his pocket.

Gould's allies buried Roosevelt's report, but he became a hero in the New York City media. "Mr. Roosevelt accomplished more good than any man of his age and experience had accomplished in years," rhapsodized the *New York Post*.

But Gould was far beyond the reach of mere journalism and law. Gould himself acknowledged that he was "the most hated man in America," and everyone delighted in seeing him getting busted in the chops.

In 1880 he purchased Lyndhurst, a Gothic Revival castle on 550 acres overlooking the Hudson River, in Tarrytown. It offered him security from the roiling mob, tranquility, a place for his extensive art collection. Most important of all, he had time to expand the estate's greenhouses into a horticultural paradise, where he could putter away endlessly with his beloved orchids.

Gould was just fifty-six at his death in 1892. The newspaper tributes were not complimentary, although the *Times* did point out that he "never gave himself the trouble of making any false pretenses."

His estate came to $84.3 million, and only two members of the Vanderbilt family had ever left larger estates at this point in American history. The entire fortune remained within his family.

A few sentimental $1,000 bequests he had made to friends and associates were disallowed. They were so uncharacteristic of Gould the court must have thought he had gone temporarily mad.

THE SITES

Lyndhurst Lyndhurst remains the showcase of what the Gould fortune acquired. The core of the home dates from 1838 and was built by the Paulding family, prominent in this part of the Hudson Valley since Revolutionary times.

Gould was its third owner, and it was he who expanded and furnished it with the priceless antiques, woodwork, stained glass, and art that fills it today. It has survived almost intact, a lasting monument to America's most excessive era, because of the determination of Gould's daughters.

His heirs could not agree on disposition of Lyndhurst, and finally, against the wishes of Helen Gould, it was put up for sale. She could not bear the thought of parting with this house that had been so dear to her father. So with her portion of the inheritance, she bought it herself.

Helen's obsession with preserving Lyndhurst perfectly was shared by her younger sister, Anna. After Helen's death in 1938, the house could not be sold in an America still not fully recovered from the Great Depression. So Anna, who was now the Duchesse de Talleyrand-Perigord, bought it in turn from her sister's estate.

With her health failing in 1961, Anna decided that rather than selling the house to strangers she would bequeath it to the National Trust for Historic Preservation. Even then, the Trust had to fight off challenges from other Gould heirs to keep the place. But it succeeded, and

Lyndhurst now is one of the jewels of its collection of historic great houses.

Lyndhurst is located at 625 S. Broadway, off U.S. 9, just south of the Tappan Zee Bridge. It is open Tuesday through Sunday and on Monday holidays, 10 a.m. to 5 p.m., May through October; weekends only, rest of year. The last tour leaves 45 minutes before closing during the peak season, 90 minutes during the rest of the year. Admission $9; children under seventeen $3. (914) 631-4481.

Jefferson, Texas One of Gould's favorite tactics as a rail tycoon was to threaten to destroy any town that didn't bend to his will. He would reroute his tracks and leave it without service. The phrase "Grass will grow in your streets" was one of his favorites.

Sometimes it worked. But it didn't in the case of Jefferson, Texas. When the town declined to locate a roundhouse there, Gould moved his main line, but not before staying overnight in Jefferson and scrawling his favorite threat in the guest register of the hotel.

Jefferson managed to survive, though. The hotel he stayed in, the Excelsior, is still standing at 211 W. Austin St., with its register on display. Tours are given daily, at 1 p.m. and 2 p.m. Admission $2; children under eight $1. (903) 665-2513.

Just to rub it in, Jefferson also purchased Gould's private railroad car, the Atalanta, and moved it here. The luxurious car was built in 1890 and has been restored to its appearance of that era. It contains four bedrooms, a kitchen, a butler's room, and a dining room. It is parked at 200 W. Austin St. and is open daily, 9:30 a.m. to noon and 2:30 p.m. to 4:30 p.m. Admission $1. (903) 665-2513.

Jefferson is located 15 miles north of the U.S. 59 exit of I-20, 57 miles northwest of Shreveport, Louisiana.

BILLY THE KID

There are flowers on William Bonney's grave, left by visitors to his burial place behind the Old Fort Sumner Museum. Coins, too, have been tossed atop the fenced-in sarcophagus, like those thrown for luck in shopping mall fountains or at the shrines of martyrs.

It is hard to say what goes through the minds of tourists who leave these tokens. It has to be intended as more than simple evidence of their passing through. It takes planning and effort to go out and buy flowers. So it must be a mark of respect: Homage to Billy the Kid, patron saint of juvenile delinquents everywhere.

He was the model, an American original. It isn't likely that he actually gunned down twenty-one men, one for each of his years, by the time of his death in 1881. That is a later, pulp fiction invention. More likely it was only a half dozen or so, and some of them probably had it coming.

Still, in cold fact, he was a teenaged killer, no less than the drive-by shooters who plagued urban streets eleven decades after the Kid's demise. It is unlikely anyone will leave coins for luck at their graves.

Western historian Peter Lyon described Bonney (which was not his real name) as an "adenoidal moron." He certainly looks the part in the only known photograph of him. He cocks his head at the camera, his mouth fixed in a smirk, his

American Stock/Archive Photos

left hand balancing a rifle which he holds by its muzzle. He is dressed in a cowboy's heavy winter clothing, but the short-brimmed hat he wears gives him the look of a tough city kid posing for an amusement park snapshot.

Don C. Trenary, a Western historian, points out that he most often shot from ambush and calls him an "unprepossessing little assassin." It doesn't quite convey the stuff of timeless heroism.

Yet the Kid lives on as a genuine folk celebrity. Paul Newman and Robert Taylor have portrayed him on the screen. Big stars for a big role.

A nineteenth century ballad cautions us: "There's many a man with face fine and fair / Who starts out in life with a chance to be square. / But just like poor Billy, he wanders astray /And loses his life in the very same way." Any tough athlete whose first name is Billy is still liable to bear the nickname of the Kid, and it is meant as a compliment. He is engrained in our popular culture; careless youth, frontier style.

He probably entered the world as Henry McCarty, a name that never would have earned him immortality. His birthplace usually is given as New York City, in 1859. The family moved to Kansas four years later, and his father died somewhere in the West. At least, there was no Mr. McCarty around when his mother married William Antrim in Santa Fe in 1873. The family then moved to the mining boomtown of Silver City, New Mexico.

His mother died of tuberculosis the following year, his stepfather left town, and at the age of fourteen young Henry, who had adopted the last name of Antrim, was on his own. For a while he seemed to be on an honest path. He moved in with a local family and got a job as a dishwasher in a hotel. Then he became involved in what seems to be a childhood prank, stealing some clothes from a Chinese laundry.

The sheriff, thinking to put a fright into the lad, locked him in jail overnight. But young Henry, in a pattern that would become familiar and increasingly deadly, shinnied up the chimney in his cell and escaped.

He was next heard from in Camp Grant, Arizona, in 1877. The Kid managed to get into a gambling fight with a blacksmith named Windy Cahill, who outweighed him by a few dozen pounds. While in the midst of being pummeled by the enraged Cahill in a saloon. Henry somehow got a gun and killed his attacker with a bullet through the heart.

Antrim was arrested and placed in the guardhouse of a nearby

Army fort. But soldiers who had witnessed the fight thought that he was merely acting in self-defense and arranged for his escape. The Kid fled back to New Mexico on a stolen horse, having killed for the first time at the age of seventeen.

He made his way to Lincoln County, picking up the tag of the Antrim Kid somewhere along the way. But when he sought employment with rancher and merchant John Tunstall he was calling himself William Bonney. Where he came up with that name is anyone's guess. Some historians surmise it was his mother's maiden name. But it was the name that would soon become the most feared in the territory.

It was early in 1878, and the trouble that always seemed to be hovering over the Kid now burst open in earnest He had stepped into the middle of a murderous range war and was about to become its symbol. His employer, Tunstall, a wealthy young Englishman, had arrived in New Mexico in 1876 with ambitions in ranching and real estate.

He had formed a partnership with local businessman and lawyer Alexander McSween, and the men opened a store in the county seat, Lincoln. Unfortunately, that put them in direct competition with Lawrence G. Murphy and J. J. Dolan.

With tight political connections and a distinct lack of scruples, Murphy and Dolan were the leading economic force in the county. When McSween was hired to settle the estate of Murphy's ex-partner, Emil Fritz, who had died in Germany, the bad will between the two factions boiled over.

Murphy accused the attorney of embezzling funds from the estate, although bank and probate fees had eaten away most of the money. Murphy, nevertheless, managed to attach most of the assets of McSween and Tunstall through his political connections. Included in the order were the cattle on Tunstall's ranch, even though he had no connection with the lawsuit.

On February 18, 1878, Tunstall rode out to talk with a posse, made up predominantly of hired gunmen sent out to seize the cattle. Billy Bonney was in the group accompanying him. Without warning Tunstall was gunned down, shot in the chest and, while lying helpless, in the back of the head. Posse members reported he was killed while resisting arrest.

In the few weeks that he had worked for Tunstall, the Kid had developed a strong affection for his employer. The Englishman had given him a saddle and a horse, the first time anyone had ever given him anything. Being a helpless witness to his murder sent Bonney over the edge. With other friends from the Tunstall ranch, he began a campaign of retribution that soon escalated into an all-out battle against the law.

In a matter of weeks, Sheriff William Brady, who had directed the murder of Tunstall, was gunned down in the streets of Lincoln, shot from ambush with eight bullets in him. Several members of his posse soon joined Brady in the afterlife and the Kid was suspected of having a hand in most of the shootings.

News of the rampage made it back to Washington, and President Rutherford B. Hayes decided to send out a new territorial governor to restore order. His choice was a former Civil War general with literary aspirations. Indiana-born Lew Wallace had already started to write the manuscript of *Ben Hur*, the best-selling work of American fiction in the nineteenth century. He would finish the novel while serving as governor in Santa Fe.

Wallace's primary job, however, was getting things calmed down in Lincoln County. A member of the Tunstall faction had succeeded Brady as sheriff, and the Kid surrendered to him, pleading not guilty at his arraignment for murder. But Wallace's predecessor unwisely set the election aside, and the next sheriff once again belonged to the Murphy-Dolan group, which was intent upon hanging young Bonney.

In July, the showdown came. The Kid and eighteen others were trapped in the McSween house in Lincoln by the new sheriff and his gunmen. The deputies occupied the Murphy-Dolan store, diagonally across the street. The ensuing gunfight went on for two days, with bullets flying all through the town. It ended only when the sheriff's men managed to set fire to a wing of the McSween house.

According to some reports, the newly widowed Susan McSween calmly played patriotic airs on the piano as the flames crept closer to her. She indignantly denied these stories in later years, after she had remarried, ran one of the territory's largest ranches, and was known as "The Cattle Queen of New Mexico." "No one could be that stupid," she said.

The sheriff was killed in the battle along with McSween, but the Kid managed to escape in the darkness. In a move still swathed in controversy, Wallace then apparently offered Bonney an amnesty if he turned himself in. At least, that's how the Kid interpreted it. But when members of the Murphy-Dolan gang were set free and swore to kill him in retribution, Bonney decided to get out of Lincoln.

He thought the amnesty offer held good, even after embarking on a two-year campaign outside the law. He engaged in a series of holdups and rustling ventures, crossing into Texas several times to sell illegal stock. So when Wallace offered a $500 reward for his capture in 1880, the Kid felt cruelly betrayed.

By this time the law had a new face in Lincoln County. Sheriff Pat Garrett had been born in Alabama, but like many southerners who grew up in the economic ruin left by the Civil War, he headed west. After a stay in Texas, Garrett came to New Mexico. As a man who knew how to use a gun, he found employment as a lawman. His first job was to bring in the Kid.

Garrett was told Fort Sumner was a good place to look. The former Army post was situated in the Pecos Valley, in an area called the Bosque Redondo (Round Grove). The spot had been well known for centuries, first visited by the exploring expedition of Francisco Vasques Coronado in 1541. Later it was a Comanche camp and a trading post.

The Army came in 1862 and set up what amounted to a concentration camp for the Navajo tribe. As the Civil War began, Federal forces were faced with a Confederate invasion of New Mexico and were uneasy about having the unfriendly Navajo nation on their western flank. So veteran scout Kit Carson was sent into the Indian heartland. In a brutal campaign, the Navajo were burned out, starved, and forced to march hundreds of miles to Fort Sumner.

They were preyed upon there by Comanche and Kiowa raiders and were unable to adapt to the new climate. After six terrible years the Navajo went on strike, refusing to plant crops. Faced with the prospect of mass starvation, the Army let them return to their homeland and closed up the fort.

The property then became part of the holdings of Lucien Maxwell, richest man in the territory. Through marriage he had acquired the largest hereditary land grant in New Mexico, more than 1.7 million acres, extending into Colorado. He made disastrous investments in gold mines, railroads, and banks, but still died a wealthy man in 1875.

His son, Peter, inherited a twenty-room mansion near the site of the old fort. Somehow the rich young heir struck up a dangerous friendship with Billy Bonney, and the Kid made the Fort Sumner area one of his hangouts.

Garrett rode into the town on December 19, 1880, and waited with his deputies. That evening, the Kid and five other men entered Fort Sumner, and Garrett ordered them to halt. Tom O'Folliard, one of Bonney's closest friends, chose to draw, instead, and was shot down. He died two hours later. The others rode east, with Garrett and his men in pursuit.

They tracked the group to an abandoned rock house at a place called Stinking Springs. Quietly, they surrounded the place, and when Charlie Bowdre, wearing a hat much like the Kid's, came to the door the next morning he was shot. Seeing that he was outnumbered, Bonney surrendered to Garrett and was taken to the jail in Las Vegas, New Mexico.

T. W. Garrard, reporter for the local paper, eager to interview the notorious gunman, described him as being about 5-8 and 140 pounds, "a frank, open countenance, looking like a school boy, with the traditional silky fuzz on the upper lip . . . quite a handsome looking fellow, the only imperfection being two prominent front teeth slightly protruding like squirrel's teeth."

Bonney said his arrest was all a mistake. He was actually a rancher and sometime gambler. "I don't blame you for writing of me as you have," he told the reporter. "I don't know as anyone would believe anything good of me anyway. Everyone seems to think I was some kind of animal."

The Kid was chipper because he thought his amnesty agreement with Wallace was still good. But that wasn't Wallace's understanding at all. The governor, instead, ordered Bonney to stand trial in Mesilla, a Mexican village near Las Cruces, far away from Lincoln, where many jurors would have been swayed by past passions and loyalties.

On April 10, 1881, he was convicted of Sheriff Brady's murder and sentenced to be hanged. He was then returned to Lincoln for execution.

The Kid wrote several indignant letters to Wallace, reminding the governor of his promise. Then in May he took more direct action. Slipping off the handcuffs in his cell at the courthouse (which had once been the Murphy-Dolan store), he shattered the skull of deputy J. W. Bell, took his gun, and finished off the helpless man with a quick shot.

When deputy Bob Olinger heard the noise he came running to the courthouse. The Kid was waiting for him at an upstairs window. "Hello, Bob," he said, and killed him with two blasts from a shotgun. He then ordered a clerk to bring him a file and a horse ("I am fighting for my life and must be obeyed," according to the report in the Las Vegas, New Mexico, *Gazette*), unshackled himself, and rode into the mountains.

Garrett once more took off in pursuit. This time there would be no talk of amnesty. Bonney had deliberately killed two deputies, and all hands were now raised against him. With nowhere to run, the Kid made his way back to his friend Peter Maxwell's house at Fort Sumner.

Garrett and two deputies caught up with him there on July 14,

1881. Waiting until dark. Garrett left his assistants as guards outside the Maxwell house and then slipped inside to Peter's bedroom. Speaking in a whisper, Garrett asked if the Kid was in the house. Maxwell sized up the situation and decided to tell the truth.

"He's not far off," he told Garrett. A moment later, a soft tread was heard on the porch outside. "That's him," breathed Maxwell.

Bonney had seen the guards outside but assumed they were Maxwell's employees. When he stepped into the bedroom and saw a third figure standing in the shadows, he knew something was up. "Who's there?" he asked, drawing his gun. They were his last words. Garrett opened fire, and the Kid went down with a bullet through the chest. He died in a matter of minutes.

Billy the Kid was buried in the old fort graveyard, sharing a plot with his cohorts, O'Folliard and Bowdre. The stone erected over the grave reads: "Pals."

The first "authentic" biography of Bonney appeared within a month. It was soon followed by an expanded, hugely inaccurate version published by the country's top mass circulation magazine, The Police Gazette. The legend was greatly embellished, and for the first time the Kid took on the aura of a Robin Hood figure, fighting against economic injustice.

Garrett, seeing a chance at cashing in, contributed his own biography of the man he had killed entitled *The Authentic Life of Billy the Kid*. "The Kid had a lurking devil in him," he wrote. "It was a good-humored jovial imp or a cruel and bloodthirsty fiend, as circumstances prompted. He always laughed when killing but fire seemed to dart from his eyes."

By building up the reputation of Bonney, the lawman seemed to feel he could finance his own ventures into mining and ranching.

There were songs, novels, and a long-running Broadway play that opened in 1906. The legend grew. Billy was really an Ivy League graduate seeking adventure. No, he was an Apache. He was "exceptionally intelligent, carefree, attractive." Best of all, as with so many legendary figures, he was still alive.

Stories circulated that Garrett had allowed him to escape and that the Kid lived on another forty years in Texas. His tombstone, in fact, was stolen in 1950 and turned up in Granbury, Texas, twenty-six years later. The town insisted it had a right to it because the "real" Billy the Kid was buried there.

Stung, Fort Sumner reclaimed the marker and began referring to its site as "Billy's Real Grave." The stone was stolen once more and eventually had to be protected by an encircling iron fence. That's where the flowers and the coins are left today.

Garrett outlived his famous adversary by nearly twenty-seven years. In February 1908 he was shot from ambush, near Las Graces, by Wayne Brazel, a sheepherder he had offended. By that time *Billy the Kid* had been playing on Broadway for two years and Bonney belonged to legend.

THE SITES

Fort Sumner The Fort Sumner State Monument is 6 miles south and east of Fort Sumner, New Mexico, by way of U.S. 60 and New Mexico 212. The grave site is behind the Old Fort Sumner Museum, at the state monument entrance. There is no charge to visit the grave and it is open daily, dawn to dusk. Lucien and Peter Maxwell are also buried here and so is Joe Grant, one of the notches on Billy's gun.

The museum itself contains exhibits relating to the Kid's career, copies of his letters to Lew Wallace, and memorabilia relating to the legend surrounding him. It is situated where the Maxwell house, the place where he was killed, once stood. The house itself was washed away by Pecos River floods in the 1890s. The museum is open daily, 9:30 a.m. to 4:30 p.m. Admission $3; children under twelve $2. (505) 355-2942.

One-quarter mile away is the visitor center for the State Monument, which details the story of the mistreatment of the Navajo at the Bosque Redondo. The fort buildings no longer exist, but a short walking loop takes you around the site and markers point to where they once stood. The visitor center is open the same hours as the museum. Admission is $3. (505) 355-2573.

Lincoln To reach Lincoln State Monument, take U.S. 380, 10 miles west of U.S. 70. The entire town of Lincoln (with a population of one hundred) is now a historic district, with many of the buildings looking just as they did when it was the Kid's home. The Old Lincoln County Courthouse was built in 1873 by L. G. Murphy as his "Big Store" and was the area's economic fulcrum. It was here that the Murphy-Dolan faction barricaded themselves during the shootout of 1878. Converted to a courthouse three years later, it was where Bonney was imprisoned while waiting to be hanged, and where he gunned down two deputies during his escape. An excellent museum sorts out the confusing political alliances and issues that led to the Lincoln County War with evocative old pictures and original belongings. Upstairs is where the Kid was jailed, and the path of his escape is also plotted. The court was moved to Carrizozo in 1913, but the original courtroom has been restored. The Tunstall store, opened by the Kid's benefactor in 1877 as a competitor to Murphy-Dolan, is just across the street and a few steps west. It actually was operated as a store for eighty years and was not sold to the state until 1957. The site of the McSween home next door, burned down in the big gunfight, is also marked.

Combination tickets to these two places and other historic sites in Lincoln unrelated to the Billy the Kid story may be purchased for $6 at the Lincoln Trust Historical Center. Buildings are open daily, 8:30 a.m. to 5 p.m. (505) 653-4372.

Mesilla The historic village of Mesilla is located off I-10, south of Las Cruces. This historic village was settled by Mexican loyalists who didn't want to remain in the United States after the rest of New Mexico was lost in the Mexican War. Nonetheless, they were taken over by the Americans anyhow after the Gadsden Purchase in 1854. It was here that Governor Wallace ordered the Kid to stand trial for the murder of Sheriff Brady. He was convicted and returned to Lincoln for hanging. The former Mesilla Courthouse is now a souvenir store on the southeastern corner of the historic plaza. It is open daily 10 a.m. to 4 p.m. and contains a few exhibits on the trial. Admission is free. (505) 523-5562.

Silver City Not much remains of the Kid's boyhood days in Silver City, thanks to the forces of nature. The house he lived in as a boy, on Broadway at Main, was destroyed by torrential rains in 1895. The entire street caved in, sank 55 feet, and now forms a park called the Big Ditch. There is a small exhibit on the Kid at the Silver City Museum, at 312 W. Broadway, housed in the town's landmark mansion, built in 1881. His mother, Catherine Antrim, is buried in Memory Lane Cemetery. The Museum is open Tuesday to Friday, 9 a.m. to 4:30 p.m.; weekend 10 a.m. to 4 p.m. Admission $3. (505) 538-5921; www.silvercitymuseum.org. The town is also worth visiting for the art galleries and craft stores that line Broadway, Bullard St., and Yankie St.

Stinking Springs Stinking Springs is near Taiban, 14 miles east of Fort Sumner. An historical marker on U.S. 60 east of the town marks where

Billy and his gang were captured after a brief shootout with Pat Garrett, in December 1880.

Tascosa Tascosa, Texas, is 22 miles north of I-40 from Vega and can be reached by way of U.S. 385 and Farm Road 1061. This ghost town of the Texas Panhandle was one of the wildest cattle towns in the West in the 1870s and 1880s. The Kid was a frequent visitor between 1878 and 1880, dealing in stolen stock and frequenting its saloons in association with some of the era's most lawless individuals. The site, ironically, is now occupied by Cal Farley's Boys Ranch, a place were troubled juveniles are given a second chance at life. There are historical markers around the town-site and the Tascosa Museum tells about its storied past. The museum is open daily 8 a.m. to 5 p.m. Free admission. (806) 372-2341.

ANNUAL EVENTS

Old Fort Days The town of Fort Sumner holds Old Fort Days during the second week in June. Western-style entertainment and a race to Billy the Kid's tombstone are just some of the events held annually. (505) 355-7705.

Old Lincoln Days The historical town of Lincoln celebrates its heritage during the first weekend in August with Old Lincoln Days. Events include the "Last Days of Billy the Kid" pageant and a crafts show. (505) 653-4025.

"The Real Billy the Kid" Outdoor Pageant Caprock Amphitheater, which is located south of I-40 from San Jon by way of New Mexico 39, houses "The Real Billy the Kid" outdoor pageant. The pageant runs from late June to late August on Fridays and Saturdays. (800) 724-0500.

Billy the Kid—Pat Garrett Historical Days Every third Saturday in July, Billy the Kid—Pat Garrett Historical Days are held in Ruidoso, 32 miles southwest of Lincoln on U.S. 70. Tours of nearby sites associated with the Kid are offered, and a chili cook-off is also sponsored. (800) 252-2255. This event is sponsored by the Billy the Kid Outlaw Gang, an organization dedicated to keeping the history of Bonney alive. You can call for information on activities and membership at (505) 389-5169.

Billy the Kid Festival To reach Puerto de Luna, home of the Billy the Kid Festival, travel south of I-40 from Santa Rosa by way of New Mexico 91. The festival takes place the first Saturday in October. The

Kid was friendly with merchant Alexander Grzelachowski, the most influential citizen of this town, which was once a county seat but is now almost deserted. He spent his last Christmas Day here in 1880, and that holiday is re-enacted as part of the festival. There are also tours of the Grzelachowski home and store. (800) 635-8036.

RELATED SITES

Old Aztec Mill Museum The town of Cimmaron, New Mexico, was built by Lucien Maxwell in the days when he was the richest man in the territory. It became one of the territory's most notorious settlements, a haunt of the Southwest's roughest characters. When no one had been shot for three days, the local paper saw fit to mention it in a front-page story. It was also a favorite stop of Buffalo Bill Cody and Kit Carson. Maxwell built one of his stately homes here in 1864. The house is gone but a gristmill next door is now an historic museum with exhibits on the Maxwell family, which played such an important role in Billy the Kid's demise. The museum is open Monday to Saturday, 9 a.m. to 5 p.m., and Sunday, 1 p.m. to 5 p.m., June to August; weekends only in May and September. Admission $2. (505) 376-2913.

Lew Wallace Study and Museum Lew Wallace's hometown was Crawfordsville, Indiana. It was here he did most of his writing, including the bulk of *Ben Hur*. Initial reviews of the book were not favorable. Wrote one New Mexico critic: "I protest as a friend of Christ that He has been crucified enough without having a Territorial Governor after him." But *Ben Hur* has become an American classic. The museum at Wallace's study, a building strongly influenced by his experience as U.S. minister to Turkey in the 1880s, contains exhibits on the history of the book as well the general's career in New Mexico. It is open Wednesday to Saturday, 10 a.m. to 5 p.m.; Tuesday and Sunday opening at 1 p.m. Admission $3. (765) 362-5769; www.ben-hur.com.

HATFIELDS AND McCOYS

There are those who say it started with a stolen pig. Still others trace it back to an election day in 1882, when a member of the Hatfield family was murdered by three McCoys. Some people claim there was a woman to blame.

Or if you want to go way back there is always the Civil War, when Devil Anse Hatfield led a band of raiders who supported the South and killed a McCoy who was loyal to the Union. Or maybe it went back even farther than that; back to the medieval traditions of clans in the British Isles from which both families had sprung before they began their long, arduous journey to the Cumberland Mountains and the valley of the Tug Fork of the Big Sandy River.

This was, and continues to be, a hard country. The Shawnee held on to it long after they had lost everything else in Kentucky and Virginia, and it took tough, remorseless men to wrest it away from them.

The first wave of settlers who came through the Cumberland Gap after Daniel Boone moved on to the lush Bluegrass fields of central Kentucky. Late arrivals took what was left, these valleys, and scratched out a living from their rocky soil.

Later on, it became coal country, and when mining began to slump the entire economy of the region slid into the empty pits. In the late 1960s, newspaper publisher Harry Caudill wrote a book called *Night Comes to the Cumberlands*, a pessimistic appraisal of what the future held for the area.

Various federal programs aimed at alleviating poverty in Appalachia helped to soften the glum forecast. The roads have been vastly improved in the last twenty-five years, ending the isolation that once separated this remote corner from the rest of America. Some new employers have been persuaded to come in. Pikeville, Kentucky, home of the McCoys, is now regarded as an exemplary small town.

But the violence remains part of the tradition, and until recent years longtime residents have been reluctant to talk about the legendary feud. It was just family trouble, better left in the past. They blamed it for the negative picture of the region in the rest of the country; the stereotypical hillbillies who, in the words of the 1940s hit song, were always "Feudin', a'Fussin' and a'Fightin'."

As the area sought to rebuild its economic base, however, it discovered that visitors were quite interested in the Hatfields and

McCoys. Only in the 1990s, a century after it ended, did the Cumberlands begin to come to terms with its past and turn it into an attraction.

If you look at a dozen different sources you will come up with fifteen different versions of the feud's origin and main events. Some say one hundred people died in the decade of the most intense fighting, although the actual number is probably closer to a dozen.

But all agree the figure at the center of the feud was Anderson Hatfield, also known as "Devil Anse." He was "six feet of devil and 180 pounds of hell," according to one of the Hatfield sons. From his home in Logan, West Virginia, he ruled his clan and made life miserable for anyone who crossed them.

Devil Anse had thirteen children, and Randolph McCoy, the patriarch of his clan, fathered sixteen. So there was plenty of raw material to carry on the fight for a good many years.

Several historians focus on the stolen hog episode of 1878 as the start of the feud, simply because it seems such a ludicrous way to begin something that would cost so many lives. Floyd Hatfield, a cousin of Anse's, was accused of stealing the two porkers by Randolph McCoy, and the matter went to court.

Unfortunately for the cause of justice and for the McCoys, the presiding justice of the peace was Ellison Hatfield, Anse's brother. He

The Hatfield Family. Archive Photos

ruled that the Hatfields had more credible witnesses and that, moreover, they were better armed. Case closed.

Actually, the pig incident was the second time the McCoys felt poorly used by the courts. Six years before, Anse had filed a land ownership suit against the widow and thirteen-year-old brother-in-law of Asa Harmon McCoy, the man he was accused of killing during the Civil War. Hatfield won a 5,000-acre judgment from the friendly court. The pig incident simply added fuel to the already seething hatred felt by the McCoys.

It wasn't until the 1880s, however, that things really heated up. First came the matter of Johnse Hatfield and Roseanna McCoy. Some have tried to turn this into a Romeo and Juliet-of-the-Hills sort of affair. A highly romanticized movie version in 1949 even had the two lovers bringing peace to the families by riding between the two gun-toting factions.

Other historians insist just as strongly that it was their forbidden love that touched off the feud.

Roseanna was then a woman of twenty-one, about three years older than the smitten Johnse. She was soon great with child, a matter of great discomfort to Randolph McCoy, who brought her back to Pikeville from West Virginia.

The two never married, although Johnse wasn't terribly picky and eventually had four wives (not at the same time, however), including Roseanna's cousin, Nancy McCoy. But while the relationship certainly didn't help matters between the families, it didn't cause the feud, either.

In August 1882 Ellison Hatfield, the judge in the notorious stolen hog case, became overly happy while celebrating election day, near what is now Buskirk, Kentucky. He unwisely picked a fight with three McCoys, who stabbed him severely.

When he died a few days later, several Hatfields crossed into Kentucky from West Virginia and seized the offending McCoys. Under Anse's direction, the three were tied to a tree and dispatched with a fifty-shot volley. This, understandably, touched off the worst of the fighting.

The two sides raided back and forth across the state boundaries, mostly firing shots from ambush. Neither state was able to put a stop to it. Kentucky put a price on the Hatfields and sent bounty hunters across the line to seize them, but that didn't work, either.

Finally, on New Year's Day, 1888, came the crowning incident. A group of Hatfields crossed into Kentucky and attacked the home of

Randolph McCoy. The house caught fire and his daughter, Alifair, ran outside to douse the flames, knowing that there were strong prohibitions against shooting a woman, even in a blood feud.

Nonetheless, she went down with a fatal wound to the abdomen, and when her mother rushed to her aid she was clubbed unconscious with rifle butts. That seemed to remove the last vestige of restraint from both sides. Killing a woman had violated every feuding code, and now it was an all-out war.

Three weeks later, a band of fifty McCoys went into West Virginia, intent on shooting down any Hatfield they saw. By this time, the feud had become major national news, and reporters from the big city papers had found their way to the area to write the stories that would make the names of Hatfield and McCoy the very definition of a family feud.

The governors of both states called out their National Guards to restore peace. More than that, there were now economic stakes at risk. Coal operators and railroads were ready to move into the area, but only if this murderous vendetta was settled. The feud was holding back progress.

Ironically, the individual who stepped forward to resolve matters was Perry Cline, the McCoy relative who had lost his land as a teenager to Anse Hatfield in the controversial lawsuit of thirteen years before. Cline was now a young attorney with powerful connections in Pikeville. His guardian was John Dils, Jr., who ran the county political machine and stood to profit handsomely from corporate investment in the area. In 1889, they were ready to exact legal revenge.

First the two men got an acquittal for the McCoys, who had been arrested by Kentucky troops in the fight. Then they obtained the first conviction of Hatfield. Ellison Mounts, the nephew of Devil Anse, received the death penalty for the murder of Alifair McCoy.

Mounts was hanged in Pikeville in 1890. With the exception of sporadic eruptions over the next several months, the feud was over.

Both of the clan leaders died peacefully in bed at an advanced age. Anse Hatfield was eight-six, and Randolph McCoy, who lost five children to the blood feud, lived to be 103.

A few years before his death, a theater promoter had offered Hatfield a sizable amount of money to tour the vaudeville circuit. He figured it would be a major attraction. Anse considered it for a while and then turned it down. He said that leaving home would simply have made him too nervous.

THE SITES

Pikeville The area is still in the process of figuring out what it wants to do with the Hatfield-McCoy legacy. Promises of a local history museum, probably located in Pikeville, have been made and a new hiking trail along the crest of the Cumberlands has been named after the feuding families—although it does not lead to any of the places associated with them.

The site of Ellison Mounts' hanging, the event that ended the feud, is marked in Pikeville, on Kentucky Ave. and High St. It is on a hillside below Pikeville College, and is a bit hard to find. Take Hambley Blvd., the main road through town, and once past the downtown area watch for Kentucky Ave. coming in on the left. It's a one-way street, and just before its junction with High St. you'll spot the marker on the right.

Dils Cemetery The Dils Cemetery is the resting place of the McCoys. As you mount the stairs from the road to this hilltop burial ground, the monument to Randolph McCoy is directly to the right. Next to it is the grave of his daughter Roseanna, who died, disappointed in love, at the age of thirty in 1889. The cemetery is reached by taking Huffman Ave. from downtown, turning left on U.S. 119, and then taking an immediate right on Chloe Creek Rd. There is parking in a lot on the right, and stairs leading to the graveyard can be found right across Chloe Creek Rd.

Matewan Matewan was once a thriving railroad town in the midst of the West Virginia coal fields. It is best known as the site of the 1920 clash between the striking United Mine Workers and detectives brought on by the mine owners. Seven detectives, two miners, and Mayor Cable Testerman were killed in the battle that raged across the main street and onto the railroad tracks of the town. The chief of police, Sid Hatfield, was shot down by vengeful detectives the following year when he showed up for a court hearing in McDowell County.

Both Hatfields and McCoys lived in Matewan. There are, in fact, commercial buildings named after both families along its main street. The Matewan Development Center, in the McCoy Building, has exhibits on both the feud and the labor strife. It is open Monday to Friday, 9 a.m. to 5 p.m.; Saturday, 10 a.m. to 4 p.m.; Sunday, noon to 4 p.m. Donations accepted. (304) 426-4239.

The place where Ellison Hatfield died of his stab wounds from the McCoys is marked just across the railroad tracks from downtown, at West Virginia 49 and Warm Hollow Rd.

Sarah Ann Town Cemetery Devil Anse Hatfield wound up with the most imposing of all the memorials for those involved in the feud. A life-size statue of the clan leader stands beside his grave at the Sarah Ann Town Cemetery, on West Virginia 10, just south of Logan.

ANNUAL EVENT

Hatfield-McCoy Bluegrass Festival Matewan closes up its one street and celebrates the Hatfield-McCoy Bluegrass Festival each June. There are crafts, music, and historical displays. The date varies, so it's best to check in advance with the Tug Valley Chamber of Commerce at (304) 235-5240.

The Hatfields and McCoys Beckley is a fairly good distance from the West Virginia stomping grounds of the feuding families. But it is there, at Theatre West Virginia's Cliffside Amphitheater, that the outdoor musical pageant *The Hatfields and McCoys* is held each summer. It is performed in repertory with another musical historical drama, *Honey in the Rock*. The shows are held at 8:30 p.m., Tuesday to Sunday, from mid-June to the last weekend in August. For a schedule, ticket prices, and reservations call (800) 666-9142; www.theatrewestvirginia.com.

The theater is located 15 miles east of Beckley, which is, in turn, 55 miles south of Charleston on I-77.

JESSE JAMES

In the spring of 1882, Bob Ford was the most astonished man in America. He thought that he was going to be a hero. After gunning down the feared outlaw and killer Jesse James, Ford felt that reward money and acclamation would come his way.

He found himself, instead, on the wrong end of a legend. Within days of his death, James was transformed from outlaw to martyr. The bank robberies, the innocent bystanders shot, the terror his wild riders had spread were all forgotten. He had turned into a Missouri Robin Hood, and Ford was the "dirty little coward" who laid poor Jesse in his grave.

It wasn't as if Ford had done the manly thing in killing James. As much as some people would have enjoyed seeing Jesse behind bars, the idea of being shot down by a trusted friend while straightening a picture on your own living room wall did not quite square with heroic behavior.

But Jesse James had been a wanted man for more than sixteen years, ever since his gang had held up their first bank in the nearby town of Liberty (and killed a teenaged college student who happened to get in their way). It was thought that the time had finally come when members of the gang, maybe even Jesse himself, could be convicted in a Missouri courtroom. Public opinion was slowly swinging against him in a state still torn with bitter memories of the Civil War. The governor had placed a $10,000 price on his head to hasten the process along.

Ford's single gunshot ended all that. Even Jesse's enemies were appalled at the manner of his demise. "Jesse James was a wonderfully lawless, bloodthirsty man," said William A. Wallace, the prosecutor who was trying to break up the James Gang. "But that gave Ford no right to assassinate him. It was one of the most cowardly and diabolical deeds in history."

It also stunned the nation. "Jesse, By Jehovah," read the page one headline in huge type in the hometown St. Joseph newspaper. By the end of the year, Jesse's grave and boyhood home had become the top tourist attraction in the state, with his mother, Zerelda, taking in a quarter from everyone who wanted a look. She also sold authentic pebbles, which she sent a neighbor-boy down to the adjacent creek to fetch, from his grave.

Hagiographic stories about him were printed quickly in the Eastern press. He was no simple thug, but the last Confederate, a man driven to life as an outlaw because of the wrongs done to his family.

The train robber was actually the defender of widows and orphans; the steely-eyed killer, an avenger of lost causes.

More than a century of mythmaking has only enhanced his story. Jesse James remains the most enduring symbol of the American outlaw, the man who chose to defy rules and conventions to fulfill his own destiny. Almost never is he depicted gunning down unarmed men. But he did that, too, and often.

It is fair to say, however, that he was a product of his times. The scars left by the Civil War in western Missouri were as dark and bloody as any place in America. Vengeance towards a government that had taken land and possessions away was a powerful motivating factor among dozens of young men who, in other times, probably would have lived unexceptional lives as small farmers and store owners.

But that rationale was no more valid than it is today when applied to poor urban neighborhoods. Even in the best of times, Jesse James would have been a farmer you wouldn't have cared to cross.

He grew up in Kearney, Missouri, just northeast of present-day Kansas City, which

Jesse James Museum

was barely a river landing then. His father was a minister who left the family to save the souls of gold miners in California. He didn't succeed in saving his own, though, dying of cholera within weeks of reaching the Mother Lode country in 1848.

As a teenager he knew the terror of the night raiders. Jayhawkers and Red Legs rode across the border from Kansas to avenge the arson and death inflicted on them by Bushwhackers who supported the South. On one occasion, his stepfather had been lynched in front of his home and was cut down just in time by Jesse's mother. Jesse himself was lashed.

His older brother, Frank, went off to join Quantrill's Raiders. Frank rode on the murderous raid on Lawrence, Kansas, and stayed at his leader's side when Quantrill was killed in Kentucky. Jesse joined the guerillas, too, and by the time he was sixteen had participated in the Centralia Massacre. Bushwhackers under Quantrill's deranged assistant, Bloody Bill Anderson, stopped a train carrying Union soldiers in Missouri and shot down two hundred of them, including those who had surrendered.

Jesse took a bullet in the lung, a wound that almost killed him, while trying to surrender in the final days of the war. It hampered his breathing for the rest of his life. It did result, however, in his marrying a cousin, Zerelda Mimms, who helped nurse him back to health.

Quantrill received a fatal wound in May 1865 and the war ended for Frank James. He came home to Missouri. Most of the Bushwhackers picked up their lives and started over. But the James brothers could not. Instead, they sat and conspired with a small group of other Confederate veterans who would not return to a normal life.

On February 14, 1866, they struck. Riding into Liberty, location of the richest bank in western Missouri, they pulled off what is described as the first daylight bank robbery in America.

In a pattern that would be repeated many times, they used speed, the threat of brutality and the frightening sound of galloping horses and gunmen screaming the high-pitched Rebel yell to cow resistance. It was the same technique that Quantrill employed to intimidate the towns he raided and Jesse had been an apt pupil.

They got away with over $70,000, a staggering amount for the time; so large that the bank never recovered and had to go out of business.

George Wymore, a student at nearby William Jewell College, happened to be walking towards the courthouse square just as the robbers came racing out of the bank. He panicked and started to run to spread the alarm. He was shot down in his tracks and his body left lying on the snowy streets as the raiders departed.

The Valentine's Day holdup stunned Missouri. The fact that a bank, a symbol of stability and security, had been robbed was shocking enough. But even though the area was accustomed to violent death, the idea of an inoffensive young man being shot down during an ordinary crime shook the area. It indicated that these were desperate men who were to be feared, which is exactly what Jesse James intended.

There is no proof that he shot Wymore. But he was regarded as the best shot of the group and was known already as a man who did not shrink from killing to make a point.

"The usual defense of the outlaws," wrote prosecutor Wallace in later years, "that their robberies and homicides were committed in just revenge upon Northern men for mistreatment received by them or their relatives during the Civil War . . . is overwhelmed by the evidence. Every bank robbed by them, with possibly two exceptions, belonged to Southern men. . . . The truth is, too, that the persons killed in these bank robberies were Southerners. We had as well admit the truth, they robbed for money, not for revenge."

Greenup Bird, the head cashier, told police that the men looked familiar. In fact, as he was being shoved into the bank's vault, one of the robbers had joked: "Don't you know every bird should be caged?"

But he couldn't place who it was. Or, if he could, he wasn't saying. With the killing of Wymore, the gunmen had made their point, and it was a powerful statement. Don't get in our way! As the robberies mounted, investigators were never able to make positive identifications. No one wanted to take the chance.

In the instances when a name was given up, there was no shortage of those who provided alibis, "proving" that the accused was hundreds of miles away at the time.

The group hit two more Missouri banks within the next year, using the same method of operation. But in Richmond, Missouri, on May 23, 1867, they encountered resistance for the first time. The townspeople shot back. The mayor, the town jailer, and his young son were all killed, and the gang rode out unscathed.

The killings, however, aroused the state. Three men suspected of having been on the raid were eventually lynched. But the names of the James Brothers were never spoken aloud, although everyone seemed to understand that they were the leaders.

Jesse, in fact, made a point of being baptized at Kearney and sang a few times with the church choir.

By the mid-1870s, the situation had become ludicrous. It was as if Missouri was living with a dirty little secret it dare not voice. The state was gaining a national reputation as a center of outlawry, and in the gubernatorial election of 1874 the Republicans made suppression of these bandits a campaign issue. They charged the Democrats with shielding them from the law.

This was a highly inflammatory issue, since the Democrats were linked with secession. Many former guerillas did indeed support the

James Gang. But the far larger number of ex-Confederates in Missouri spoke out against them.

The gang extended its reach all the way to a bank in Russellville, Kentucky, and that brought the Pinkerton Detective Agency into the case. But still Jesse eluded any attempt to apprehend him. He was married openly in a church ceremony in Kansas City, even though he was by then a wanted man.

Jesse was a fair-skinned man of about average height for those times, about 5-9 with a slight built. He was several inches shorter than Frank, with no facial resemblance whatsoever to his older brother. Everyone who met him remarked on his deep blue eyes, which turned steel gray when he was angered. No one ever wanted to see them turn gray.

For most of his life he was clean-shaven, although in his last years he grew a dark beard as a token towards disguising a face that was growing familiar on wanted posters. But photo reproductions were of poor quality and, even if they had wanted to, those who encountered him may not have been able to make an identification. His neighbors in St. Joseph professed amazement that they had been living so near the famous robber.

Having perfected bank robbery, the gang turned to trains in 1875. They deliberately wrecked a Rock Island express in Iowa, killing the engineer. Then six months later, just to vary the pace, they held up an old-fashioned stagecoach in Arkansas.

For a while, every holdup in the south central states was attributed to the James Gang. But they were active enough in reality to keep the pot stirring.

Several Pinkerton men who tried to work undercover were gunned down by gang members when local residents informed on their activities. Jesse himself is credited with the shooting of James Whicher, one of the agency's top detectives, in 1874.

But that act had severe consequences. Now the Chicago-based organization, apparently working closely with the federal government, was grimly determined to hunt the killers down. The Pinkertons were told that the James Brothers planned to visit their mother at her Kearney home in January 1875. They arrived by secret train and prepared an ambush.

Frank and Jesse were nowhere near the place, but the Pinkertons attacked anyhow. An incendiary device was thrown through a window of the farmhouse and extinguished. Another one followed, and this one exploded. Jesse's young half-brother, Archie Samuel, was killed, and his mother had her arm blown off.

The Pinkertons, realizing their mistake, ran off. But the publicity was so harmful that most of Missouri rallied behind James, enabling him to continue his career for several more years, even after gunning down a neighbor whom he suspected of assisting the detectives.

By now the gang had decided that it needed one spectacular job to secure its finances. Jesse selected a target far from the old familiar places. The First National Bank of Northfield, Minnesota, was hundreds of miles from home. In this unsuspecting little town, he felt a holdup would be easy.

On September 7, 1876, Jesse, Bob Younger, and Charlie Pitts rode into Northfield, wearing long white dusters to conceal their sidearms. Over a leisurely breakfast, they posed as cattle buyers who were in the area to close a deal.

Then they strolled over to the bank, and, while other gang members watched the street, they announced the holdup. But despite the guns that were being leveled at them and a knife held to one man's throat, the three employees refused to cooperate. One of them rushed out the door and despite being wounded by Younger managed to spread the alarm. The cashier was shot dead by Jesse when he reached into a drawer.

The bandits finally scooped up some cash, but the delay was fatal. Northfield was up in arms. By the time the gang reached the street, guns were firing at them from every direction. Clell Miller and Bill Chadwell fell with fatal wounds. Jesse and Frank; Pitts; and the Youngers, Bob, Jim, and Cole, all were wounded. Some were almost incapacitated.

The James Brothers managed to escape the pursuing posse and after ten days crossed into the Dakota Territory. But Pitts was killed and all three Youngers captured. The gang had been annihilated. It was the worst miscalculation of Jesse's career. There was no sympathy wasted on them by Minnesotans, no friendly farm nearby at which to hide. The gang members were not heroes to the North country.

"I tried a desperate game and lost," said Bob Younger. "My brothers and I are rough boys and used to rough work and therefore must abide by the consequences."

He died in prison thirteen years later, while his brothers served out their full twenty-five-year terms. Jim killed himself shortly after his release while Cole went on to become a revivalist preacher, touring the country to warn about his misspent life. He outlived everyone else in the gang, dying near his old home in Lee's Summit, Missouri, in 1916.

For three years, the James Brothers disappeared. They made their way to Mexico for a while and then hid out in Nashville, Tennessee. It was then that Jesse first used the alias of Howard, the name he would die with.

In 1879, a train was held up near Glendale, Missouri, a job with all the earmarks of the old James Gang. They had recruited a new set of hard riders, young boys seeking adventure, not old enough to harbor grudges from the war. One of them, Dick Liddil, lived with the sister of the two Ford brothers, Bob and Charlie. They never rode with the gang, but functioned as hangers-on and go-furs. Another of the new boys, Bill Ryan, was captured after the Glendale job, and Wallace prepared to put him on trial.

The James brothers weren't too concerned about that. There was no chance of convicting a member of the gang. Not in Missouri. And they still had some old scores to settle, too.

Again Jesse made a bad decision. On July 15, 1881, the gang boarded a Rock Island train out of Kansas City, in Gallatin, Missouri. They held up the passengers and killed one of them, Frank McMillan. But witnesses said later that it was obvious they were after someone else.

When conductor William Westfall saw the men who had boarded his train, he gasped. "You're the one I want," said Frank James and shot him. Westfall turned to run and the elder James fired again. The conductor stumbled but continued scrambling away. Then Jesse fired one bullet through the man's head.

According to railroad records, Westfall had worked on the special train that brought the Pinkertons to Kearney on the night Zerelda James's home was bombed. The James Brothers somehow had found out.

But this killing once again turned opinion against the gang. Prosecutor Wallace, realizing that this was his chance, cannily made sure that a number of illustrious former Confederate officers were in the courtroom when Ryan went on trial. Wallace was threatened with death if he went ahead, and the James Gang set off fireworks in the nearby woods as a signal that they were watching.

But the jury convicted Ryan, one of the most stunning verdicts in Missouri legal history. Wallace called it "the supreme hour in my practice as a lawyer."

Almost immediately, the James Gang started to crumble. Big reward money was placed on their heads and the fear factor was gone. Jesse killed Ed Miller, whom he suspected might turn him in, and Liddil shot down Wood Hite, who was a cousin of the James's. Fearing for his life, Liddil then turned himself in and gave up the names of everyone else in the gang.

Shortly after that, Bob Ford made a trip to the home of Governor Thomas J. Crittenden. He wanted to make sure the $10,000 reward on Jesse would be good, dead or alive. The governor assured him that he could collect either way.

On April 3, 1882, he chose dead. He called upon the unsuspecting James at the outlaw's St. Joseph home, where Jesse was living under the name of Howard, and shot him in the back.

Jesse James was thirty-four years old. It had been a life spent almost entirely in murder and thievery, violence and blood feuds. Yet within weeks he was being mourned as a hero. His devoted mother put up a grave marker that read: "In loving remembrance of my beloved son. Murdered by a traitor and coward whose name is not worthy to appear here."

Frank James, terrified that someone else would come gunning for him, surrendered. He was put on trial for the murder of McMillan. Wallace was confident that he could get another conviction.

But once more opinion had swung back to the side of the remaining James brother. When the defense put Confederate hero General Joseph O. Shelby on the stand, the game was over. In Shelby's emotional, if somewhat inebriated, testimony, Frank came across as the last Southern trooper. He was acquitted and lived on until 1915, without ever serving a day in jail.

Instead, Frank and Zerelda James became keepers of the flame, ceaselessly expanding the legend of Jesse. In time, he boosted the admission charge to the old homestead to fifty cents a head and charged extra for taking pictures.

But there was no stopping the motion pictures made about Jesse. One of the first, in fact, starred the bandit's son, Jesse James, Jr., who had been an infant when his father died. He left his job as a Kansas City attorney to play the role of his father in a 1920 Western.

"Missouri has been living down the James Boys for nearly fifty years," sternly editorialized the *Kansas City Journal*, "and had pretty well succeeded until this new outbreak. Of course, young Jesse conceives this as an opportunity to prove that his father and uncle were driven into banditry by social and political oppression. But he is adding nothing to his reputation for good citizenship by lending himself to this precious piece of profiteering at the expense of truth and historical accuracy."

But three years later, when a book appeared called *Strenuous Americans*, which meant to "embody all that is American in the American character," Jesse was the second name listed; right between Brigham Young and P. T. Barnum.

The legend seemed to gather force in the 1930s, when the dislocations of the Depression made anyone who held up banks seem like a heroic figure. A string of movies in which Jesse figured as one great guy appeared.

In 1948, near the centennial of his birth, an electrifying announcement was made. Jesse hadn't died at all. It was part of a clever plan, a way for him to disappear and lead a normal life. That was some other guy in the coffin.

The real Jesse James had been living near St. Louis under the name of J. Frank Dalton, and since he was one hundred years old he felt it was time to tell the truth. Reporter Robert Ruark was sent out by the *St. Louis Globe-Democrat* to interview the old fellow and he thought his story was pretty convincing. No less an authority than *The Police Gazette* proclaimed that he was the real thing.

Dalton decided to hold a "bandit reunion" at the Meramec Caverns, which promoted itself as one of Jesse James's hideouts. It was given national coverage, and Dalton died a happy man in 1950.

His story was riddled through with inconsistencies and errors of fact. But it wouldn't go away. Finally, in 1995, Jesse's descendants ordered that his body be exhumed to prove once and for all that it was the real bandit buried in Kearney.

The bones were submitted to DNA testing and the evidence was conclusive. It was he. Whoever Dalton may have been, he wasn't Jesse James.

There was one additional oddity about the test. In old photographs of Jesse in his coffin, a bullet hole appears over his eyebrow. It was assumed that this was the exit wound of the shot that killed him and a hole in the wall of his home was shown off as the place where the bullet had come to rest.

Over the years, so many visitors to the home had gouged out a chunk of the wall that a hole the size of a softball had been left there. But the exhumation proved that the bullet had remained inside his skull. The mark on his eyebrow was simply an old scar. So all those people across America with pieces of Jesse's bullet hole in their possession really have nothing but a piece of old wallpaper.

As for Bob Ford, he lived on as if under the curse of Cain. A pariah in Missouri, he moved to the mining town of Creede, Colorado, and opened a saloon, while living in constant fear that someone from the old days would find him and even the score for Jesse.

On June 8, 1892, someone did. Ed O'Kelly walked into Ford's establishment carrying a shotgun. "Been waiting for this, ain't you, Bob Ford?" he said and fired one round into his face.

O'Kelly was arrested and placed under guard to prevent a lynching. "I don't rob and I don't insult women," he told officers, "but I kill rats like Bob Ford."

He was convicted of murder and sentenced to life in the state prison. But thousands of pleas for clemency were sent from Missouri, and his sentence was reduced. He \ released in 1902 after serving ten years.

Two months after his death, Ford's body was taken back to Missouri for reburial. It was the only way he ever could have returned to his home state.

THE SITES

Jesse James Farm and Museum The Jesse James Farm and Museum is billed as the oldest paid tourist attraction in Missouri. It's been satisfying the curiosity of visitors to Kearney since 1882, when it opened for business a few weeks after Jesse's unfortunate death.

For its first thirty-three years the farmhouse was operated by his mother, Zerelda, and then Frank James, who both lived on the premises. Jesse's older brother, in fact, died of a stroke on the bedroom floor. It is now a state facility and very well run. The resident historians are authoritative, informative, and even-handed when it comes to describing the lives and careers of the James family.

The central portion of this cabin was built in 1842, when Reverend Robert James and his wife, Zerelda, arrived on the Missouri frontier from Kentucky. Frank was born early the following year, and Jesse came along in 1848, a few months after his father had died in California. Zerelda then married Dr. Reuben Samuel, a physician, who moved into the house.

The family was hardly a pack of semi-literate hillbillies. Frank liked to quote Shakespeare and while Jesse was a bit short on formal education he seemed to be quick-witted. Zerelda was a strong-minded, strapping woman, nearly 6 feet in height, with a will to match.

The back portion of the house contains the kitchen, where the bomb that cost Zerelda her arm was thrown. Many of the furnishings and carpeting are family originals.

Jesse originally was buried in back of the house, but the gravesite was moved to Mount Olivet Cemetery, in Kearney, in 1902 so it could be better protected. A museum placing Jesse's career in historical perspective is located near the parking area and contains several exhibits of family memorabilia. Mt. Olivet Cemetery is on Missouri 92 at Missouri 33, in Kearney. The farmhouse is a five-minute walk away in a setting that preserves its sense of isolation.

The farm is located east of I-35, by way of Missouri 92 and Jesse James Rd., about 28 miles northeast of downtown Kansas City, Missouri. It is open daily, 9 a.m. to 4 p.m., May through September; Monday to Saturday, 9 a.m. to 4 p.m., and Sunday, 12 p.m. to 4 p.m., rest of year. Admission is $7; under fifteen $3.75. (816) 628-6065; www.jessejames.org.

The Jesse James Home The Jesse James Home is now in its third location in St. Joseph. It was originally situated on a hill just outside the downtown area. Then in 1939 it was moved to the U.S. 71 Beltway, where it operated as a tourist stop on the grounds of a gas station and café. In 1977 it was moved back into the city, two blocks from its original site, adjacent to the Patee House, the city's historic grand hotel.

It was to the Patee (then known as the World's Hotel) that Jesse's wife and children were taken following the shooting. The hotel was the original headquarters of the Pony Express, and the Jesse James House is run in conjunction with the historical complex, at Penn and 12th Sts.

The modest frame bungalow has been restored to its appearance of the day of the shooting in 1882, including several pieces of family furniture. The room in which Jesse was killed by Bob Ford, with the picture he was straightening deliberately left hanging crooked, is described in a tape-recorded message. The house also contains several displays relating to the 1995 exhumation of Jesse's body, with a collection of items removed from the original coffin.

The house is open 10 a.m. to 4 p.m., Monday to Saturday; opening at 1 p.m. on Sunday. Admission is $2; students $1. (816) 232-8206.

Jesse James Bank Museum When the James Gang robbed the Clay County Savings and Loan in Liberty, the bank could never recover its losses. There was no federal insurance in those days, and it went out of business in 1868, two years after the holdup, paying depositors sixty cents on the dollar.

The brick building, which first opened in 1858, is now the oldest structure on the town's Courthouse Square. It subsequently housed two other banks, a variety of commercial ventures, and has been a museum since 1965. No significant alterations were ever made to it, so the interior remains almost precisely the way it looked when the James Gang rode up on Valentine's Day, 1866.

A guide narrates details of the holdup in the bank's main business area, and a back room contains exhibits on the career of the James Gang.

The Jesse James Bank Museum is open Monday to Saturday, 9 a.m. to 4 p.m. Admission is $3; under fifteen $1.50. (816) 781-4458. It is located at 103 N. Water St., east of I-35, by way of Missouri 152, about 16 miles northeast of downtown Kansas City, Missouri.

The 1859 Jail and Marshal's Home Although Frank James was never sentenced to any time in jail, he did reside in the Independence Jail while awaiting trial in 1882. Things were made as comfortable as possible for him, considering the surroundings. During his few months spent here, the jailer permitted several amenities, such as carpeting and personal effects, denied to most inmates.

The jail had been built in 1859 and was notorious during the Civil War as a place of internment for Southern sympathizers, or those suspected of disloyalty. It continued as a jail and the residence of the local marshal until 1933.

Visitors may tour the private quarters of the marshals who lived here, the cells (including the one that was set aside for Frank, made up to look as it did when he occupied it), and an annex which contains displays on the history of the building.

The 1859 Jail and Marshal's Home is located in downtown Independence, at 217 N. Main St., just south of Truman Blvd. It is open Monday to Saturday, 10 a.m. to 4 p.m.; Sunday, 1 p.m. to 4 p.m.; April through October. Closed Mondays in March, November, and December; closed the rest of the year. Admission $3; children under sixteen $1. (816) 252-1892.

Northfield Historical Society The town that smashed the James Gang in 1876 is justifiably proud of the achievement. Northfield, Minnesota, preserves the memory of the fatal raid in the building that used to be the First National Bank. It is now the Northfield Historical Society Museum, at 408 Division St.

The museum is open Tuesday to Saturday, 10 a.m. to 4 p.m., and 1 p.m. to 4 p.m., Sunday. Admission is $2; children under thirteen $1.50. (507) 645-9268; www.northfieldhistory.org. Northfield is located east of I-35, on Minnesota 19, about 40 miles south of St. Paul.

Jesse James Wax Museum The strange story of J. Frank Dalton and his claim to be Jesse James is one of the odder manifestations of the legend surrounding the outlaw. The DNA testing on Jesse's remains in 1995 put the final hammer to Dalton's tale. Nonetheless, at the Jesse James Wax Museum they are sticking to Dalton's story. In fact, it is billed as "the most authentic story ever told," which is quite a claim.

It may be silly, but the museum is a great example of an old-fashioned roadside attraction built along what used to be the Mother Road, U.S. Route 66. It now stands just off I-44 at the Stanton exit, 46 miles west of the St. Louis Beltway (I-270). Inside are wax images of the aged Dalton, the young Jesse, and several other figures in the story.

The museum is open daily, 9 a.m. to 5 p.m. Admission is $4; children under eleven $2. (573) 927-5233.

Meramec Caverns Nearby is another classic roadside attraction that has cleverly linked itself to Jesse James's reputation. Meramec Caverns was a local landmark for decades. With the advent of the automobile, the entrance room to the underground system was used for dances by youths from nearby towns.

In the 1930s, a local entrepreneur, Lester B. Dill, got the idea of opening it for tourists. But business was slow. Then he came across an historical article that indicated Quantrill's Raiders had blown up a Federal gunpowder mill in the cave. Knowing that Jesse rode with Quantrill for a time, Dill surmised that he knew about the cave and may well have used it as a hideout on a few occasions.

At least, that's what the highway signs said. Dill put up hundreds of signs along U.S. 66, all of them prominently featuring the James angle, and his cave became one of the big tourist stops on the highway west. Actually, the material relating to the outlaws is just a tiny part of the ninety-minute tour, and the spectacular Stage Curtain formation is worth seeing. But Jesse is who brings them in.

The Caverns are 3 miles off I-44 at the Stanton exit. They are open daily, 9 a.m. to 5 p.m.; until 7 p.m., May through Labor Day.

Admission to the guided tour is $15; children under eleven $8. (800) 676-6105; www.americascave.com.

ANNUAL EVENTS

The Life and Times of Jesse James *The Life and Times of Jesse James* is presented at the James Farm in Kearney, Missouri. The historical drama is performed in the evening, Friday through Sunday, August to Labor Day. Call (816) 628-6065 for times and ticket information.

Russellville Festival The tactic of thundering into a town and intimidating it into compliance was used repeatedly by the James Gang and usually with great success. But not always. One of the first towns to offer large-scale resistance was Russellville, Kentucky, in May 1868.

When the cashier of the Long and Norton Bank managed to get out of the building, despite being wounded and pistol-whipped by Cole Younger, he alerted the community. By the time the other bandits were ready to escape, they had come under fire. One citizen was wounded in the exchange of gunfire, and the rest took off in pursuit of the gang.

But Jesse always made sure that his men were supplied with the best horses available and that they were well rested. The gang made its escape over the Tennessee border, well ahead of the Russellville posse. Pinkerton agents managed to arrest just one of the raiders.

Russellville salutes its show of resistance on the second weekend of October with a festival that is combined with a celebration of tobacco, the major crop in this part of Kentucky. There is a reenactment of the holdup, antique shows, entertainment, and tobacco displays. Call (270) 726-2206. Russellville is on U.S. 68, 30 miles west of the I-65 exit at Bowling Green.

Defeat of Jesse James Festival Northfield gets into the spirit with its Defeat of Jesse James festival, held the weekend after Labor Day. There is also a raid re-enactment here, as well as outdoor food booths, an art show, rodeo, and parade. Call (800) 658-2548.

BLACK BART

Not many of the bad guys in American history could ever be described as lovable. Maybe Butch Cassidy on a good day. But most of the others, despite reputations that were greatly laundered after their deaths, were surly devils.

The exception, despite his menacing moniker, was Black Bart—dandy, poet, humorist, man about San Francisco, and stagecoach robber. You've got to love him.

His real name was Charles E. Bolton, and when he wasn't holding up Wells Fargo stagecoaches he worked as a mining engineer. He frequently dined in the same San Francisco restaurant favored by several of the police investigators who were scouring California for him.

Between 1875 and 1883, he held up twenty-eight stages. He never fired his gun and made a very favorable impression upon passengers, many of whom remarked on his gentlemanly demeanor. The fact that he rarely took anything from them but only grabbed the express company's strong boxes may have helped enhance his image.

He left almost no clues. But he did leave poems.

His best-known composition went:

I've labored long and hard for bread,
For honor and for riches.
But on my corns too long you've tred,
You fine-haired sons-of-bitches.

These literary efforts were always signed: "Black Bart, PO-8."

The work that went into ending his eight-year criminal career would have been worthy of Sherlock Holmes; only that detective would not make his first literary appearance until nine years after Bolton's arrest. It was James Hume, a Wells Fargo investigator, who cracked the case at last.

Bolton's success was based on careful study. It was not easy for a lone man on foot to hold up a horse-drawn coach. But he was a frequent visitor to California's mining country and, using his training as an engineer, he made a careful study of the places where a coach would be most vulnerable—near the crest of long inclines, or around a sharp curve, where a man could wait in concealment for the coach to slow down.

His first job was on July 26, 1875, when he hit the stage from Copperopolis. This Calaveras County mining town, one of the leading sources of copper for the Union Army in the previous decade, was already in decline. Cash boxes were being sent out with less frequency. But

Bolton seemed to know this one was coming.

Driver John Shine, who would become a state senator, said later that just as he approached the summit of Funk Hill an astonishing figure suddenly appeared in the road. He wore a white duster, and a flour sack with holes cut for eyes masked his face. He had a derby hat setting rakishly atop his head. He also held a shotgun.

"Throw down the box," he ordered Shine. From the edge of his vision, Shine could see the muzzles of several other guns pointed at him from behind boulders and trees. He decided quickly to comply.

Only later, when the strongbox was long gone, along with the several thousand dollars it contained, did Shine return to the spot of the holdup. He noticed that the concealed gunmen hadn't moved. On closer investigation they proved to be sticks, propped up by the canny Bolton.

In the next few years, several other robberies followed, all across the mining district. Bart also ranged into the north, through the Russian River country and up as far as Willits.

He never got away with a major haul. In his entire career, it is estimated that he garnered only about $18,000—although that wasn't bad money for the 1870s.

Wells Fargo Bank

His first poem, quoted at the start of this chapter, was dropped off following the robbery of the Duncan's Mill coach, in August 1877. After that, the verses became a regular part of his modus operandi. The newspapers loved the story. Not only was this man sticking it to Wells Fargo, he was jeering at the company in rhyme.

Wells Fargo was stung and assigned a team of detectives to the case. They found next to nothing. He wore coverings over his boots so his heels left no markings. Since he traveled on foot and quickly made his way into mountain country after a holdup, there were no tracks to follow.

Moreover, there was no pattern to his holdups. Sometimes months would go by between them and then several would occur in a short time span, but many miles apart. The express company was baffled.

In 1882, however, it appeared as if Black Bart's luck was running out. One stage driver, anticipating a problem, kept a rifle at his side, and when the robber did appear he got off a quick shot that creased his scalp.

Then on November 3, 1883, after a long period of inactivity, Bolton returned to Funk Hill, the site of his first crime. It was as if he was trying to regain confidence by going back to his initial success. But this time, it was his undoing.

The driver deliberately had bolted the strongbox beneath the passenger compartment. While Bolton waited for it to be released, a trailing rider came upon the scene. He fired three shots at the robber who fled into the underbrush.

He left behind a handkerchief. According to some accounts, he had used it to wrap a hand wound he received from one of the gunshots. But others say he simply suffered a panic attack and took off without noticing it was gone.

Detective Hume examined it carefully and found that it contained a laundry mark in one corner, with tiny lettering that read FXO7. At that time, he knew that only San Francisco laundries marked their items in such a manner. However, there were ninety-one laundries in the city.

Hume was given an investigative team to visit each one of them. After a week, the search party was rewarded at Ferguson and Bigg's California Laundry. The owners identified the handkerchief as belonging to a dignified gentleman named Charles Boles, who lived in a nearby hotel.

When confronted by the detectives, the suspect drew himself up to his full height, flashed his diamond stickpin and heavy gold watch, and identified himself as T. Z. Spalding. But a signed family Bible and some unfinished poems in the same handwriting as those left at Black Bart's crimes gave the game away. This was Bolton, and Bolton was Black Bart.

He was indeed a man with legitimate business interests and some education, a Civil War veteran from Illinois. But whenever money ran low, he replenished his supply in the most effective way he could. He added that he had never even loaded his shotgun when he went on a job. He didn't want to risk harming anyone.

Bolton was sentenced to six years at San Quentin Prison, but was released after a bit more than four, in 1888. The reporters who swarmed around him noted that he had aged considerably in confinement. He was partially deaf, stooped, and his hair had turned completely white. But his wit remained undimmed.

"Gentlemen, I am through with crime," he said. One newsman asked if he intended to keep writing poetry.

Bolton laughed. "Didn't you just hear me say that I was through with crime?" With that he walked away and vanished from history.

Later that year, another Wells Fargo stagecoach was robbed and a poem left behind. It was quickly assumed that Black Bart was at it again. But Hume said it was an obvious hoax.

"This poem," he said, "is not up to Bolton's standards."

THE SITES

Wells Fargo Exhibit Wells Fargo was willing to let bygones be bygones. In fact, there was even a rumor in the years after Bolton's release from prison that the company had pensioned him off with the proviso that he stop holding up its stagecoaches. Several New York newspapers ran that story at his reported death in 1917.

Like his career in crime, however, Bolton proved elusive even in death. There was no confirmation of his obituary. In fact, his old adversary Hume said that he heard Bolton had bought it seventeen years before on a hunting trip in the Sierra.

Wells Fargo features an exhibit on Black Bart in its historical museum at its San Francisco banking headquarters, at 420 Montgomery St. The museum contains various displays on the Gold Rush era and the role the company played in the opening of the West, as well as on Bolton's one-man campaign against Wells Fargo.

The museum is open Monday to Friday, 9 a.m. to 5 a.m. Free admission. (415) 396-2619.

Willits Visitors to Willits are still shown a cluster of rocks reputedly used by Black Bart for concealment in one of his stagecoach ambushes. They are located 11 miles south of the city, on old U.S. 101. Look for the marker. Willits is 135 miles north of the Golden Gate Bridge.

Funk Hill Although Copperopolis did not produce a metal as glamorous as gold, it is still one of the more picturesque old mining towns of the Mother Lode country with a wealth of buildings from the 1860s. It is located 12 miles west of Angels Camp, on California 4. The site of Black Bart's first and last holdups, at Funk Hill, is 4 miles east of the town.

THE DALTON GANG

It was the phony whiskers that did it. The Dalton Boys were not the brightest pennies in the stack, but when they decided to hold up two banks at once, in broad daylight, in the middle of their old hometown, they realized that the job called for special measures.

After all, it wouldn't do to be recognized too quickly. Their former neighbors in Coffeyville, Kansas, knew what the boys had been up to for the last two years. Trains, banks, horse rustling. They were famous. Maybe not as famous as their cousins on their mother's side, the James and Younger boys. But that would surely come.

Bob Dalton himself, who devised the double bank holdup scheme, declared that this job would "beat anything Jesse James ever did."

So on October 5, 1892, three of the Dalton Brothers—Bob, Grat, and Emmett—along with Dick Broadwell and Bill Powers, rode into the unsuspecting Kansas town, intent on holding up both the C. M. Condon and First National Banks.

Shortly after they dismounted, the three Daltons put on the false whiskers, obtained for the purpose of concealing their identities. Looking more like the Marx Brothers than the Dalton Brothers, they advanced on the banks.

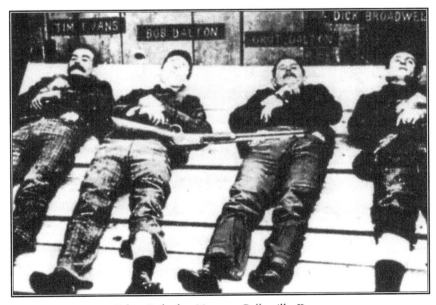

Dalton Defenders Museum, Coffeyville, Kansas

There they were observed by Alex McRenna, a resident of the town. Normally a group of riders carrying Winchester rifles would not have aroused his suspicions. Men riding in from the Oklahoma Territory, just a few miles to the south, was a common enough occurrence. Most of them, given the sort of place the Territory was, would be armed.

Even when these men cradled their weapons and began to run towards the middle of town, McKenna didn't react. But when he saw the beards, he knew something funny was happening.

Even before the five gang members had entered the banks they had targeted, McKenna was running down the street to spread the alarm. "It's the Daltons," he hollered. The very obviousness of their disguises had given the game away.

The Daltons hadn't started out this way. Although the eight brothers were raised on glowing tales of their illustrious outlaw kin, three of them lived quietly as farmers with their mother in the family's new home, near Kingfisher. Oklahoma.

Four of them had served as deputy marshals, working for Judge Isaac Parker's famous court in Fort Smith, Arkansas. Frank Dalton was gunned down in 1887 in performance of his official duties. Bill Dalton had made his way to California and was elected to the state assembly.

The remaining Daltons grew dissatisfied with life as lawmen. The pay was lousy; working conditions were even worse. There were constant hassles with bureaucrats who tried to disallow their expenses— $2 for an arrest and six cents a mile transportation costs.

Emmett also worked as a cowboy on the Halsell HX Bar Ranch, near Guthrie, Oklahoma. This was a sprawling cattle operation along the Cimarron River, and it seemed to attract an especially rough group of riders. Many of them were dodging their pasts, and others were looking for future trouble.

A remarkable number of cowboys from this ranch went into outlaw work, and several of them rode with the Daltons. When it came time to organize, Emmett would know just where to recruit.

In the meantime, the three Daltons decided to quit the law and try some free-lance rustling in the Indian Territory. But they botched the job. With a posse in pursuit, Bob and Emmett decided it was an excellent time to pay brother Bill a visit in California. Grat was arrested but turned loose for lack of evidence and he, too, headed for the Pacific Slope.

This was one instance where a little California dreaming was disastrous. On February 6, 1891, the Southern Pacific train was held up near what is now the town of Earlimart. In a pattern that would become a Dalton signature, Bob forced the fireman, carrying his coal pick, back to the express car and had him break open the door. The gang was then able to loot at leisure.

The fireman made the mistake of trying to get away, and he was shot down. While Bob had previously killed a cowboy with a long criminal record back in Oklahoma, this was his first fatal shot while carrying out a criminal act. There would be more.

The robbery came apart when Grat's horse was injured. A posse was able to pick up his trail and, to its surprise, found that it led right to the home of State Assemblyman Dalton. Both men were arrested, while the other two Dalton brothers hastened back to Oklahoma.

Bill had an alibi and was released, although his political career came to an untimely end. Even in California, this sort of family behavior was frowned on. But Grat was given twenty years in prison. On his way there, however, he managed to get away by diving head first out the window of a moving railroad car.

He rejoined his brothers and for the next seventeen months they became the terrors of the Southern Plains. The Daltons already were wanted men in one state and one territory. There was no turning back. So with some of Emmett's old friends from the HX Bar Ranch, they started checking train schedules.

Broadwell and Powers rode with them. So did "Blackface" Charley Bryant, nicknamed for a permanent powder burn on his face. So did Bill Doolin, who would go on to have the longest career of all of them.

They held up a Santa Fe train near what is now Perry, Oklahoma, and killed a member of a pursuing posse. During another Santa Fe holdup, at Red Rock, Oklahoma, Bryant gunned down a young telegraph operator who was trying to send an alert.

The gang members would go undercover after a robbery, either getting jobs as ranch hands or hiding out in caves along the Cimarron. But Bryant's distinct facial identity made him readily identifiable and Marshal Ed Short found and arrested him at Hennessey, Oklahoma.

Short intended to take his man to Wichita, Kansas, by train but one stop along on the trip, at Waukomis, Bryant got his hands free enough to grab a gun. He and Short exchanged shots, and both men were killed.

The gang was now reduced to six men, but they were about to pull their biggest job. On July 14, 1892, they hit the Katy Line express at Adair, Oklahoma. What made this holdup remarkable was that lawmen were waiting for them. Their move had been anticipated, and several Indian police and U.S. marshals were riding in a passenger car.

What they hadn't expected was that the Daltons would take control of the station at Adair and pull off the robbery while the train was making a regularly scheduled stop. It wasn't until the express car had been entered in the Daltons' usual manner, with the aid of the fireman's ax, that the police woke up.

But when the lawmen jumped off the train, they found themselves on the opposite side from the gang. While the Daltons backed up a wagon and loaded it with the money, the police were trying to shoot under and between the cars. They didn't hit a single outlaw, but one of their bullets managed to kill the town doctor, who was sitting in his office one block from the depot.

The gang members dropped from sight for about ten weeks. Bob had assumed the leadership role, and he knew there was nothing that could be done until the pursuit cooled down. But he had big plans.

It was while he was in hiding after the Adair holdup that Bob devised the Coffeyville plan. The Daltons knew every street in town, he reasoned. The two-bank job was feasible, and with the money they got, everyone could leave Oklahoma and get a new start. Besides, it had never been done before. That appealed to Bob most of all.

On October 2, the men left their hideout near Tulsa and began riding north. Things went smoothly until the morning they neared Coffeyville. Then Doolin's horse went lame. He needed a fresh mount, so while the other five rode ahead he stayed behind to steal another horse, promising to join them as quickly as possible. That bit of luck saved his life.

The men left their horses in an alley behind 8th Street, agreeing to meet there after the job was done. Bob estimated it would take no more than ten minutes.

Bob and Emmett took the First National Bank, while Grat and the other two men entered the Condon establishment. But while they were inside, McKenna was running through the streets, crying out their presence.

The cashier at Condon's Bank was smarter than his adversaries, too. He insisted there was a time lock on the vault and it could not be opened for another three minutes. That was a lie. It was already open. But Grat decided to wait it out.

Meanwhile, the townsfolk were grabbing their guns and racing towards the bank. Every second the cashier delayed sealed the gang's fate.

Bob and Emmett took care of their business more smoothly, but even by the time they emerged gunfire already had started. To get back to their horses, the five gang members had to race through a murderous rain of lead.

Bob, a deadly shot, carried a Winchester, and as he and Emmett raced for their horses he turned to gun down three townsfolk. But as the two groups of gang members neared their goal, the firing increased in intensity. John Kloehr, owner of the livery stable and the best shot in Coffeyville, led the barrage.

Powers was hit in the back, a wound that would kill him, and Grat went down with a deadly wound also. But when the town marshal, Charles T. Connelly, ventured too close the dying Dalton brought him down with his last shot.

Broadwell had managed to reach his horse but could not survive his wounds. His body was found on the trail, less than a mile outside of town.

Meanwhile, Bob and Emmett had come under unrelenting gunfire in the alley. Kloehr finally brought Bob down with a shot to the stomach. As he struggled to go on fighting he was delivered a death wound to the back.

Emmett, although gravely wounded, had reached his horse and rode back to his brother. Bob, however, already was beyond help and another rifle blast knocked Emmett from the saddle.

With more than a dozen wounds in his body, Emmett was judged to be dying by the town physician. That saved him from being lynched by the enraged populace. Four outlaws and four citizens had been killed, and three more Coffeyville residents were wounded.

In one regard, Bob Dalton had, indeed, beaten his cousins. The gunfight in Coffeyville was even deadlier than the one that had destroyed the James Gang and sent the Youngers to prison, in Northfield, Minnesota, sixteen years before.

As Doolin rode towards town, he was greeted by hysterical horsemen shouting out news of the fight and the deaths of the four gang members. Doolin turned around and galloped towards Oklahoma, hiding out at the HX Bar Ranch.

He was joined shortly thereafter by Bill Dalton, returned from California. After an unsuccessful attempt at settling down as a rancher, the last Dalton brother joined the new gang put together by Doolin. They extended the family's criminal history to September 1895.

Dalton was then hiding out at a ranch west of Ardmore. His wife had gone into town to pick up a shipment of liquor for him, and when suspicious lawmen demanded to know its destination she broke down and told them where Dalton was. He was shot and killed while trying to escape.

Less than a year later, Doolin, too was killed in a confrontation with the famed marshal Heck Thomas. That was the real end of the Dalton Gang.

Emmett served fourteen years in prison and was pardoned in 1907. He moved to Los Angeles and became a successful businessman in real estate. He never failed to point out that he made more money in a single real estate deal than he had in his entire career as an outlaw.

"I have been through it all," he said in an interview in 1923. "I know a dollar honestly earned is worth $10,000 obtained by fraudulent means. When once a man has stepped over the at-times indistinct line that divides right from wrong, there is no comeback."

Emmett wrote a book about his life, *Beyond the Law*, and took a featured role in the silent picture that was made from it. It was later redone as a talkie called *When the Daltons Rode*.

He toured the country to speak on the futility of breaking the law and died a wealthy man in 1937.

The name of the Daltons long outlived him, though, and it remains a synonym for groups that scoff at the law. When several Philadelphia Phillies, for example, in the early 1960s proved so unruly that the team manager had to hire a private detective to tail them, they called themselves the Dalton Gang.

The Sites

Coffeyville, Kansas Coffeyville is now a bustling little city of 13,000 people, about three times its size in 1892 when the Daltons rode in. But that long ago morning remains a visible presence there.

Condon Bank, at 811 Walnut St., is restored to look just as it did on the day of the raid. That is where the quick-thinking cashier, C. M. Ball, thwarted the holdup by making up the story about a time lock. It is now called the Perkins Building and is open Monday to Friday, 9 a.m. to 5 p.m. Free admission.

Death Alley, where the thick of the gunfight took place, runs west of Walnut, between 8th and 9th Sts. Various markers there point out the site of the old jail and where both outlaws and Coffeyville residents fell.

Emmett Dalton returned to Coffeyville in 1931 to a cordial reception and visited the graves of his brothers, Bob and Grat, in Elmwood Cemetery. It is located on S. Walnut St. A carved hitching post marks the spot of the Dalton graves.

The entire story of the battle is best told in the Dalton Defenders Museum, at 113 E. 8th St. It contains original photographs, belongings of both the gang and the men who defeated them, guns used in the fight, one of the bank safes, and saddles. The museum is open daily, 9 a.m. to 5 p.m.; closing at 7 p.m. from Memorial Day to Labor Day. Admission $3; children under eighteen $2; children under thirteen are free. (620) 251-2550.

Coffeyville is immediately north of the Oklahoma state line, 75 miles north of Tulsa by way of U.S. 169.

Dalton Gang Hideout There was also a Dalton sister. Her name was Eva, and in 1886 she moved to Meade, Kansas, with her husband, John Whipple. Her brothers often paid her visits, and as their reputations grew darker the neighbors grew more suspicious.

Finally, the Whipples moved away, and when the home was sold at a sheriff's sale a 95-foot-long tunnel between the house and the barn was discovered. No one was quite sure what its purpose was, but in Meade the place is now known as the Dalton Hideout. That may be a stretch, because most of their trips to Meade were made when they were still on the right side of the law. Nonetheless, it's a good story.

The Dalton Gang Hideout is located on Pearlette St., 4 blocks south of U.S. 54. It is open Monday through Saturday, 9 a.m. to 5 p.m.; Sunday, 1 p.m. to 5 p.m. Admission is $2. (800) 354-2743. Meade is 43 miles southwest of Dodge City, by way of U.S. 283 and 54.

Dalton Cave An authentic Dalton hideout was near Mannford, Oklahoma, along the Cimarron River, just west of its junction with the Arkansas. The Dalton Cave is one mile west of the town on Oklahoma 51. This was part of the Creek Nation, and a friendly Indian farmer sheltered and fed the gang after the train robbery at Adair. It was also while staying here in the summer of 1892 that the raid on Coffeyville was planned. Mannford is 27 miles west of Tulsa.

ANNUAL EVENT

Dalton Defenders Day Coffeyville just can't get enough of those Daltons. The Saturday closest to each October 5 is now Dalton Defenders Day. There is a recreation of the famous gunfight, music in the streets, an art fair, and an antique show. Call the Chamber of Commerce at (620) 251-2550.

JUDGE ROY BEAN

He was, by his own declaration, "the law west of the Pecos." This was west Texas in the late nineteenth century, a place where law of any kind was something of a rarity. The cities and centers of government in what was then the nation's biggest state were hundreds of miles away. On its meandering course through Texas's wildest, most sparsely settled region—a chunk of land that in itself was larger than most Eastern states—the Pecos River was a symbol of the harsh reality of life.

In fact, the river's name became a verb. To "pecos" an individual meant to shoot him, load the corpse with rocks, and drop it in the river.

So the activity of Roy Bean was not altogether inconsistent with bringing civilization to a wild place. Still, his courtroom was not quite the sort of place that the framers of the Constitution had in mind. None of the Bill of Rights were in effect unless Judge Bean said they were, and a little ethnic intimidation and economic coercion were regarded as perfectly natural.

Paul Newman, doing his best to look fat, drunk and grubby, portrayed him in a movie, *The Life and Times of Judge Roy Bean*, in the 1970s. But even an actor as accomplished as Newman couldn't bring himself to get quite as disgusting as the real thing. Inevitably, the image that emerged was greatly sanitized.

Bean arrived in west Texas, seeking his destiny with the Southern Pacific Railroad construction crews, in the early 1880s. He was already a man pushing the age of sixty and had seen more than his share of hard times and bad men.

He was born in Kentucky, one of three brothers, and followed his older sibling, Sam, to Mexico in 1848. That stay was shortened when a saloon fight in Chihuahua ended in the death of Roy's adversary. He then drifted to California and New Mexico, working occasionally as a lawman and more often as a barkeeper—a rather common mix of occupations in the Old West.

Working as both a lawman and a barkeeper was the career path followed by Wyatt Earp and Wild Bill Hickok. But while those two made their mark as marshals and gunmen, Bean aspired to a higher calling.

First, however, he had to get through the Civil War. Bean turned up in Texas during that conflict as a member of a plundering group called the Free Rovers. Its members fancied themselves a Confederate guerilla outfit but managed to keep just about all of what they stole.

He then lived for a while in San Antonio and gained valuable courtroom experience as the defendant in a string of lawsuits involving his many failed business enterprises.

Bean then hit upon his special calling. He linked up with railroad crews as they headed west and set up saloons at their construction camps. The first such business was at a place called Vinegaroon, a local slang term for a scorpion.

He performed so ably in this capacity that the railroad gangs elected him justice of the peace by acclamation. Bean liked the sound of that. After many years of having the law after him, he was now the man who decided what the law was. This was a definite improvement.

He moved on to another camp, one located in a Rio Grande town named Langtry. In later years, Bean asserted that he had named the place after the love of his life, Lily Langtry, the famous actress and very close friend of the Prince of Wales (the future King Edward VII).

She was regarded as the greatest English beauty of her time. The famed portraitist James Whistler described her as "the loveliest thing that ever was. She is perfect."

Bean never actually met the Jersey Lily. It was a case of worship from afar. Very afar. He didn't even manage to get the spelling of her name right when he opened his saloon—and courtroom—The Jersey Lilly, three months after her American debut in 1882. Moreover, most

Judge Roy Bean on horseback. Western History Collections, University of Oklahoma Libraries

historians agree that the town of Langtry had been named prior to Bean's arrival for a railroad official.

Nonetheless, Judge Roy declared the name of the town was a heart offering for Lily Langtry, and no one cared to debate the point. He was, after all, the law.

He had repeated his previous electoral success in Langtry and was named juris prudence. He quickly put up signs advertising his services as a Notary Public and a dispenser of cold beer. The latter service took precedence. Trials would frequently be interrupted to allow the judge to serve some brew to spectators, witnesses, or anyone else who happened to wander by.

Many of his legal decisions reflect the presence of such a diversion.

In one frequently cited ruling, a corpse was found in Langtry with $40 in one pocket and a gun in the other. The case was brought to Bean. He declared the deceased guilty of carrying a concealed weapon, fined him $40, and kept the money.

In another instance, in which a Chinese railroad worker had been gunned down, the judge ruled that there was "no law in Texas which prohibited killing a Chinaman." He acquitted the gunman. There was some documentation that the killer's friends had threatened to destroy the judge's bar and mess him up pretty badly, as well, unless he rendered that verdict. But, unfortunately, this was not an atypical racist judgment.

Bean knew next to nothing about the law and cared even less. He owned one official legal reference book, which he placed on his desk with a six-shooter laid conspicuously atop its cover.

He also kept on the bench a book marked "statoots," which contained laws that the judge especially liked, even though they may never have been passed by any legislature. The book included his interpretation of the rules of poker, too.

The fines he handed out frequently involved buying a round of drinks for everyone in the bar . . . er, courtroom. If rail passengers dropped in, ordered a drink, and handed the judge a large bill with which to pay for it, they were often told that no change was available. When the unfortunate passenger protested, he would be told to get back on the train or face some jail time for non-payment.

Bean finally discontinued this gambit when Southern Pacific officials protested. Since that was the only line in town, even the law had to back down.

Although he was licensed to perform marriages, he had no legal authority to grant divorces. This did not stop him. Bean figured if he could make a marriage he could unmake it, too. The fee was $5 for either service.

Despite his odd judicial decisions and excessive drinking, Bean was a softy when it came to Miss Langtry. Whenever her name was mentioned, a round of drinks was bought for the house—although Bean himself rarely paid for them.

He sent the actress an invitation to come visit, casually mentioning that he, after all, had named a whole town for her. Unsurprisingly, he never received a reply. When she appeared in San Antonio in 1888, Bean took the train to see her perform. But he lacked the courage to actually go backstage and talk to his ideal. (Or maybe he was just in shock. The headline on a sentimental article written by producer David Belasco on the occasion of Langtry's death in 1929 read: "She Would Gladly Have Traded Her Beauty for Great Stage Talent, But It Was Not To Be So.")

Bean continued blazing a trail through the judicial wilds for twenty-one years. By the end of his career, with west Texas safely civilized, relatively speaking, the white-bearded judge was something of a tourist attraction. Passengers would stop off to visit the saloon and mock trials would be held to entertain them. As long as they bought drinks and toasted Lily Langtry, the judge was content.

Bean died in 1903, reportedly after a night of revelry in San Antonio. He lapsed into a coma on his return home and died in a back room of the Jersey Lilly.

Despite his fierce veneer and the rough country in which he dispensed justice, there is no evidence that Bean actually ordered the execution of anyone. He believed in the healing powers of strong waters rather than rope.

A few months after his death, Lily Langtry finally did visit her town. She toured the saloon, heard the stories of the judge's devotion to her, and proclaimed herself deeply touched. Then she boarded the train and left Langtry forever.

THE SITES

Langtry, Texas Had it not been for Bean's brilliant judicial career, Langtry would probably have shared the fate of countless other rail camps—obscurity, oblivion, and obliteration.

Instead, it is a Texas historic site, complete with a visitor center and paintings depicting major events in the judge's life. The Jersey

Lilly still stands, and visitors can enter the old shack to see where "the law west of the Pecos" was administered, as well as the bar where Bean handed out beer and justice in equal portions.

A small museum displays a few of the judge's belongings, as well as mementos of the movie, which was shot elsewhere. A garden containing a large sampling of southwest Texas's desert plants surrounds the museum. Bean is buried in the nearby town of Del Rio, and Langtry, who ended her life as Lady de Bathe, rests at the place of her birth, the Channel Island of Jersey.

The town of Langtry is located on U.S. 90, on the road to Big Bend National Park, about 220 miles west of San Antonio. The museum is open daily, 8 a.m. to 5 p.m. Free admission. (915) 291-3340.

RELATED SITES

Pecos, Texas Pecos is another Texas town closely associated with the brand of law handed out by Judge Bean. The West of the Pecos Museum, in the former Orient Hotel, has exhibits on the wild frontier history of this town. The hotel, built in 1896, is an attraction in itself. The town was the home of the legendary cowboy Pecos Bill, and its annual July 4th rodeo, dating back to 1884, is the oldest one in the state.

Pecos is located 177 miles northwest of Langtry. The West of the Pecos Museum, on U.S. 285 at 1st St., is open Monday to Saturday, 9 a.m. to 5 p.m., and Sunday, 1 p.m. to 4 p.m. It is closed the week before Christmas. Admission is $4; those over sixty-five $3. (432) 445-5076; www.westofthepecosmuseum.com.

JOAQUIN MURIETA

There is no definitive evidence that he ever existed. His story may be the composite biography of five different bandit leaders during California's Gold Rush era.

Yet a dozen towns in the Mother Lode country claim his legend as their own. His name appears on Spanish Colonial-style suburban subdivisions across present-day California. And to the state's Mexican-American population, Joaquin Murieta remains a hero, as real as the sunrise, a symbol of defiance and hope in the midst of despair and oppression.

To the Anglos of the 1850s, Murieta's name meant something else. He made no claims on them for ethnic justice but merely sought to steal their hard-won gold.

When the state organized a special body of rangers to capture Murieta, the Anglos cheered. When the head of the bandit chief was exhibited at gatherings around California, they gathered to gawk and sigh in relief.

California had been wrested away from Mexico after resident Americans instigated the Bear Flag Revolt in 1846. Under terms of the treaty ending the Mexican War, it became a part of the United States on February 2, 1848.

Just nine days before that date, however, gold had been discovered on John Sutter's land on the Sacramento River. Within a year California had become the site of the greatest gold rush the world had ever seen.

There was, however, a problem. The population was still largely Mexican, and the Anglos were not happy with the prospect of sharing

Western mining camp. National Archives & Records Administration

the gold fields with them. So a tax of $20 a month was placed on "foreign" prospectors. The tax effectively excluded all Mexicans, whose country this had been just a few months before, from the gold field because they did not have the money to pay.

To make it even worse, Europeans were not regarded as foreigners for purposes of the tax. So Hispanic resentment was running high. In one camp, a battle was fought between Americans and Chilean miners.

When stories began to spread through the Mother Lode country about the exploits of a bandito, there was a quick stirring of excitement in the Mexican community. His band seemed to be everywhere.

The band was in Marysville, north of Sacramento, where they had robbed and killed seven miners in twelve days. They were in Shasta County, in the far north, raiding farmhouses. They were holding up stagecoaches near Fresno.

All of the attacks were led by someone named Joaquin.

That name rang a bell in several of the mining camps. In Murphys, they recalled a Joaquin who used to deal faro at the hotel. Looked like a dangerous man. This was probably him.

That sounded familiar, only it was in San Andreas where he worked. Or maybe it was Mokelumne Hill, in Calaveras County. Lots of Mexicans there, just looking for trouble.

The stories grew, intertwined, fed back on one another. It was forgotten that Joaquin was a fairly common name among California's Mexicans. Or that as many as five separate bands seemed to be involved with these crimes. Or that many of the holdups were clearly the work of Anglo bandits, drawn to the gold fields for loot.

By 1853 it was firmly established in the minds of most Californians that the looting was all the work of one Mexican. And he had to be stopped. So the legislature introduced a bill offering a reward for the head of Joaquin.

It was then pointed out to the lawmakers that offering a capital bounty on someone with such scant identification was probably dangerous, not to mention unconstitutional. So the legislature sat down and amended the bill to call for the capture of Joaquin Murieta, although no one by that name was known to anybody there.

Captain Harry Love was hired to head the pursuit. He had been a former chief of spies for General Zachary Taylor during the Mexican War, with the rank of captain. He drifted to California after the war, and, with his knowledge of Spanish and methods of gathering information among Mexicans, seemed to be the best man to get the right Joaquin.

He was given $5,000 and told to put together a posse. Governor John Bigler threw another $1,500 of reward money into the pot for any Joaquin, dead or alive.

In June 1855, Love and his men, acting on a tip, managed to trap a group of suspected bandits at Arroyo de Cantua, on the rugged eastern slope of the Coastal Range. Several members of the group surrendered, but two of them decided to run for it.

One of them, identified as Manuel Garcia, was shot to death as he tried to mount his horse and ride off. When they examined the body, Love's men found with growing excitement that there were only three fingers on one of the hands. They knew that a henchman of one of the bandit leaders was rumored to be called "Three-Fingered Jack."

The posse then turned its attention to the other dead bandit. The prisoners acknowledged that he was their leader and that his name was Joaquin.

Everything fit. Love, a man of action, decided that it would be a waste of time to drag the body to the nearest town. Instead, he ordered Garcia's short-digited hand to be severed and the corpse of Joaquin to be decapitated. After all, the orders of the legislature had been for a head, nothing more.

Love preserved the grisly trophies in jars of alcohol, and a priest who claimed to know Murieta made the identification. After the clergyman signed an affidavit, the reward money was turned over to Love.

No one paid any attention to one of the Mexican prisoners who insisted the dead Joaquin's last name was Valenzuela. A San Francisco newspaper, Alta California, said the entire action was a fraud and that if Joaquin Murieta really existed this was not him. However, most Californians were convinced that justice had been served.

One year later, a writer named John Rollin Ridge published an epic called *The Life and Adventures of Joaquin Murieta, the Celebrated California Bandit*. It was typical of the lurid, semi-fictitious claptrap that nineteenth century readers seemed to welcome upon the death of a prominent person. And twentieth century readers, too, for that matter.

Ridge's work was a highly sentimentalized version of events. His Joaquin Murieta was born in Sonora, Mexico, and made his way to the gold fields in 1850. Anglo miners raped his wife, hanged his half-brother, and beat Murieta severely.

With that set-up, Ridge seemed to anticipate the plot line of most of Clint Eastwood's early movies. Murieta vowed revenge and one by one managed to pick off and kill those responsible for the criminal acts.

When all the members of the lynch mob had been slain, Murieta realized he could not give himself up without facing a rope. So he organized the dispossessed Mexicans into a band of outlaws and embarked on the campaign of crime, which Ridge transformed into a battle for social justice.

Although Ridge made most of it up, his book seemed to validate Murieta's existence. For the next fifty years, his severed head was a staple attraction in California. It was placed on permanent display in San Francisco, where it disappeared in the 1906 earthquake.

The other four bandits supposedly named Joaquin disappeared from memory. Their stories were all conflated into Murieta's. Some of the state's most respected historians, Hubert H. Bancroft and Theodore Hittell, treated Murieta as a real person in their accounts of the Gold Rush era.

The great twentieth century Chilean poet, Pablo Neruda, also wrote about Murieta, which seemed to further legitimize the story.

Of course, the inevitable legends grew. The head in the jar was not that of Murieta, at all, because the real Joaquin Murieta was never captured. Realizing that the reports of his death finally gave him the chance at a normal life, he faded into a quiet retirement and disappeared.

But that would be a legend about a legend, and with that we leave the realm of history.

THE SITES

Murieta Rocks When Captain Love attacked the bandit camp at Arroyo de Cantua, it seemed to authenticate the place as Murieta's hideout. It certainly looks like a bandit's stronghold. The rocky outcropping commands a view of the surrounding country for miles around, making it a bit hard to understand how Love could have taken him by surprise so thoroughly.

The place, still called Murieta Rocks, is on California 198, south of the town of Priest Valley and east from the San Lucas exit of U.S. 101. This remains one of the wildest areas of the Coastal Range. It is difficult to believe that you are about midway between Los Angeles and San Francisco, just a short drive from the freeways that cut across contemporary California.

This is, instead, a glimpse at an older California. The location alone brings Murieta's story very much alive. There is an historic marker and a good view of the rocks from Highway 198, 11 miles north of Coalinga.

Murphys Another place where the tale of Murieta is especially vivid is in the mining town of Murphys. This place lies a bit off the heavily traveled Mother Lode Highway, California 49, and is somewhat less visited than many of the towns on that road. It is 9 miles east of Angels Camp, on California 4, in Calaveras County.

More than forty original buildings have survived in Murphys, which is named after the brothers who founded the place, John and David Murphy. Most of the structures date from the mid-1850s, a bit after Murieta was reputed to have worked here. In fact, the register of the Sperry Hotel, built in 1856, contains the signature of Charles Bolton, who was better known as Black Bart.

Despite any palpable reminder of Murieta, Murphys is one of the most atmospheric of Gold Rush towns, and it is easy to imagine how it looked in the days when his legend was made.

JACOB WALTZ AND THE LOST DUTCHMAN MINE

Never was a mountain range more accurately named than the Superstitions. The peaks that seal off the eastern edge of metropolitan Phoenix have been the source of legend and mystery for centuries.

The tales go back long before the arrival of the Anglos, when the land was owned by Mexico but belonged to the Apaches. Even then it was believed that there was treasure, a fortune in gold, somewhere in those Arizona hills.

But since 1891 and a deathbed revelation by an eighty-one-year-old prospector named Jacob Waltz (or Wolz) all those stories have focused on one fantastic treasure trove—the Lost Dutchman Mine.

The treasure has been known as the Dutchman only since 1895. That's when a feature article by *San Francisco Chronicle* writer P. C. Bicknell first used the name and linked Waltz to the legendary Peralta gold mine. Since then, the Lost Dutchman has inspired more dreams of avarice than any other place in America.

The dreams are drenched in blood, because Waltz killed for his gold; not once, but, if the stories are to be believed, repeatedly—first to learn of its whereabouts and then to keep that location a secret. After he found the treasure, sometime in the early 1870s, there were those who tried to follow him into the Superstitions. Eight of them never came out, including his own nephew. Waltz apparently did not believe in sharing.

The legend began in the late sixteenth century when Spanish Jesuits first arrived in the area. Some of the Indians whom the priests converted at their missions returned the favor by leading them to veins of gold.

The Indians believed that these hills had been a place of refuge from a great prehistoric flood. Those who escaped the waters were allowed by the gods to stay there, as long as they remained silent. But if they spoke they were turned to stone, which accounts for the strangely shaped rock formations in the area. The mountains were believed to be sacred, and the Indians were not amenable to trespassers.

Sometime in the early nineteenth century, however, members of a Mexican family named Peralta supposedly found the old Jesuit mines and began transporting the riches home to Sonora.

But one of their biggest caravans was ambushed by the Apaches around 1850 and wiped out. A handful of the Peraltas managed to escape, so goes the story, and kept the memory of the fabulous mines alive. Contemporary researchers have found evidence of mining equipment and remnants of a terrible battle at the traditional massacre site.

From there the stories trail off down various paths, and down one of them trudges the white-bearded, stocky figure of Waltz. According to the historical record, the German immigrant, known as "The Dutchman," arrived in the Salt River Valley in the late 1860s from California.

He supposedly gained the confidence of some young Mexicans who said they knew the location of the Peralta find. They took Waltz into the Superstitions and were never seen again.

Every so often, for the next twenty years or so, the Dutchman would turn up in Phoenix, buy some food and whisky with gold, and then disappear back in the mountains. He became a familiar figure in the frontier town but did not encourage inquiries into his activities.

In 1891, he came to the home of Julia Thomas, one of the few people he had befriended. Old and sick, he told her the location of his gold strike before he died. But when Thomas and some friends tried to follow the old man's instructions, a key element, the pointing branch of a palo verde tree, could not be found.

The story was merely a local curiosity until Bicknell's article appeared. That brought the Lost Dutchman to national attention and touched off a treasure hunt that has never ended. Bicknell himself devoted years of his life to the search, relying on clues given to him by Thomas.

Arizona Historical Foundation, University Libraries, ASU

He was convinced the key to the gold was Weaver's Needle. This thumb-like rock formation, named for frontier scout Pauline Weaver, was a familiar landmark at the edge of the Superstitions, along the Old West Trail (U.S. 60). Thousands of subsequent searches for the mine have followed Bicknell's information and used the Needle as the central reference point.

But no one has cashed in. The nearby community of Apache

Junction, now a Phoenix suburb, still celebrates Lost Dutchman Days every winter, and visitors fan out into the hills to try their luck at defying Waltz's ghost.

Yet there are those who have insisted all along that Waltz was nothing but an old fraud, just another bragging prospector who found an occasional nugget but never the fortune he claimed. They scoff at the stories about the Peralta treasure and call them simply part of the mystique of the Superstitions. It never existed, they say, and Waltz was a harmless old man who survived on his fantasies.

But many public figures, including former Arizona Attorney General Bob Corbin, were believers. In a 1985 interview with the Associated Press, Corbin said he had been a weekend searcher for twenty-five years and that he thought that eighty or ninety deaths were connected with the Lost Dutchman Mine.

Although no one has come away with the gold, stone tablets found in 1952 by a vacationing family are thought by some historians to bear a cryptic map, drawn by the Peraltas. This discovery has been enough to extend the legend for another half a century.

Even if the mine were found at last, the U.S. Wilderness Protection Act of 1964 would not allow it to be worked. No new claims can be filed in the Superstitions. It would be just as if the Lost Dutchman Mine didn't exist.

But it would probably take more than a mere federal law to hold back the gold that has filled the dreams of so many for so long.

THE SITES

Superstition Mountains Museum The old mining town of Goldfield is located 4 miles north of Apache Junction on Arizona 88, the Apache Trail. Before this highway was completed in 1905, as part of the Salt River Valley dam project, the Superstitions were one of the least accessible parts of America. That was part of the Lost Dutchman's allure. The Superstition Mountains Museum tells the story of the Dutchman and other legendary mines in the area. There are also tours of area mines, many of which were passed right over by seekers intent upon finding the Lost Dutchman in the 1890s. The museum is open daily 10 a.m. to 5 p.m. year round. Admission is free. (480) 677-6463.

Lost Dutchman State Park Located off Arizona 88, Lost Dutchman State Park in Goldfield offers hiking and camping in the heart of the area associated with the mine. In late winter and early spring, interpretive programs relate the legend of the Lost Dutchman, with park staffers playing the role of figures in the Jacob Waltz story. The park is open daily from 8 a.m. to 6 p.m. There is a $3 vehicle fee. (480) 982-4485.

Jacob Waltz Memorial A salute to the man who launched thousands of fantasies, the Jacob Waltz Memorial is in Apache Junction. The memorial stone pays tribute to Waltz, and the attached plaque tells the story of the mine that plays such a large role in the history of Apache Junction. It gives no clues on where to find the mine, though. The memorial is at U.S. 60 and the start of the Apache Trail, Arizona 88.

ANNUAL EVENT

Lost Dutchman Days Apache Junction celebrates Lost Dutchman Days during the last weekend in February. The Days offer an old West festival, rodeo, barbecue, entertainment, and treasure hunts. (480) 982-3141.

SOAPY SMITH

The fortune hunters who went to the Klondike in the late 1890s faced many obstacles. There was the bitter cold, the trek across Chilkoot Pass, the isolation and distance from the amenities of civilization.

But before conquering Mother Nature, they had to get by Soapy Smith. Never was the gateway to a treasure guarded more ferociously than by Soapy and his army of thugs in Skagway, Alaska.

There was, in truth, a good deal of charm about the man. Some of his cons were even ingenious.

To take advantage of patriotic fervor among the miners, he set up a Spanish-American War recruiting station in Skagway. When a young volunteer came in he was told that he would have to get undressed for the physical exam. When he did, one of Soapy's boys stole his clothes.

Soapy set up a telegraph office where homesick prospectors could wire messages back to friends and family. No one seemed to notice that no telegraph wires led to Skagway.

It is no wonder that a century after his death he remains Alaska's most celebrated character. But he was hardly a harmless bunco artist, a W. C. Fields prototype in a parka. There is a violent side to Soapy's story, and even though present-day Skagway celebrates him in music and theater, the Skagway of 1898 was delighted to get rid of him.

Jefferson Randolph Smith first attracted notice in the gold fields of Colorado. He was described as coming from an "aristocratic" Georgia family in some accounts—although why a Georgia family would give its son two names celebrated in Virginia is a bit of a puzzle.

But that was his story, and he was sticking to it. He also told people that he had worked as a cowboy and lost his money in a crooked card game. Burning with an urge for revenge, he decided to cheat the world.

He first turned up in Denver, where he earned his nickname. He would stand on a street corner selling bars of soap that he claimed were wrapped in currency, bills of various denominations up to $100. Some of them actually were, but those bars were sold to shills who returned the money to him later. All the others were wrapped in worthless paper.

"It was a good living for all concerned," wrote one of Soapy's biographers, Don C. Trenary, "and even added in a slight measure to the cleanliness of the community."

His associates were not always the sharpest of knives. One of them, Icebox Murphy, earned his nickname by breaking into a butcher shop and blowing up the refrigerating unit because he thought it was the safe.

But Soapy did quite well with his scam until the authorities caught on and ran him out of Denver. He moved on to Creede, Colorado, one of the richest silver camps in the state's history. It was a roaring camp of 8,000, at the peak of its prosperity, when Soapy arrived in 1893. Its vein of ore was so pure that it continued producing after the Silver Panic of that year had shut down all other mines in Colorado.

Smith found ready customers for his soap gag in Creede and also "discovered" a petrified man, which he put on display for a fee. The fact that it had been sculpted from cement in Denver wasn't noticed until Soapy had made his haul.

But Creede went into decline, and, looking for new pastures, Soapy boarded a steamer bound for Alaska. He arrived in October 1897, just as the excitement of the gold strike in the Klondike was building to its peak.

The gold fields were actually located in Canada's Yukon. But Skagway was the closest port of entry, where adventurers left the boat dock with packs on their backs to labor across 3,550-foot Chilkoot Pass, the last half-mile at a 45-degree angle. About 30,000 of them made the trek that winter.

Soapy Smith (center). Denver Public Library, Western History Department

This strike smelled like opportunity to Soapy. With the absence of any effective law-enforcement agency, he quickly organized the thugs who already were in residence; opened a saloon, hotel, and other less legitmate entersprises; and began preparations to pluck the prospectors.

One of his first acts was to send agents back to Seattle to circulate among the miners. They told the newcomers that they were organizing miner companies to get a better rate for transporting their gear to the Yukon. The pigeons would sign for the freight bill and as soon as the ship landed in Skagway the gear would be escorted to one of Soapy's various enterprises.

One way or another, the miner would be separated from his cash. Unable to pay the freight charge he had signed for, he had no alternative but to go back home. Soapy then resold his gear at an inflated price.

The card table at his saloon had a hidden compartment from which the house dealer could remove any card he needed. A real estate office was actually a blind to get prospective property-buyers inside. The office manager would then get into a fight with the buyer on some pretext, the lights go out, and the sucker would wake up a few hours later with a bump on his head and his cash gone.

When an evangelist landed in Skagway, good citizen Soapy said religious endeavors needed to be encouraged. He gave the minister a $300 contribution. Inspired by his example, other citizens came by the preacher's tent and built his take up to $3,000. Then, during the sermon, one of Soapy's gang came by and stole it right back.

Smith was smart enough to understand, however, that philanthropy is sometimes necessary to build good public relations. He was regarded as a soft touch for any bum with a hard-luck story and gave away hundreds of dollars a week.

He set up a fund to care for abandoned sled dogs. On July 4, 1898, he organized the biggest Independence Day celebration in Alaska's history, with parades and music and speeches. It was also a gala event for Soapy's corps of pickpockets.

But public opinion was slowly starting to shift. Eight bodies found in the area were popularly attributed to be victims of Soapy's gang, miners who had made the mistake of trying to fight back. The amiable con man now was seen as leading a reign of terror.

A few days after the Independence Day bash, a miner named J. D. Stewart returned from the Klondike. He was unwise enough to enter a saloon and show off $2,800 worth of dust he had accumulated there.

With no further ado, the bag of dust was taken from him, and Stewart was beaten and thrown out in the street. That bold act of robbery was finally too much for Skagway. A vigilance committee was formed, called "The Hundred and One," who issued a warning for "all confidence, bunco and sure-thing men to leave Skagway."

Soapy took this personally. When he heard this group had actually called a meeting, he went into a tirade, threatening to shoot any man who tried to arrest him. Then he decided to march on the meeting at the town wharf with twelve of his gang members and break it up himself.

Mining engineer Frank Reid, who was known for integrity and bravery, had been named leader of The Hundred and One. He came forward to confront Smith.

Soapy brandished a rifle and quickly pressed it against Reid's abdomen. The engineer swept it aside and went for his own gun. Both men fired, and an instant later both crumpled to the ground, mortally wounded.

Reid was given a hero's funeral. "He gave his life for the honor of Skagway," reads the inscription on his tombstone.

Smith's body lay where it fell for several hours, with no gang member daring to claim it. Finally, a woman who had been helped out by Soapy when her husband died came for the corpse and arranged for the funeral.

At the service, one of Smith's favorite sayings was repeated: "The way of the transgressor is hard-to quit." It was also pointed out that he had been kind to dogs.

THE SITES

Skagway, Alaska The brief gold rush era passed through Skagway a long time ago. It is now a tiny village of about seven hundred souls, at the northern end of the Alaska Marine Highway. It can be reached overland on a branch road from the Alaska Highway, but most often it is visited as part of a shore excursion on cruises up the Inland Passage.

Klondike Gold Rush National Historical Park preserves several sites associated with Soapy Smith and the events of 1897–98. Park headquarters is a restored railroad station at Broadway and 2nd Ave., and the visitor center recounts the story of the trek across Chilkoot Pass and the adventurers who came this way. It is open daily, mid-May to mid-September. Free admission. (907) 983-2921; www.nps.gov/klgo.

Gold Rush Cemetery Gold Rush Cemetery, located a few blocks from the middle of town, contains the grave of both Smith and Frank Reid. One of the more popular excursions from Skagway is a tour of the nearby waterfall named in Reid's honor.

White Pass and Yukon Route Train Ride A sense of the natural obstacles the miners were up against can be appreciated with a ride on the White Pass and Yukon Route. Opened in 1900, it retraces the route to the Klondike taken by the gold-hunters. The three-hour narrated excursion runs to the top of White Pass and goes by most of the landmarks of the region. Trains leave from the Klondike Gold Rush National Historical Park visitor center daily, mid-May to mid-September. For schedule and fares call (800) 343-7373.

Related Site

Soapy Smith's Restaurant Soapy also left a distinct mark on Denver, his original base of operations. A bar and restaurant is named Soapy Smith's in his honor. It is situated in one of the city's oldest downtown buildings, at 1317 14th St. Memorabilia of Soapy's era in the city is displayed. (303) 534-1112.

Annual Event

Days of '98 Soapy is also the star of a show that runs throughout the summer months. *Days of '98* is presented at the Eagles' Hall, at 6th and Broadway in Skagway. It features period song, dances, and comedy patter with Smith as the lovable leading man. The show goes on at 12:50 a.m., 2 p.m. and 8:20 p.m., mid-May to late September. Call for prices and information at (907) 983-2545.

LIZZIE BORDEN

She was innocent. The all-male jury said so in under an hour, and most of that time was spent chatting sociably so as not to look as if they hadn't given the matter due consideration.

The verdict was applauded in most of the media and public opinion was in agreement.

And yet if you asked most Americans today who took an ax and gave her mother forty whacks, the answer, of course, would come back Lizzie Borden. She has been convicted by posterity.

Lizzie Borden took an ax
And gave her mother forty whacks.
When the job was nicely done,
She gave her father forty-one.

Of course, that rhyme didn't help. Sung to the tune of the 1890s hit "Ta-rah-rah-boom-de-ay," the familiar Lizzie Borden doggerel is almost as well known a century later as it was right after the double homicide of Andrew and Abby Borden in their handsome Fall River, Massachusetts, home.

There has been a ballet about the crime and an opera and the inevitable made-for-TV movie. Numerous books. The vast majority of these works begin with the assumption that Lizzie did it.

It is a case that has strange contemporary echoes of the O. J. Simpson trial and the Jon Benet Ramsey murder. It also involved elements of social standing and police bungling. And although a song from the Broadway show *New Faces of 1952* tells us that "You can't chop your momma up in Massachusetts and then blame all the damage on the mice," Lizzie may have gotten away with doing just that.

It happened on August 4, 1892, a sultry Thursday in that mill town on the Taunton River. The Bordens were among the wealthiest families in Fall River,

The Fall River Historical Society

although it might be a stretch to call them among the most respected.

Andrew Borden had the reputation as an overly sharp businessman who would cut corners. He was even accused, when he started off as an undertaker, of cutting the feet off corpses to fit them into undersized caskets. As a director of several banks he was known as a bloodless man who gave no leeway and would not hesitate to foreclose.

His first wife had died thirty years before, after bearing him two daughters who survived past infancy. Emma was forty-two, and Lizzie was a rather plain young woman of thirty-two. Both had passed the marriageable age and were resigned to a life of spinsterhood and church work.

They detested their stepmother of twenty-eight years, Abby, a roundish woman who weighed over two hundred pounds. Lizzie also resented their home. It was in a no longer fashionable part of town. Most of Fall River's upper crust had moved "on the Hill," an address that Borden's income could easily have afforded. But a penny-pincher in his home life as well as his business dealings, he insisted on hanging on to the old house, which lacked such conveniences as electricity and a bath.

He doted on his daughters, however, supplying them with fine clothes, foreign travel, and all the good things Victorian ladies required. Nonetheless, this was a home that later ages would describe as a tad dysfunctional.

Things started going haywire after dinner on August 2. With Emma away on a visit, Mr. and Mrs. Borden experienced severe stomach pains and vomiting. Lizzie said she felt a little queasy, too. It was chalked up to some bad fish prepared by their housekeeper, Bridget Sullivan.

Later that evening, Lizzie spent some time with a friend, Alice Russell, and told her of threats being made against her father by "his enemies," and suspicions that there had been burglary attempts at their home. "I feel as if something is hanging over me that I cannot throw off," she said.

Two days later, Andrew Borden left for his office after breakfast at about 9:20 a.m. and Abby went upstairs to do some light housework. Bridget went outside to wash the windows, leaving Lizzie in the kitchen sipping coffee.

Because of the heat, Andrew decided to take an early break for lunch and returned home at 10:45. When Borden asked his daughter about Abby's whereabouts, he was told she was off visiting a sick friend. But his wife was already dead. She was lying in a pool of her own blood in an upstairs bedroom.

Andrew decided to lie down on the living room sofa for a short nap.

He never woke up. Shortly after 11:00 a.m., Bridget was summoned by Lizzie screaming, "Father is dead! Somebody came in and killed him!"

Borden's face had been chopped up beyond recognition, with ten ax blows (not forty-one) delivered to his head. Bridget went upstairs and there she discovered the corpse of Abby. Those who saw Lizzie's reaction to this additional bit of news said later that she remained remarkably calm.

Reports of the incredible double murder swept across Fall River. But the police displayed remarkable forbearance. No search of the house was made for thirty-two hours after the bodies were discovered and Lizzie was not questioned until three days later. *The New York Times* attributed the delay to the "high social standing of the parties involved."

Nonetheless, on the day of the funerals, Lizzie was arrested. There were just too many contradictions in her story.

If she had been in the house, how could she have been unaware of her stepmother being murdered upstairs? Where was she when her father was being murdered? At various times she said she was out in the barn loft gathering sinkers for a fishing line or eating pears; another time she said she was in the backyard. But a cursory look at the loft indicated that the dust had been undisturbed on its floor.

There was also a matter of an ax head that police found in the basement, rubbed in ashes to make it appear old and with the handle broken off.

The nation's press reacted with outrage, condemning the police for picking on a poor little orphan. "The only person that the government can catch is one whose very innocence placed her in its power," harrumphed the *Boston Globe*, which maintained her innocence throughout the proceedings. "The poor defenseless child ought to have claimed by very helplessness their protection."

The American public simply was unable to entertain the idea that a properly brought up young woman could have brutally murdered her stepmother and then calmly sat around awaiting the arrival of her father so she could do the same to him.

The inquest on August 10 was the only time Lizzie ever testified directly. "Were you always cordial with your stepmother?" she was asked. "That depends upon one's idea of cordiality," she replied.

"Would it take you all that time to eat a few pears?" "I do not do things in a hurry," responded Lizzie.

There was also testimony from a local pharmacy that Lizzie had been shopping for poison shortly before the Bordens had come down with their stomach problems. The judge therefore decided to hold Lizzie for a preliminary hearing.

He was pilloried in newspapers, by ministers, by the newly emerging feminist organizations, and the Women's Christian Temperance Union. She was called a sacrificial lamb and it was reported, inaccurately but with great horror, that she was confined to a jail cell. Many suggested that it was obvious the Irish servant girl had done it and wondered why she hadn't been arrested, although there was never any evidence or motive pointing that way.

The preliminary hearing began three months after the murders and produced a major bombshell. Through the entire debate over Lizzie's guilt or innocence, her defenders had insisted that if she had done it there would have been blood on her dress. But there was none found on any piece of clothing in the house, and the blue dress she said that she had been wearing was spotless.

But at the hearing, her friend, Alice Russell, testified that she had seen Lizzie burn a blue cotton dress three days after the murders. Lizzie explained that it had been soiled with brown paint. The prosecutors pointed out that dried blood would appear to be brown.

Her attorney's summation reiterated the sheer impossibility of imaging a woman "whose baby fingers have been lovingly entwined around her father's brow" picking up a weapon and killing him. Yet the judge, his voice breaking with emotion, said that if it were a man standing in the courtroom and the same evidence had been presented against him, he would have no choice but to bind him over for trial. And that's what he did with Lizzie.

The trial began in New Bedford in June 1893 and was a sensation. Lizzie was defended by a former governor of Massachusetts, George Robinson. The presiding judge, Justin Dewey, had been elevated to the bench by Robinson.

While the prosecution was ably handled by a future U.S. Supreme Court Justice, William Moody, he had no chance. Robinson's closing oration concluded, "If this little sparrow does not fall unnoticed then, indeed, in God's great providence, this woman has not been alone in this courtroom." Judge Dewey's instructions to the jury were practically a direction for an innocent verdict.

And so it was returned, to the exuberant joy of the courtroom spectators and most of the nation.

Nonetheless, according to historian Kathryn Allamong Jacob, after the verdict things began to change. Lizzie quickly bought a big new house "on the Hill" and directed that hereafter she be referred to as Lisbeth.

She dropped out of her church, although its minister had been among her most fervent defenders. When a book was published containing her inquest testimony, which had been suppressed at the trial, she bought up all the copies and destroyed them.

She was dropped by the respectable families of Fall River and her sister moved out of town. By the time of her death, in 1927, she had become a recluse and public opinion had undergone a complete reversal.

Not even a painstakingly documented book by Edward Radin, Lizzie Borden: The Untold Story, published in 1961, has done much to change that appraisal.

Maybe if "whacks" hadn't rhymed so conveniently with "ax," it would have been different. But that wicked little poem survives as history's verdict on Lizzie.

The Sites

The Borden Home For a century after Lizzie Borden moved out of her father's home, the residence remained in private hands. But since the mid-1990s it has been a bed and breakfast, albeit one of the more curious of its kind in New England.

The first floor has been returned to its appearance of the 1890s. Overnight guests have the option of staying in the Andrew and Abby Borden Suite, the Lizzie Borden Suite, or the John Morse Room, in which Mrs. Borden was hacked to death. Morse was Lizzie's uncle, who had frequently spent the night in what was then the guest bedroom. Rooms on the third floor are named after Bridget Sullivan; the family attorney, Andrew Jennings; and the district attorney, Hosea Knowlton.

Tours of the house, at 92 2nd St., Fall River, are given daily. (508) 675-7333; www.lizzie-borden.com.

Fall River Historical Society More Lizzie memorabilia is contained at the Fall River Historical Society. The museum has exhibits relating to the double homicide and trials, along with the more staid events in the town's history.

Moreover, the museum is located "on the Hill," Lizzie's favorite neighborhood, at 451 Rock St. It is south of U.S. 6 and east of Massachusetts 79. The museum is open Tuesday to Friday, 9 a.m. to 4:30 p.m.; weekends, 1 p.m. to 5 p.m., June through September; closed on weekends, April, May, and October through December. Admission $5; children under fourteen $3. (508) 679-1071; www.lizzeborden.org.

JOHN D. LEE AND THE MOUNTAIN MEADOWS MASSACRE

On the morning of March 23,1877, John D. Lee stood to face a firing squad in a southwestern Utah field known as Mountain Meadows.

Almost twenty years before, as a pioneer leader of the Church of Latter Day Saints, Lee had participated in the most heinous event in Mormon history. Now he stood unblinking in the sun and faced his executioners.

"I do not fear death," he said. "I shall never go to a worse place than I am now in. Evidence has been brought against me which is as false as the hinges of hell, and this evidence was wanted to sacrifice me.

"I declare I did nothing designedly wrong in this unfortunate affair. I did everything in my power to save that people, but I am the one who must suffer. Having said this, I feel resigned. I ask the Lord, my God, if my labors are done, to receive my spirit."

In a few moments, the fatal shots were fired, and precisely where Lee's soul ended up was between him and his Maker. Mountain Meadows, depending on your point of view, had either been avenged or had claimed its final victim.

For generations afterwards, the Mountain Meadows Massacre of 1857 was seldom mentioned in Utah. It was regarded as a hideous stain on the history of the Latter Day Saints.

Eighty-two unarmed members of a California-bound wagon train were slaughtered here by Mormon settlers, who then tried to fix the blame on Paiute Indians. Seventeen small children were spared and taken in by nearby families, before being returned to relatives in Arkansas.

Lee, one of the leaders of the massacre, lived as a fugitive for seventeen years in some most remote corners of America before being apprehended by federal officials in Arizona. Whether he was justly executed, or whether he took the fall for higher church authorities, remains a topic of fierce debate among historians.

"The complete, the absolute truth of the affair can probably never be evaluated by any human being," wrote Juanita Brooks, author of *The Mountain Meadows Massacre*, the first authoritative account of the affair. "Attempts to understand the forces which culminated in it and those which were set into motion by it are all very inadequate at best."

To try to grasp the reason for the actions of Lee and his neighbors in 1857, it is necessary to understand the persecution the Mormons had experienced since their inception. Facing unrelenting hostility from neighbors who resented their teachings and their prosperity, the Latter Day Saints, under the leadership of founder Joseph Smith, had been forced to relocate repeatedly—from New York to Ohio to Missouri and back to Illinois.

They built the community of Nauvoo on the banks of the Mississippi River, and by 1842 it was the largest town in Illinois. But two years later, Smith was imprisoned on trumped-up charges in a nearby town and shot to death by a mob.

His successor, Brigham Young, realized the of the church would find peace only beyond the reach of settlement, and began planning a daring overland trek to Utah. In 1847, the first of the Mormons reached the Salt Lake Valley and began to build the community of Deseret, where they could practice their religion in peace.

Within a decade, they were thriving. Settlements reached across the fertile valleys of the Wasatch and across the desert basin of what is now Nevada. But in 1857, alarmed by reports of polygamy and apparent defiance of American laws by territorial courts, President James Buchanan ordered U.S. forces, under Colonel Albert Sidney Johnston (soon to become a brilliant general of the Confederacy), to put down this supposed Mormon rebellion in Utah.

Haunted by memories of past victimization, the Latter Day Saints prepared to resist force with force. Young declared martial law and said all invaders would be repelled.

It was into this seething mixture of anger and religious righteousness that the hapless Baker-Fancher party stumbled. They had started in Arkansas and planned to graze their stock in Utah before undertaking the harrowing desert crossing to California.

Salt Lake City, Utah. National Archives & Records Administration and
The Dictionary of American Portraits

183

John D. Lee was living near Cedar City at the time, a farmer who was also a local political leader and magistrate. He was forty-five years old, had joined the Church as a young man and witnessed the tragedy in Nauvoo. Lee had come to Utah with the original Mormon party and was a dedicated, active member of the Church. He stood ready to answer Brigham Young's call to take up arms in defense of Deseret.

Traveling with the emigrants in the Baker-Fancher group was a small bunch of roughnecks and troublemakers. They raided Mormon farms as they passed through, stealing stock, insulting women, and abusing the Paiute, who were allies of the Saints. In the mind of Lee and many other leaders, this unruly group became a symbol for the murderous mobs of Illinois and Missouri and the invading army that was marching against them even now.

They sent messengers to Salt Lake City for instructions. Young had learned that the immediate threat of armed invasion had passed. Johnston's force did not have the supplies to get to Utah by winter. He sent back orders to let the California wagon train pass through.

But it was too late. Lee and his cohorts already had taken matters into their own hands.

They encouraged the Paiute to attack the wagon train on the morning of September 7. Lee wrote later his hope was the Indians would be able "to do the work." Instead, they were beaten off after killing seven emigrants. But as one of the party tried to escape the attack he was gunned down by a Mormon settler in plain sight of both sides.

This left Lee and his men in a "sad fix," he said. They agreed that the Paiute could not be counted on to finish the job and that now it would not be advisable to leave witnesses to what had happened.

Lee insisted to the end that his group only felt they were carrying out the wishes of the Church leadership and that defying such orders could have meant his own death. Nonetheless, the plan he devised was especially cold-blooded.

He entered the emigrant camp under a flag of truce and told them that his men would escort them past the Indians to safety. But they had to stack their arms so as not to arouse the suspicions of the Paiute. "I knew that I was acting a cruel part and doing a damnable deed," Lee wrote just before his death in a book called *Mormonism Unveiled*.

On the morning of September 11, the unsuspecting travelers marched single file from the protection of their wagons. As soon as they were in the open, the Mormons opened fire. Within minutes, the meadow was filled with the dead. Only children too young to speak were spared.

Lee and other leaders agreed to blame the massacre on the Indians and never to discuss what had occurred. "We took the most binding oaths to stand by each other . . . to keep the matter a secret from the entire world."

Nonetheless, word trickled out and when Johnston's army arrived in Utah the following year the investigation led to Lee. He fled the territory, living for a time among the Havasupai tribe, on the floor of the Grand Canyon.

After a few years, he moved to a place on the Colorado River and operated a ferry service. It became known as Lees Ferry and was an important transportation link between Mormon settlements in Utah and northern Arizona, the only crossing of the river for hundreds of miles.

Unfortunately, the ferry became too well known. Investigators had never given up their pursuit of him and in 1874 he was arrested in Utah and charged with the killings at Mountain Meadows.

Lee was tried by a Utah court, which ended in a hung jury. Retried in 1876 he was found guilty and executed the following year, insisting to the moment of his death that he was merely carrying out the orders of the Church hierarchy.

The episode remained an undigested lump in Utah history for more than a century. With their early years so filled with instances of persecution, it was hard for Mormons to acknowledge that members of the Church had behaved in such a murderous manner.

Moreover, the Latter Day Saints were still regarded with distrust by the outside world well into the twentieth century. Lee's book, which purported to reveal the malicious secrets of the Church, had a receptive audience who were willing to believe almost anything about the Mormons. One of the most famous Sherlock Holmes mysteries, *A Study in Scarlet*, employed vengeful Mormons from Utah as the villains. Mountain Meadows would only clinch the case against them in the minds of their enemies. So Lee was buried and the story interred with him.

Only in 1990 was a sort of reconciliation made. At the 133rd anniversary of the massacre, descendants from both sides met at Mountain Meadows to unveil a memorial to the dead. Names of the victims were read by Judge Roger V. Logan, Jr., of Harrison, Arkansas, who was related to twenty-one of them.

Church President Gordon B. Hinckley spoke of "a bridge built across a chasm of cankering bitterness."

Also on the program was the president of Brigham Young University who noted that "whatever drove the actions of those who came here before, ours must be driven by something higher and more noble."

His name was Rex E. Lee, and he was a direct descendant of the man who was shot for what happened here.

THE SITES

Mountain Meadows Memorial Mountain Meadows Memorial is 29 miles north of I-15, from St. George, by way of Utah 18. An elliptical-shaped granite slab was erected in 1990 to honor the memories of eighty-two emigrants who were killed here by the Mormon group led by John D. Lee.

Lees Ferry Lees Ferry is off U.S. 89A from Marble Canyon, just south of Glen Canyon Dam. Lee came to this place in 1872, at the confluence of the Colorado and Paria rivers, to operate a ferry. His first boat was a vessel named the *Emma Dean*, abandoned by the pioneering expedition of Major John Wesley Powell, who led the first exploring party into the Grand Canyon. Lee replaced it with a larger vessel, capable of carrying four wagons across the river and requiring four men to operate. Lees Ferry became the key crossing on the road to Mormon settlements in northern Arizona, and after his execution it was kept up by his widow and then by the Church. A ferry operated here until 1929, when it was replaced by Navajo Bridge, on U.S. 89A. It is now an almost abandoned outpost in the midst of canyon country.

Supai Supai, headquarters of the Havasupai Indian Reservation, can be reached only by muleback. A road through the neighboring Hualapi reservation runs northeast from Arizona 66, just east of Peach Springs, and reaches the rim of the Grand Canyon at Hualapi Hilltop. From there it is an 8-mile descent to the Canyon floor. This is where Lee hid for many years after he was charged with the Mountain Meadows massacre in 1858. It is one of the most isolated and spectacular settings in the country and the tribal office can arrange for tours to some of the least known parts of the Grand Canyon. Tribal offices can be reached at (928) 448-2121.

Related Sites

Joseph Smith Home The home of Joseph Smith is located on Stafford Rd., south of Palmyra, New York, which is north from exit 43 of the New York Thruway on New York 21. Here is where the founder of the Mormon religion lived as a young man and received the inspiration to begin the Church. It is open daily from 9 a.m. to 6 p.m. Free admission. (315) 597-4383.

Latter Day Saints Visitor Center The Latter Day Saints Visitor Center in Nauvoo, Illinois, is a restoration of the Mormon community of the 1830s and 1840s. Nauvoo is 12 miles south of Fort Madison, Iowa, on the Illinois Great River Road. The center, at Main and Young Sts., explains how the community was destroyed and Smith assassinated, forcing the trek to Utah. It is open daily from 9 a.m. to 5 p.m. Free admission. (217) 453-2237.

St. George Mormon Temple St. George Mormon Temple, completed in 1877, is the oldest in Utah. St. George is off exit 8 of I-15 in extreme southwestern Utah. Non-Mormons may tour the adjoining tabernacle, with its 140-foot high steeple, and the visitor center at 450 S. 300 East St., which explains the Church's beliefs. Open daily from dawn to dusk. Free admission. (435) 673-3533.

Annual Event

Supai Peach Dance A Peach Dance is held at Supai every August. Lee, one of the few white men known to have lived among these people, taught the tribe how to cultivate peaches and the crop still plays an important role in Havasupai life. Tribal offices can be reached at (928) 448-2121.

JUDGE ISAAC PARKER

Congress set aside the land that is now Oklahoma as the Indian Territory in the late 1830s. It was an answer to the irksome problem of what to do with Native Americans who had been thrown off their ancestral lands in the settled states of the South and Midwest.

Choctaws, Cherokees, Creek, Chickasaw, Kiowa, Seminole, Wyandotte—they would all come here, either voluntarily or through forced removal, and the land would belong to them forever. Forever, as it turned out, meant until 1906, when Congress directed that the Indian lands were to be absorbed by the Oklahoma Territory.

During the almost seventy years that the Indian Territory existed, several of the sovereign tribes created institutions to govern themselves effectively. But there was one big problem. The Indian justice system had no jurisdiction over whites.

In practical terms, that meant that the territory was outlaw country. It became a refuge for hard cases and lawbreakers from all across the West. Belle Starr ran what amounted to a resort for fugitives at her Younger's Bend ranch on Cherokee land. Others simply preyed at will on Indians and whites alike.

Then Judge Parker came to the bench in Fort Smith, Arkansas.

He was appointed to the newly created U.S. Court for the Western District of Arkansas, which meant the Indian Territory, by President Ulysses S. Grant in 1875. Parker was then thirty-seven years old.

In the latter part of his twenty-one-year tenure in this court, he is described as looking a bit like Santa Claus. He had a white beard, pink cheeks, a cheery demeanor, and was a bit overweight. He was a dedicated family man and a member of the local school board. He also scared the daylights out of some of the worst killers in the West.

Although personally he did not favor capital punishment, he did not hesitate to send more than eighty men to their deaths on his gallows.

His court was unique in American legal history because there were no appeals. Only a presidential pardon could reverse Parker's sentences for the first fourteen years he presided at Fort Smith.

On the other hand, he was sent there by Grant with orders to straighten out a highly dangerous situation. Over the years, sixty-five federal marshals working for Parker were killed on their official duties. The judge was not inclined to show mercy to men who had given none themselves.

Parker was caricatured by his opponents as the "hanging judge," a man who casually passed out death sentences for the malign pleasure it gave him. He was depicted as an enforcer of crude frontier justice, ignoring Constitutional niceties in order to quick-march defendants to the hangman.

In reality, Parker was a conscientious official who always was concerned about the legitimacy of his court. He knew that his authority rested on a perception of fairness, and he was backed overwhelmingly by the people of Arkansas and Indian officials. They understood that he was enforcing the provisions of tribal treaties.

Many of his opponents had darker motives, though. What they really wanted was a quick takeover of the Indian Territory for white settlement. When they argued that Parker's executions were an argument for extending "civilizing influences" into the Territory, they meant white settlers.

Parker, however, was a staunch advocate of Oklahoma entering the Union as an Indian state. He argued that position vehemently in front of the Judiciary Committee of the U.S. House of Representatives in 1895.

Fort Smith National Historic Site

"They have every element which is involved in civilization and they are using those elements from the neighbors and friends of the good people of the surrounding states," he said. "They have the confidence and respect of the people, and I say, 'Let them alone.'"

It was a losing battle, though. By the 1890 Census, white settlers already outnumbered Native Americans in the Indian Territory by two to one. The margin was growing with every year and the pressure to allow more whites in was irresistible.

Parker's public relations problem was also, in large part, because of his choice of executioner. George Maledon was as grim as Parker was affable. He seemed to take professional satisfaction in hanging men as efficiently as possible and was proud of having sent more men to their deaths than any other individual in American history.

Maledon oversaw the construction of a gallows that could handle twelve hangings at once. It ran 20 feet long and 30 inches wide and it was a source of deep disappointment to the executioner that the maximum number he ever dispatched at one time filled only half its capacity.

He did it twice, and both times the performance was the sensation of the social calendar in Fort Smith. The sextuple hangings drew a crowd of 5,000 spectators, who watched in awe as the murderers were dispatched to their Maker.

"Their necks were broken and all died without a struggle," a contemporary reporter wrote about the first such affair. But the Eastern press covered the event thoroughly and luridly, and it gave Parker a reputation for cruelty that he never lived down.

Parker, to be sure, was not an advocate of progressive criminology. He understood that young men could be led astray and many youthful offenders were sentenced leniently in his court. But adult killers could expect no such treatment.

"Your crime leaves no ground for the extension of sympathy," he told one defendant. "You can expect no more sympathy than lovers of virtue and haters of vice can extend to men guilty of one of the most brutal, wicked, repulsive and dastardly deeds known in the annals of crime. Your duty now is to make an honest effort to receive from a just God that mercy and forgiveness you so much need."

To the infamous killer Cherokee Bill, he said: "The crime you have committed is but another evidence, if any were needed, of your wicked, lawless, bloody and murderous disposition. . . . Your case is one where justice should not walk with leaden feet. It should be swift. It should be certain. As far as this court is concerned, it shall be, for public justice demands it."

After that, hanging must have been a relief.

In 1889, Congress subjected Parker's decisions to review by higher courts, and in 1896 it abolished his job altogether, creating three new federal districts in Oklahoma. Parker lived only two months longer than his court, passing away of Bright's disease.

One of the instances in which Parker's death sentence was reversed was the case of gambler and pimp Frank Carver. This was an especially keen disappointment to Maledon, because Carver had been convicted of killing his daughter, who had been working as a prostitute in Muskogee.

Maledon probably felt the sting of the court's demise more sharply than anyone. He had developed a powerful affection for his gallows and even tried to buy it—Lord knows for what purpose—from Fort Smith. But the city refused and had the contrivance destroyed.

He did manage to take away part of the main beam and bits of the ropes used to hang forty-four men, including Cherokee Bill and his first six-man job. He then went on tour as part of a carnival sideshow attraction, showing off his instruments of death.

When asked if he had ever felt remorse over his official duties, Maledon replied: "I've never hanged a man who came back to have the job done over."

He was a sentimentalist to the end.

THE SITES

Fort Smith National Historic Site Fort Smith National Historic Site preserves the site of the military outpost built at the edge of the Indian Territory and the courtroom used by Judge Parker.

The junction of the Arkansas and Poteau rivers was recognized as a strategic location as early as 1817, when Major Stephen Long established an outpost to keep the peace among the Osage and neighboring tribes. A settlement grew up around the fort, and with the establishment of the Indian Territory it was expanded in 1838.

Zachary Taylor commanded the fort just before the Mexican War, and it was also a point of departure for California-bound wagons after 1848. The barracks, commissary, and the foundations of several other buildings remain from that outpost, which was closed in 1871.

Parker arrived four years later and set up his court in the former barracks. It was enlarged in 1887 to the dimensions that are shown in the present restoration. The furnishings are original, but Maldeon's gallows are a reproduction. There is a visitor center with displays on some of the bad guys who met their ends here and a ten-minute audio-visual show.

The site is on Rogers Ave. at 3rd St. It is open daily, 9 a.m. to 5 p.m. Admission is $2; children under sixteen free. (479) 783-3961; www.nps.gov/fosm.

BUTCH CASSIDY

Of all the outlaws who were posthumously transformed into engaging rogues, Butch Cassidy may come closest to actually filling the role.

He robbed banks. He also robbed trains, ranches, and anything else he came across. But even the lawmen who pursued him admitted Cassidy had a good heart, and that going straight was just a bit difficult for him. There is no record of him shooting anyone, and he apparently avoided cohorts who were too eager to use a gun.

Trigger happiness was one of his complaints about the Sundance Kid and one of the reasons their relationship was not quite as cozy as the famous movie linking their names.

Cassidy and his Hole-in-the-Wall Gang, later known as "The Wild Bunch," were one of the more imaginative and wide-ranging outlaw bands of the 1890s. But by the 1960s, they had been largely forgotten.

Although fondly recalled by a few Western cultists, they weren't in the same league with celebrity outlaws such as Jesse James or Billy the Kid. Few of the general histories even mentioned them.

But the great success of the 1969 film, *Butch Cassidy and the Sundance Kid*, rescued them from obscurity. Communities all across Utah and Wyoming soon began to eagerly promote their tie-ins with Cassidy and his pals. The Wild Bunch had become bankable attractions.

The film was something of a landmark, because it was the first Western in which unrepentant bad guys were depicted as heroes. Of course, it helped a lot to have Robert Redford and Paul Newman, two of the top box office draws in Hollywood history, in the title roles. Redford's obvious affection for the character he portrayed, and his use of the Sundance name for many of his own enterprises, only strengthened the appeal.

"Butch Cassidy was a likeable desperado," said the film's director, George Roy Hill. "Screen Westerns before that had become American morality plays. Villains were black-hearted, one-dimensional characters who paid for their crimes before the hero walked into the sunset.

"As a character study, Butch Cassidy couldn't have been put on the screen before then."

The film shared many of its attributes with *Bonnie and Clyde*, made the year before with the same sort of sympathetic portrayal of the outlaws in its title. An America going through the convulsive social upheavals of the late sixties was willing to accept films in which conventional morality was turned upside down.

Cassidy's real name was George Leroy Parker, and Sundance was originally Harry Longbaugh—hardly the sort of names you'd want to put on a marquee.

While still in his teens, Parker joined a gang of rustlers in Utah led by Mike Cassidy. When the leader disappeared, Parker assumed his last name. The Butch was added during one of his attempts at honest labor when he got a job in a butcher shop in Rock Springs, Wyoming.

Longbaugh apparently chose his name while doing an eighteen-month stretch for horse-stealing in the Crook County, Wyoming, jail. He liked the name of the county seat, Sundance, and simply appropriated it.

Cassidy had been riding the outlaw trail for a good twelve years before Sundance joined him in 1899. In an interview given in 1977, when she was ninety-four years old, Cassidy's

American Heritage Center/Wyoming Territorial Prison Corp.

sister, Lula Parker Betenson, said that her brother's best friend actually was Elzy Lay. (That wasn't his real name, either, by the way. It was William Ellsworth.)

"He talked a lot about his friends and said there were a lot of them," she recalled. "But that Elzy was the best, always dependable and levelheaded. Sundance liked his liquor too much and was too quick on the trigger."

Cassidy was born to a Mormon family in the ranching community of Circleville, Utah (where his sister was still living when she was interviewed 111 years later).

At the start of his career, in the late 1880s, his base of operations was Utah. There he operated from the remote Robber's Roost country, south of Castle Dale, in the rugged, trackless country called the San Rafael Swell. Later on, he moved to Brown's Hole, a valley hidden away in the Uintah Mountains, where the states of Utah, Wyoming, and Colorado come together.

His gang robbed banks in Denver and Telluride, held up the Denver and Rio Grande express near Grand Junction, and started up a protection racket in which local ranchers had to pay them not to steal their cattle.

But returning over the same territory to collect these payoffs was not a wise policy. On one of these trips, the Wyoming law was waiting. After getting his forehead creased with a bullet, Cassidy was arrested. He was sentenced to two years in the Laramie Penitentiary, the only jail time he is known to have served. And he didn't even serve all of that.

After eighteen months, at a hearing for parole, Governor William Richards asked Cassidy if he intended to go straight. He considered for a moment and then offered the governor a deal. He couldn't promise complete abstention, but promised not to commit any more crimes in Wyoming.

That sounded good to Richards, probably on the assumption that if Cassidy served his full term he couldn't have cut that good a deal for the honest citizens of his state. So Butch was freed in January 1896.

But he had never actually promised to leave Wyoming. Instead, he headed for the Hole-in-the-Wall country, in Johnson County, and made it his headquarters during the gang's most notorious era.

With his buddy Elzy Lay and a few other close companions, they hit banks in Idaho, Utah, and South Dakota for major scores in the next two years. The key to their success was Cassidy's insistence on careful planning.

A typical example was their raid on the Denver and Rio Grande train in Castlegate, Utah. Cassidy had arrived in town incognito several weeks before the planned robbery and got work doing odd jobs around the railroad station. So when the mail and express sacks were unloaded on April 21, 1897, no one paid much attention to him loafing around the station.

In fact, the first anyone noticed Cassidy was when he stuck a gun in the ribs of the paymaster. Lay and Frank Caffey soon joined him and relieved the shocked guards of about $8,000.

One of the great advantages of being an outlaw in the era before mass communications was that no one was really sure what you looked like. They told the story for years in Price, Utah, about how a gunman identified as Cassidy was laid out in a local funeral home, and among the mourners who rode in to pay his respects was Cassidy himself.

After robbing a Nevada bank, he and Sundance sent its president photographs of themselves from an amusement park gallery. There was little chance of being identified later—the West was a very big place, and they knew where to hide.

Hole-in-the-Wall was situated just off the Bozeman Trail, which is now Interstate 25. Like the modern highway, it offered quick access to most major towns in the area, and hard-riding men could cover a lot of territory in a hurry.

On June 2, 1899, the gang made its biggest score. They stopped the Union Pacific express at Wilcox Station, near Rock River, Wyoming. Decoupling the baggage car and moving it across a trestle, they then dynamited the bridge to cut off pursuit and gathered up $30,000 in bank notes.

This job broke the promise Cassidy had made to the governor about taking his work beyond Wyoming's border. More than that, it got the Wild Bunch noticed by the Pinkerton Detective Agency, which began the relentless pursuit that would soon end the careers of most of the gang's members.

This is when Cassidy and Sundance split off from the rest of the gang in an effort to elude the untiring, Pinkerton—organized posses. Cassidy's old friend Lay was captured in New Mexico and sent to the Territorial Prison for seven years. He served his time, went straight, and lived until 1934.

Cassidy managed to avoid capture, however, and after a year he and Sundance formed the gang again. In quick succession in 1900–01, the Wild Bunch held up another Union Pacific train in Wyoming, the bank at Winnemucca, Nevada, and the Great Northern Flyer in Montana. Total haul: $120,000.

This brought the posses back after them, with some of the best trackers in the country at their head. The story was covered avidly by the big city dailies in the East. The frontier era was supposed to be over and yet here was this band of outlaws who didn't seem to hear the news. The Wild Bunch was a sensation.

And then they disappeared.

What happened is still a matter of debate, because neither Cassidy nor Sundance was positively identified again, alive or dead. They, apparently, fled to Fort Worth, Texas, where Sundance was attracted to a young woman named Etta Place.

The three of them went on to New York City, and by the end of 1901 reportedly were living in Argentina. Then the legends begin.

According to one version, they lived as ranchers for a time but couldn't resist the lure of easy money in banks. After four years, they fled to Chile with the law at their tails.

Etta returned to the United States, but the two outlaws were then reported in Bolivia, holding up the payrolls of tin mines. Finally, on November 6, 1908, they were trapped in the town of San Vicente and killed in a gunfight with Bolivian soldiers.

Then there is the other version of the story. In 1972, a hotel fire in Missoula, Montana, took the life of Robert Longbaugh. He claimed to be the son of the Sundance Kid and left behind an account of attending Cassidy's funeral in Spokane, Washington, in 1937.

According to his story, a man named William T. Phillips arrived in that city in 1910 and started a business to make and sell adding machines. He was an expert in Western lore and wrote a biography of Cassidy. Apparently, he confided to a few friends that he actually was Cassidy.

Author Larry Pointer found the biography and was convinced Phillips was telling the truth. His book, *In Search of Butch Cassidy*, was published by the University of Oklahoma Press in 1978 and makes the case complete with photographs.

Some bones recovered in San Vicente at the traditional grave site of the two outlaws were subjected to DNA testing in 1992, but the results were inconclusive.

Cassidy's sister in her 1977 interview said she knew the truth. He visited her in Circleville many·times, she said, long after his reported death in Bolivia.

"Butch was chased all his life," she said, "so when we got the news that he was dead, we decided he would be chased no more.

"He was a perfect gentleman. He had good table manners, great regard for ladies, and always left a fancy tip. But he was sure death on banks and railroads."

THE SITES

Hole-in-the-Wall Country Hole-in-the-Wall is about as remote as it was when Cassidy used it for a hideout in the 1890s. The 35-mile gap in the Bighorn Mountains, along the Middle Fork of the Powder River, lies southwest of the town of Kaycee, along I-25, by way of Wyoming 190.

Early trappers knew the area, and it was also used as a campground by the Cheyenne and Arapaho. Its appeal was that there was only one entrance from the east, and a small group of men could hold off attackers indefinitely. It was also an ideal place for grazing the cattle that the Wild Bunch rustled during vacations from bank and train robberies.

The Willow Creek Ranch is situated in the area. It offers accommodations on a working ranch and pack trips into the most scenic portions of the Hole-in-the-Wall Country. It is open May through October. Information and reservations can be made at (307) 738-2294; www.willowcreekranch.com.

Brown's Hole Brown's Hole, in the extreme northeastern corner of Utah, is also one of the less accessible places in the West. No paved road leads into it. Fur traders based themselves there in 1837 and called their base Fort Davy Crockett, in honor of the defender of the Alamo, which had fallen the previous year.

On the eastern edge of the Uintah Range (the only major mountain range in the continental United States that runs east and west), Brown's Hole is situated along the Green River, just north of Dinosaur National Monument. The easiest way to get there is on Colorado 318, which branches off from Maybell at U.S. 40. The pavement ends at the Utah line and 8 miles of gravel road leads into the valley. You can also drive in from Vernal, Utah, on U.S. 191 and then 22 miles east on unpaved road, which begins just north of Dutch John.

The main attraction in the area is the Jarvie Ranch, built in 1881 and run by the same family for forty-three years. The original owner, John Jarvie, knew Cassidy during the outlaw's stay in the area during the late 1880s. The original ranch buildings are still intact and tours are given daily, 10 a.m. to 5 p.m., May to October. (435) 885-3307.

Crook County Museum Mementos of Harry Longbaugh's stay in Sundance, Wyoming, as a guest of the county, are displayed in the Crook County Museum. It is located on the lower level of the courthouse, at 309 Cleveland St. There are photographs and court documents relating to the outlaw, who supposedly changed his name to the Sundance Kid after his stay here. Sundance is located off I-90, in the northeastern corner of the state. The museum is open 8 a.m. to 8 p.m., June through August. Free admission. (307) 283-3666; www.crookcountymuseum.org.

Wyoming Territorial Prison Wyoming Territorial Prison, where Cassidy served his eighteen-month jail term in 1894–95, is now a living history museum. Built in 1876, the facility operated for twenty-four years, predominantly as a federal penitentiary. It has been restored to its appearance of the 1890s and also houses the U.S. Marshals Museum, celebrating the role these lawmen played in taming the West. Characters who were actually incarcerated here, including Cassidy, are portrayed by actors as visitors tour the site.

The prison is just west of Laramie, on I-80. It is open daily, 9 a.m. to 6 p.m., May through September. Admission and guided tour $5; children under eighteen $2.50; children under 11 free. (307) 745-6161; www.wyoprisonpark.org.

Trail Town Trail Town, in Cody, Wyoming, has assembled several historic buildings from around the state. Among them are the log cabin occupied by Cassidy and Sundance from Hole-in-the-Wall. To make the Robert Redford connection complete, the museum also displays the tombstone of Jeremiah Johnson, who also was portrayed by the actor. It is 3 miles west of Cody, on U.S. 14 and 20. Open daily, 8 a.m. to 7 p.m., late May to mid-September. $4. (307) 587-5302.

Western Mining and Railroad Museum Helper, Utah, is a railroad town situated in coal mining country and the combination made it an attractive lure to Cassidy's gang. The Western Mining and Railroad Museum exhibits artifacts from their robbery of the Pleasant Valley Coal Company in 1897. Helper is on U.S. 6 and 191, just north of Price. The museum is at 296 S. Main St. Open Monday to Saturday, 10 a.m. to 6 p.m., May to September; Tuesday to Saturday, 11 a.m. to 4 p.m., the rest of year. Donations accepted. (435) 472-3009; www.wmrrm.org.

ANNUAL EVENT

Cassidy Cassidy, an outdoor musical extravaganza, is performed each summer in Vernal, Utah. This is the closest city to the Brown's Hole area and is rich in associations with the Wild Bunch. The musical bills itself as the "mostly true" version of what happened to Cassidy and Sundance. It runs from late June to the first weekend in August, with performances Monday to Thursday and Saturday at 8 p.m. For reservations and ticket information call (800) 477-5558.

WYATT EARP

Any child of the 1950s who sat enthralled in front of a television set, watching the sagas of old Dodge City and Tombstone unfold, probably can still recite the words to the theme song.

Wyatt Earp, Wyatt Earp
Brave, courageous and bold.
Long live his fame and long live his glory
And long may his story be told.

In 1957, *The Life and Legend of Wyatt Earp* was the third highest-rated show on TV, trailing only *Ed Sullivan* and *I Love Lucy*. Handsome, clean-shaven Hugh O'Brian became one of the biggest stars on the tube.

There was some recognition even then that the show was probably heavier on the legend than the life. One critic called it "a fictionalized glorification of a tinhorn outlaw." The show's producer

Dodge City Peace Commissioners (left to right): Charles Bassett, W.H. Harris, Wyatt Earp, Luke Short, L. McLean, Bat Masterson, and Neal Brown.
National Archives & Records Administration

admitted: "We've got to slice the truth pretty close to make it last." For example, in real life Earp wore a bushy mustache.

Even at Earp's death, twenty-eight years before, an obituary had declared: "He personified at times the best as well as the worst of the elements involved in the civilizing of the Southwest. . . . Wyatt Earp shot his way to fame instead of notoriety only because chance favored him and at the turning point in his career his feet happened to be pointing in the right direction."

There are those who would argue even with that modest assessment Some historians feel his entire career was largely a fiction, created by his old buddy-turned-journalist, Bat Masterson. Rather than courageous and bold, they characterize Earp as a gambler and killer.

The sign placed above the coffins of the men shot down by Earp, his brothers and the gunman Doc Holliday in the famous fight at the OK Corral read: "Murdered on the streets of Tombstone."

According to legend, Earp was a deputy U.S. Marshal on October 26, 1881, the day of the confrontation. That is the version of events depicted in all major films about the fight. At the inquest that followed the shootings, however, he gave his occupation as saloonkeeper, and that was probably an elevated description. Mostly, he gambled at the Oriental Saloon.

Earp was born in Illinois, grew up in Iowa, and supported himself as a stagecoach driver, railroad worker, and buffalo hunter. It was during one of these hunts in 1872 that he met Masterson. Their paths would cross many times in the next few years.

Earp was described as one of the fastest and deadliest guns in the West, although that may be a matter of hyperbole. His worshipful biographer, Masterson, was a notoriously poor shot who preferred to club wrongdoers with his cane, hence his nickname. Any degree of skill with a gun would have impressed Bat.

Earp claimed that his first job as a lawman was in Ellsworth, Kansas, in 1873. The town was one of the railheads for Texas cattle drives, filled with rowdy cowboys and the rough characters who preyed on them. One of the roughest was Ben Thompson, a gunfighter and gambler who terrorized the place.

In a scene replayed in countless Western epics, including the TV show, Earp strode down the wooden sidewalks of Ellsworth, pistol-whipping or punching out anyone who got in his way, and disarmed the fearsome Thompson.

Such an event actually took place and was reported in the

Ellsworth newspaper. But Earp is never mentioned. There was a deputy sheriff named Hogue to whom Thompson turned over his gun. But unless Earp was disguised as Hogue, his presence escaped the attention of everyone at the scene.

After this success, he moved on to another wild Kansas cowtown, Wichita. In the laudatory biographies, Earp is described as being so fast with a gun that he rarely had to shoot anyone. Before an opponent had a chance to react he was staring down the muzzle of a six-shooter.

According to Western historian Peter Lyon, writing in 1960, Earp claimed to have arrested 800 men in two years as marshal of Wichita and shot only one of them, so great was his reputation. And that one shot was just a flesh wound!

But a check of city records indicates that Earp was hired merely as a policeman. He served one year and was fired in 1876 for taking part in an election brawl. His pay was withheld until he turned over money he had collected in fines but hadn't accounted for, and then he was arrested on a vagrancy charge.

This, however, was only prologue. Within a few weeks of his dismissal he turned up in Dodge City, where he was reunited with Bat Masterson. There was plenty of work for both of them. At this time, Dodge City was known as the wildest town in the West. It was everything Ellsworth was, times ten.

Railroad hands, cowboys, buffalo hunters, and soldiers from nearby Fort Dodge all met in a combustible mix. Political and economic power rested with the town's saloonkeepers, who took turns being mayor. They wanted a lawman who would keep the peace, while understanding that too much peace was bad for business.

There were laws against gambling in Dodge City, for example, but they were only enforced when some poor cowboy complained that he had been cheated at a card game. He would then be arrested and charged with gambling.

Masterson and his brother owned saloons and were delighted to see Bat's old pal Earp come to town. He was made a deputy marshal and supplemented his rather paltry income with gambling money. During this time the two men managed to get involved in a fight over a dance hall girl named Dora Hand, who was shot by a rejected suitor.

Earp and Masterson, joined by Charlie Bassett and a truly distinguished lawman, Bill Tilghman, pursued the gunman. He was brought back to Dodge and acquitted for "lack of evidence" through his political connections. Because of the fallout over the incident, Earp was fired.

He went to Deadwood, but returned to Dodge when Masterson was elected sheriff in 1878. This is when he struck up a friendship with the alcoholic, tubercular dentist, Doc Holliday. Although he, too, has been glorified as part of the Earp legend, Holliday in reality was no day at the beach. He had to flee his native Georgia after killing two black men and was apparently wanted for two more shootings in Texas.

But he decided that Earp was his idol, and the two men, along with Masterson, spent many cheery evenings in each other's company, gambling at the famed Long Branch Saloon. Earp, indeed, was faro banker there, a far more profitable trade than keeping the peace.

He also married teenaged prostitute Mattie Blaylock at this time. (The arrangement was under the common law.)

By the end of 1879 the entire retinue was getting restless. Masterson lost his bid for re-election, his brother had been killed by a gunman, and Earp got word from his brother, Virgil, that there was money to be made in the wild mining camp of Tombstone.

So off they went to Arizona and their rendezvous with immortality.

Tombstone was barely one year old when they arrived. The town had sprung up around the silver claim of a prospector named Ed Schieffelin. He had boldly ventured into this area, deep in Apache country, in 1877, disregarding warnings that all he would find there was his tombstone. Instead, Schieffelin hit the Lucky Cuss strike and within three years 3,000 people had poured into the mining camp.

None of Tombstone's citizens were candidates for the PTA. They flocked in from California, Australia, everywhere on the planet where men searched for gold. Many of them arrived in Tombstone after being invited to leave their former place of residence. As low as the mining camps set the bar for behavior, these characters couldn't meet it.

The group from Dodge City, apparently, felt right at home here. The saloons, bordellos, and gambling dens of Tombstone were as wild as any in Western history. The law was a petty inconvenience, observed or ignored as the occasion dictated.

Masterson drifted away in a few months, but Wyatt got a job as a stagecoach guard, while also buying a one-fourth interest in the Oriental Saloon. Virgil was named town marshal and eventually deputized his two brothers, Wyatt and Morgan.

Along with the usual shootings that arose from gambling, women, and jumped claims, there was also a feud going on between the town's businessmen and area ranchers. Clashes between the groups were common, and the Earps were frequently drawn into fights with cowboys from the Clanton ranch. Several of them ended in pistol-whippings, which irritated the daylights out of the Clantons.

Now the story gets complicated. In March 1881 there was a stagecoach holdup. The Clantons, who engaged in a bit of rustling on the side, may have been involved. But according to historian Lyon, the brains behind the heist was someone with inside knowledge of the stage line. That would have been Wyatt Earp.

This is not a widely held theory, although it was put forth in evidence during the examination that followed the shootings. According to Lyon, the reason for the growing enmity between the two groups was the desire by Earp to keep the Clantons quiet about the fact that they knew he robbed stagecoaches. On several occasions during the summer, the Earps tried to goad the Clantons and their hands into a fight. But knowing of their reputations as gunmen, along with the intimidating presence of the dangerous Doc Holliday, the cowboys backed off.

On October 26, brothers Ike and Billy Clanton came into Tombstone, along with Frank and Tom McLowry and Billy Claiborne. They were furious because Ike and Tom had both been pistol-whipped the previous day by the Earps.

Sheriff John Behan, sizing up the situation, located the Clanton group and told them to give up their guns. Billy Clanton and Frank McLowry refused, but told Behan they were all leaving town as soon as they picked up their horses at the OK Corral.

Behan left them only to see the three Earps and Holliday striding down Fremont St. towards the corral. The sheriff tried to stop them but was brushed aside.

There are a dozen different versions about what happened next. According to legend, Wyatt called out: "You men have been looking for a fight and now you've got it." In his sworn testimony, however, Wyatt said it was Virgil who hollered: "Throw up your hands! I have come to disarm you."

The two groups were only a few feet apart, facing each other in a dusty vacant lot beside the stables. Each side accused the other of drawing first. In a matter of seconds, both McLowrys and Billy Clanton were dead. The unarmed Ike and Claiborne fled the scene. Morgan and Virgil, along with Holliday, went down with wounds. Only Wyatt was still standing, a posture suited for Henry Fonda, Burt Lancaster, Kevin Costner, O'Brian, and the dozens of lesser stars who have played the role in films and TV.

The local newspaper, *The Tombstone Epitaph*, backed the Earps all the way. Wyatt and Holliday were arrested three days later, however, and charged with murder, while Virgil was fired as marshal. Magistrate Wells Spicer, after examining the evidence and hearing the testimony, came up with his verdict—which was that the Earps and Holliday were the best damn shots in Tombstone.

"They acted," said Spicer. "Their shots were effective, and this alone saved all the Earp party from being slain. . . . I cannot resist the conclusion that the defendants were fully justified in committing these homicides; that it was a necessary act, done in the discharge of an official duty.

"I do not believe that any trial jury that could be got together in this territory would . . . with the rules of law applicable thereto given them by the court find the defendants guilty of any offense."

There were those in Tombstone whose opinion differed. Sixty-four days after the gunfight, Virgil was shot from ambush in Tombstone and left permanently crippled. In March 1882, Morgan was shot through a window while playing billiards and killed.

Wyatt gave the matter some thought and decided to get out of Tombstone. He abandoned his wife, who was left penniless and committed suicide a few years later by taking an overdose of laudanum. Tombstone, far from being tamed, continued in a state of lawlessness so outrageous that President Chester A. Arthur directed that John Slaughter be sent in as a special marshal. He did the job.

Slaughter was helped by the fact that the mines began to play out and then flooded. Tombstone, its reason for existence gone, shrank to a tiny backwater.

Earp made his way to Colorado to gamble and then moved to California, where he worked as a boxing referee. He didn't have much success with that, either. He awarded a decision to Tom Sharkey in 1896 on a low blow from Bob Fitzsimmons, a foul that only Earp was privileged to see. He didn't get much work thereafter.

Eventually, things turned his way. He married San Francisco heiress Josephine Marcus, invested well in real estate and oil, and was a wealthy man at his death in 1929. It was forty-seven years after he stood in the OK Corral, but those few seconds in the blowing dust of Tombstone defined his life.

His old sidekick Masterson suffered the ultimate indignity. After a few more years of gambling and part-time law-enforcement, he wrote some pieces about his career for a newspaper in Fort Worth. They were so well received that he accepted an offer from the *New York Telegraph* in 1901 and spent the last twenty years of his life as a sportswriter.

"There are those who argue that everything breaks even in this old dump of a world of ours," he began his final article. Early arrivals at the paper the next morning found him dead at his desk, a tame end for the old man.

Much of Tombstone is now a national historic district, several of the buildings lovingly restored to their look of the 1880s. Among the regular visitors is the Notorious Clanton Gang, an organization made up of descendants of that illustrious Tombstone family and their friends.

"There has always been two sides of the story," said Gordon Clanton, a sociology professor at San Diego State University, during the 1995 reunion. "Our side is just not as well publicized. It's an open-ended story.

"The Clantons were not a whole lot more crooked than most. They all had shades of gray." The same could be said of their old antagonist, Wyatt Earp.

THE SITES

Crystal Palace Saloon Although Tombstone bills itself as "The Town Too Tough To Die," it was pretty much on its last legs by the early 1960s. The mines had long since shut down, and only a trickle of tourists, mostly those interested in Western lore, came through. One of them, however, was an attorney from Grosse Pointe, Michigan, named Harold Love.

During his stopover here in 1963 he found that the Crystal Palace Saloon was for sale. It was irresistible, and Love soon found himself the proud owner of a decrepit bar in a town nobody visited.

He decided to restore the place and began a search for the original bar, figuring it may still be somewhere in Arizona.

"It was like the artist who painted 2,500 pictures, 5,000 of which were still in existence," he recalled later. "It turned out that everybody had the authentic Crystal Palace bar. So we reconstructed it from old pictures in the *Epitaph*." The Crystal Palace, at Allen and 5th Sts., operates as a regular restaurant and bar, opening daily at 11 a.m. and is open for dinner, Wednesday through Sunday. There is no admission charge.

Love wound up buying the *Epitaph*, too, as well as Schieffelin Hall, the town's largest theater and meeting hall, and the site of the OK Corral.

The OK Corral The Corral is entered from Allen St., the town's main business thoroughfare, one block south of Arizona 80, between 3rd and

4th Sts. Wooden cutouts of the main figures in the gunfight have been set up where they stood in October 1881 while a taped narration recounts what happened there.

There are displays of antique carriages and fire-fighting equipment in this complex, as well as the last surviving prostitute crib in Tombstone. This was the lowest form of the profession. Having neither a pimp nor a job in a dance hall, these unfortunate women simply set up a stall with a bed in it along the street and serviced any miner or cowboy who came along.

Also within the Corral is the reconstructed studio of Camillus Fly, who left a striking photographic record of Tombstone in its greatest years. Along with displays of the sort of vintage equipment he used are the pictures he took of the town in the 1880s, as well as historic photographs of the Apache leader Geronimo at his surrender to federal troops.

The Corral is open daily, 9 a.m. to 5 p.m. $2.50. (520) 457-3456. A $5 combination ticket also includes admission to Tombstone's Historama and the *Epitaph* office.

Tombstone's Historama and the Epitaph Historama is an introduction to the main events in Tombstone's history, using animation and a film narrated by Vincent Price. It is located next door to the Corral and programs begin on the hour, from 9 a.m. to 4 p.m. daily.

The *Epitaph* began publication in 1880 and is the oldest continuously published newspaper in Arizona. Original printing equipment is on display here and the combination ticket entitles the visitor to a souvenir copy of the *Epitaph*'s edition that covered the gunfight. The offices are located on 5th St., between Allen and Fremont.

Tombstone Courthouse State Historic Park Tombstone Courthouse State Historic Park is located at 219 E. Toughnut St. The courthouse wasn't built until the year after the gunfight, in 1882, but its exhibits give the best historic overview of the affair, as well as showing other artifacts of old Tombstone. This building retained the Cochise County government offices until 1931, probably because other cities in the area were too frightened to try to take them away. The original courtrooms, where John Slaughter hauled in lawbreakers, remain as they were, and so does a gallows at the back of the courthouse. Open daily, 8 a.m. to 5 p.m. $2. (520) 457-3311.

Boot Hill Graveyard Boot Hill Graveyard is just west of Tombstone, on Arizona 80. Reclaimed from the tangle of weeds it had become, this historic cemetery is the final commentary on Tombstone. Here lie the gunmen, the miners, the ordinary citizens who died in one of the most colorful communities in American history—the Clantons and the McLowrys; John Hicks, shot in a saloon brawl; Joseph Wetsell, stoned to death by Apaches who didn't want to alert his friends by using guns; two unnamed cowboys who were hanged; Margarita, who was stabbed by a fellow prostitute; and, of course, here lies Lester Moore: "Four slugs from a .44, No Les, no Moore." Open daily from 7:30 a.m. to 5:30 p.m. Donations accepted. (520) 457-3300.

Dodge City Complex By the time *The Life and Legend of Wyatt Earp* and *Gunsmoke* became national TV hits, Dodge City's rousing past had long been relegated to memory. Almost no original sites associated with Earp's residence here eighty years before remained. Marshal Matt Dillon, of Gunsmoke, was wholly fictitious.

However, aroused by the renewed interest in its history, the Kansas town obliged by building a reconstruction of Front Street, the Long Branch Saloon, and Boot Hill. This is fairly hokey stuff, more Disney than Dodge. Even the graveyard is imitation. Bodies from the original Boot Hill were reinterred in a newer town cemetery in 1879, and a school was built on the site, at 4th and Spruce. It was later replaced by the city hall.

But the Front Street reconstruction captures the spirit of old Dodge City and that is what most visitors are looking for anyhow. There are some photographic displays of the old cow town and a few artifacts from its wild past

The complex is open daily, 8 a.m. to 8 p.m., from Memorial Day to Labor Day; Monday to Saturday, 9 a.m. to 5 p.m., and Sunday, 1 p.m. to 5 p.m., the rest of year. The admission price is $6 for an individual; $15 for a family during the summer; slightly lower at other times. The show at the Long Branch costs $5. (516) 227-8188.

The Dodge City Trolley offers tours to some of the town's other historical places, apart from the Front Street reproduction. Included are Santa Fe Trail locations and the site of Fort Dodge, where several stone buildings from the 1860s still stand. The trolley runs daily, 9:30 a.m. to 5:30 p.m., Memorial Day to Labor Day. Fare is $5. (316) 225-8186.

RELATED SITES

Bird Cage Saloon Another of Tombstone's most lavish saloons, the Bird Cage, has been restored to its 1880s glory. At Allen and 6th Sts., the Bird Cage is run as a museum with most of its original theatrical fixtures intact. According to legend, the performers at this place sang their ballads from inside cages, and the ballad "Bird in a Gilded Cage" was written about them. It is open daily, 8 a.m. to 6 p.m. Admission $3.50. (520) 457-3421.

San Bernardino Ranch San Bernardino Ranch, Arizona, was the home of John Slaughter, the lawman who eventually cleaned up Tombstone. He bought the place in 1884, and it contains many family belongings and original furnishings. Now a national historic site, the ranch is located 16 miles east of Douglas, by way of 15th St. and the Geronimo Trail, which is an unpaved road and passable only in dry weather. Open Wednesday to Sunday, 10 a.m. to 3 p.m. Admission $3. (520) 558-2474.

ANNUAL EVENTS

Wyatt Earp Days Tombstone has a full calendar of Old West observances. Wyatt Earp Days take place the last weekend of May. There are gunfight reenactments, chili cookoffs, and an 1880s fashion show. (520) 457-3291.

Territorial Days Territorial Days are usually held the first weekend in March and commemorate the town's founding in 1879. There are parades, antique hose cart races, and pioneer merrymaking during this event sponsored by the volunteer fire department. (520) 457-2442.

Helldorado Helldorado, on the third weekend of October, is the oldest Wild West celebration in Tombstone, dating back to 1929. It was put on then as a 50th anniversary tribute to the town's founding and was so popular it has been repeated ever since. There is a street carnival, parades, and reenactments of famous local events. (520) 457-2550.

Dodge City Days Dodge City Days, held on the last weekend of July, is the biggest celebration in the Kansas town. There are parades, a rodeo, a street barbecue, and Old West entertainment. (316) 225-8186.

YUMA TERRITORIAL PRISON

In July, the average high temperature in Yuma is 106.6 degrees. That, of course, was the month that territorial officials picked for the opening of Arizona's new prison, on July 1, 1876.

It was one week after General George A. Custer and his men had been slaughtered at the Little Big Horn. Those transported to Yuma may have felt that Custer got the better deal.

The most notorious of Western prisons, Yuma was feared not only for its extreme weather but for its isolation—on a high bluff with nothing but desert in any direction. There were Apaches to the east, Mexico to the south, and the Colorado River below. The name alone was terrifying.

In reality, Yuma was not quite that bad. Of the 3,069 men and women who were incarcerated here in its thirty-three-year history, 111 died. That was a fairly low rate by nineteenth century penal standards. Most of them succumbed to tuberculosis, but that was a disease readily contracted in those days.

Eight prisoners were killed by guards while trying to escape, although twenty-six attempts were successful. Moreover, conditions inside were fairly humane. There was a prison library, one of the first in the country, which was maintained by charging visitors twenty-five cents to enter the prison. Medical care was decent and extreme pun-

Yuma Territorial Prison State Historic Park

ishment rare, mostly involving solitary confinement in a dark cell. Many of the prisoners worked in a crafts shop, making items that were offered to sale to visitors on Sunday.

There was no death row. Executions were handled by county governments then, and even for homicides committed on prison grounds the death penalty was administered elsewhere.

Still, there was something about these cells, carved out of the rock walls above the Colorado, that inspired fear.

In 1876, Yuma was still a port town. Ocean vessels would round Baja, California, and unload their cargo onto small steamships at the mouth of the Colorado, in Mexico. Much of the prison's interior furnishings were brought to Yuma that way.

The town grew up along the emigrant trail to California, at the only place for miles where the river could be crossed. During the height of the Gold Rush, the fleet of ferries here carried 60,000 people a year. Yuma then rivaled Tucson for economic influence in Arizona. But with the coming of the railroads, its water-borne commerce was bound to decline, so Yuma's political leaders sought another source of employment.

They used their political clout to beat out the upstart community of Phoenix for the prison, and the first group of prisoners scheduled for incarceration actually helped with the construction.

Before it closed in 1909, the prison housed a wide variety of wrongdoers. There were Mormons, imprisoned for polygamy; the Phoenix superintendent of schools, convicted of embezzlement; and a journalist who was convicted for chloroforming victims and robbing them while they were unconscious.

The biggest name ever kept here was probably Buckskin Frank Leslie, who was the bartender at Tombstone's Oriental Saloon, in which Wyatt Earp owned an interest. Although involved in several killings, they were all regarded as self-defense in the climate of Tombstone. But when he shot down a prostitute in 1889 he was convicted of murder.

In Yuma, however, he was a model prisoner and worked tirelessly in the prison hospital during an epidemic. He was pardoned by the governor and left Yuma after just seven years.

Not as fortunate was Three-Fingered Jack Laustennau. He was convicted of being a labor agitator (the actual charge was inciting a riot) during the Morenci copper strike of 1903. He was not a happy inmate at Yuma and within a year had used his organizing skills to lead an unsuccessful, fifteen-man breakout attempt.

A superintendent and guard were threatened with death and then beaten unconscious. At that point, however, a convict named W. T. C. S. Buck, who was a prison cook, came racing out of the kitchen armed with several knives and cleavers. He attacked the prisoners, gave the guards a chance to get organized and won himself a pardon.

Laustennau died shortly thereafter of the effects of venereal disease while in solitary confinement.

Swede Rogers may have been the craftiest of all the prisoners here. According to the stories, he spoke five languages, but had problems going straight in all of them. Seeing that pardons seemed to accompany foiled breakout attempts, Rogers organized an escape, and as soon as his companions started to run, he joined the guards in fighting them.

Rogers had his sentence halved and was given a trusty's privileges, allowing him to leave the prison grounds to play his violin at social gatherings in Yuma.

Then there was Yuma's best-known female prisoner, Pearl Hart. She had failed in an inept stagecoach robbery in 1900, although the jury only convicted her of possessing a stolen weapon and sentenced her to five years. Apparently, her earthy appeal swayed those good citizens into voting the lesser charge. It also earned her coverage in New York's yellow press, where her exploits were magnified and glorified.

Upon her release in 1902 she became an actress in New York, although the better roles seemed to elude her. She then retired from the stage and entered obscurity.

Another of the notable women of Yuma was Mother Ingalls, wife of one of the superintendents. During one breakout attempt, she scampered up the tower and grabbed a Gatling gun from a wounded guard. When two inmates fired on her, she shot them both down and ended the uprising.

Then she climbed down from the tower and cooked lunch for her husband.

The most tragic escape attempt involved Superintendent Thomas Gates. While walking through the yard in October 1887 he was assaulted by three inmates who wanted to use him as a shield. The guards had been instructed never to give in to such coercion and they opened fire on the convicts.

Two of them went down but the third inflicted a terrible wound in Gates's neck before being shot. The superintendent nearly died from loss of blood and was forced to resign his position to recuperate.

He, eventually, returned to Yuma but was never free of the constant pain that resulted from the attack. In March 1896, Gates withdrew to his office, picked up a revolver, and put a bullet through his head.

As the prison grew more crowded and increasingly outmoded, the territory finally voted to replace it with a more modern facility in Florence. The last prisoner left in 1909 and the deed for the land reverted back to the city.

Yuma used the prison property for five years as a high school. Classes, however, were held in the recreation hall, not the cells. The school athletic teams were known ever afterward as the Criminals.

The property then sat deserted for two decades while locals carted off much of the stonework for other building projects. During the Depression, the prison bluff became known as Bums Hill because of the vagrants who took up residence in the former cells. Several Western movies, taking advantage of the authentically grim walls, were also shot on the premises.

Restoration work finally began in 1939 and the old Territorial Prison became a state park twenty-two years later, a unique museum of a legendary penal institution.

THE SITE

Yuma Territorial Prison The shudders are almost palpable among visitors at this place. They enter through the museum, built on the site of the mess hall. There are hundreds of fascinating items displayed here, including prison gear associated with both the inmates and administrators. Photographs of dozens of prisoners, snapped as they entered the confines of Yuma, compose a true rogue's gallery. Many of them are still chilling, even when viewed from the safe distance of a century, especially when combined with a description of their offenses. But most of these desperados and despoilers had their sentences shortened, and a surprising number received official pardons.

It is the main cell block and solitary confinement cells that you really come to see, though. Most are still in place, although the absence of the roof that once covered them makes them look more dreadful and exposed to the elements than they actually were. The guard tower, which sits atop the prison water tank, also is just as it was. It was from this vantage point that Mother Ingalls foiled the jailbreak. When you climb up to the roost, which commands a clear view of every corner of the yard, you can see how one little lady with a Gatling gun could be a formidable obstacle to escape.

Markers also point out where Superintendent Gates was grabbed and wounded. The adjacent cemetery contains the graves of 104 prisoners, all but seven of those who died here. Yuma Territorial Prison is located a few blocks east of downtown Yuma, at the Giss Parkway exit of I-8. Open daily from 8 a.m. to 5 p.m. Admission $3. (928) 783-4771.

RELATED SITE

Yuma Crossing State Historic Park Yuma Crossing State Historic Park is at the 4th Ave. exit of I-8 in downtown Yuma. The park is located in the former U.S. Army Quartermaster Depot, built in 1871, which supplied military outposts throughout the Southwest in the late nineteenth century. Displays explain the importance of Yuma in the transportation of those times, and even earlier, when it was part of the route of Native Americans and Spanish explorers. Open daily from 10 a.m. to 5 p.m. Admission is $3. (928) 329-0471.

PANCHO VILLA

If it had not been for a few hours in the predawn darkness of March 9, 1916, Pancho Villa's name would never appear in this book. But when his raiders struck the tiny border town of Columbus, New Mexico, leaving eighteen dead American soldiers and civilians behind them, he earned his place in the pantheon of bad guys.

Villa's forces were blamed for killing many times that number of Americans before the Columbus Raid. But that had occurred on Mexican soil, where a civil war was going on. It was understood that foreign nationals took their chances in such a situation.

Even though the American press, led by William Randolph Hearst's jingoistic *New York Journal*, huffed and puffed, the administration of Woodrow Wilson was inclined to keep hands off. Secretary of State William Jennings Bryan had even favored Villa for President of Mexico, because he heard the bandit chief was a teetotaler.

The raid at Columbus is sometimes described as the last invasion of American territory by a foreign army. That isn't quite true, because in the days following this raid Villista forces also struck four Texas border towns.

But the loss of life, the brutality of the raiders, and the involvement of American military at Columbus made pressure for retaliation inevitable. Within a week, General John J. Pershing was leading a punitive, 4,800-man military expedition across the border. The expedition wandered around for eleven months and grew to 10,000 troops. Never making contact with Villa, they fought instead with units of the Mexican army and almost instigated a war between the two countries.

Pershing finally withdrew in February 1917. But the sense in the United States was that honor had somehow been satisfied.

As leader of the state of Chihuahua's disaffected peons, Villa first allied himself with the forces that had toppled dictator Porfirio Diaz in 1910. His real name was Dorotea Arranga. But after killing a wealthy landowner's son who had either raped or seduced his sister, Arranga fled into the mountain country and adopted the name of a famous nineteenth century bandit.

After Diaz was removed and exiled, a series of assassinations and power grabs brought Villa's old rival and sworn enemy, Victoriano Huerta, to power in 1913.

Villa offered his Division of the North, the effective law in Chihuahua (which lies due south of New Mexico), to Venustiano

Carranza. For a time he was even able to capture and hold Mexico City. But when Carranza turned out to be more of a conservative than Villa liked, he turned against him, too.

Archive Photos

Villa felt he had an understanding with Wilson that the U.S. government would withhold recognition from Carranza as Mexico's legitimate president. But in October 1915 that recognition was granted.

Villa suspected that secret deals had been cut with Carranza to allow American companies to exploit Mexico's resources, which in his view would turn it into little more than a province of the United States. So he turned his forces loose on American interests in Chihuahua.

Through the late winter of 1916 there was some suspicion that Villa was planning something along the U.S. border. He was then thirty-eight years old and had been carrying on his fight against the various leaders of Mexico's government for six years.

Historians still argue about why he took the drastic step of crossing the border at Columbus. There are several possibilities.

He had suffered several calamitous defeats to Carranza and was in desperate need of fresh livestock and arms. The raiders obtained eighty-five horses and thirty mules, which made the incursion a great success.

He also came away with a quantity of Mauser rifles. This was important because when the U.S. gave recognition to Carranza, it turned Villa into an outlaw. The arms dealers from whom he had been buying weapons doubled their prices because the trade was now illegal.

Villa was also furious at what he saw as a betrayal at the battle of Agua Prieta, just across the border from Douglas, Arizona, in 1915. He had trapped Carranza's northern army there with no hope of reinforcement. But the U.S. government allowed Mexican troops to be sent from Ciudad Juarez on American railroads to break the siege.

Victory was snatched from Villa and turned into a humiliating defeat. The attack on Columbus, four months later, may have been in retaliation for American intervention at Agua Prieta.

There is also conjecture that he was working on an alliance with Germany to get arms and that the raid was meant to demonstrate that he could act as a diversion on America's southern border, delaying its ability to enter World War I.

Whatever the reason, Villa's force of 485 men came streaming across the border at 4:15 a.m. Columbus was caught entirely by surprise. Before sleeping troops of the 13th Cavalry posted at Camp Furlong could respond, the Villistas were on them.

They headed towards the center of the town, 5 miles north of the border. Fires were set in virtually every structure along the main street. Grocer James Dean was shot where he stood in the street. When the owner of Ritchie's Hotel was seized at gunpoint and told to surrender his cash, he obliged and then was murdered anyhow.

The American troops finally managed to get their machine guns working and opened a withering fire upon the raiders, many of whom had dismounted and were easy targets. As the number of Mexican casualties rose, the Villistas retreated across the border, leaving behind eleven prisoners and more than ninety dead. Of the prisoners left behind, six were hanged after a quick trial; two died from their wounds; two received prison sentences; and one, who was only twelve years old, was later freed.

Villa's men left behind a smoking ruin of a town and a wave of anger that spread across the country. Pershing was chosen as the leader who would punish this bandit killer.

Black Jack Pershing was then fifty-five years old and regarded as the most effective general in the U.S. Army. He had served effectively in campaigns against the Apache leader Geronimo and then in the Spanish-American War.

His rise was rapid, with President Theodore Roosevelt promoting him from captain to brigadier general over 862 senior officers. While war raged in Europe, the United States remained at peace in 1916, and promotions were hard to come by.

Pershing had lost his wife and three of his four children in a fire that swept through their house at San Francisco's Presidio in 1915, and he was still a man dealing with intense grief when he was named to head the expedition.

He had earned his nickname, Black Jack, because of his ability to command the Army's black cavalry divisions. One of them, the 10th Calvary, was at the core of the expeditionary force.

Pershing left Columbus on March 16. His orders were open-ended but he understood them to mean that he was to do whatever it took to bring in Villa, dead or alive.

He was equipped with some of the most modern tools in the Army's arsenal. He had motorized vehicles, tanks, and airplanes for reconnaissance in the rugged canyon country. It was the first time any of these had been used in wartime conditions by American forces. At the other extreme, the expedition was also the last time a mounted cavalry charge would be employed by the U.S. military.

The Carranza government looked on with dismay as the expedition penetrated deeper into Mexico. Although it welcomed a move against Villa, it had not counted on Pershing continuing across the frontier for 400 miles. Carranza's attitude became increasingly hostile.

In June there was a vicious clash with government forces at the town of Carrizal, in which the 10th Cavalry received twenty casualties, and for a time it appeared that war would break out between the two nations. The invasion also had the effect of solidifying popular support for Villa, who had regained his place as a Mexican national hero for his defiance of the Americans.

When Villa was handed a defeat by Carranza's forces early in 1917, the U.S. government used it as the excuse it needed to get out of a bad situation. By February 5, the last American soldier was gone from Mexico, and the Army set about to prepare itself for a far more serious expedition to France.

It would again be led by Pershing, who had acquired invaluable knowledge about the use of the instruments of mechanized war in Mexico. In that regard the expedition was not a complete waste of time.

The strife between Villa and Carranza dragged on for another three years. Finally, in 1920, Carranza resigned and Villa's long battle ended. He settled down to his mansion and ranch in the Chihuahua town of Parral.

On July 19, 1923, while being driven from his lawyer's office to his home, he was ambushed by eight riflemen. His bodyguards were killed, and Villa accelerated his Dodge touring car directly at his attackers. The car hit a tree, and, while Villa sprawled helplessly, he was shot forty-seven times.

The leader of the assassination, Jesus Salas Barrazas, was sentenced to twenty years in prison. He served six months and was released. That seemed to reflect the lingering ambivalence towards Villa on both sides of the border.

Always a hero to the peons, Villa was regarded as a dangerous man, even in death, by the Mexican government. For years it allowed no permanent memorial to him to be erected at his burial place in Parral. Only after forty years of campaigning by his widow, Luz Villa, was he reinterred in Mexico City as an officially recognized national hero.

In the United States, the enduring image of the thickly mustached horseman in the wide sombrero, weapon belts strapped across his chest, survived for decades. Wallace Beery portrayed him as a heroic figure in the classic movie *Viva, Villa,* and over the decades his popular image in America shifted to that of an earnest revolutionary against corrupt governments. Some historians point out that there is no eyewitness evidence that he even was present at Columbus, although it was always supposed that he directed the attack.

The truth, as usual, lies somewhere in between. There are many recorded instances of Villa nonchalantly shooting down unarmed prisoners. His courting technique seemingly was modeled after Attila the Hun, with rapes of girls as young as fourteen blamed on him. Besides the faithful Luz there were at least seven other women who claimed to have been "legally" married to him. His rages were violent and erratic and even close associates were never sure of their own safety around him.

"He was a jaguar," wrote his onetime secretary, Martin Luis Guzman, "whose back we stroke with a trembling hand, fearful that at any moment a paw might strike at us."

Columbus was rebuilt and now promotes itself as a retirement community in a mild climate at the "gateway to Mexico." But even in the late 1960s, almost half a century after the raid, there was deep resentment among many New Mexico residents about naming a state park in Columbus after Villa.

The bitterness of those few hours of bloodshed never has been completely erased.

THE SITES

Pancho Villa State Park Pancho Villa State Park in Columbus is 32 miles south of I-10 from Deming by way of New Mexico 11. The park is built around the U.S. Customs House, erected in 1902, and now the park visitor center. After the raid, Camp Furlong, the U.S. military base, was moved to this area. But on the night the Villistas attacked, what is now the state park was mostly open ground. The Army camp was then located on the east side of the road that is now New Mexico

11. Exhibits on the raid and a film placing it in historical context are shown at the center. A driving tour of the former Camp Furlong, which was abandoned in 1926, is also outlined. The area has been turned into a cactus garden, magnificent in late winter when the desert is in bloom, but remnants of the old post are still in evidence. Open daily, 8 a.m. to 5 p.m. Admission $3 per vehicle. (505) 531-2711.

Columbus Historical Museum Across New Mexico 11 from the state park is the Columbus Historical Museum. This museum was the former depot of the El Paso and Southwestern Railroad and contains more detailed information about what happened in Columbus on the night of the raid, as well as exhibits on the punitive expedition. Open daily, 10 a.m. to 4 p.m. Donations accepted. (505) 531-2620.

Luna Mimbres Museum The Luna Mimbres Museum, in Deming, is located on 301 S. Silver St. Deming was the command center for the expeditionary force, and many of the troops were bivouacked here before being sent across the border. Although primarily a museum of Southwestern archeology and Indian art, there are also displays relating to the Villa expedition's stay in Deming. Open Monday to Saturday, 9 a.m. to 4 p.m.; Sunday, 1:30 p.m. to 4:30 p.m. Donations accepted. (505) 546-2382.

RELATED SITE

General John J. Pershing Boyhood Home State Historical Site The Pershing Boyhood Home is in Laclede, Missouri. Many of Pershing's personal effects are exhibited here, including mementos of the Villa Expedition. Open Monday to Saturday, 8 a.m. to 4 p.m.; Sunday, noon to 5 p.m. (660) 963-2525.

ANNUAL EVENT

March Raid Day March Raid Day is held the second Saturday of March in Columbus. The Day consists of commemorative ceremonies for those killed in the raid. (505) 531-2711.

AL CAPONE

Big Jim Colosimo lacked a certain breadth of vision, and in his line of work that was a fatal shortcoming.

Colosimo ran the rackets on the South Side of Chicago. By 1920, from his headquarters at the Roma Inn and the Four Deuces Café, he had unified illegal activities in that part of town, which was known as the Levee, to a tighter extent than any of his predecessors.

A certain peril resulted from this success. Big Jim felt the need to import Johnny Torrio from New York to act as a bodyguard and advisor. Colosimo was fifty-two years old, he had just married an actress from San Francisco, and wanted to enjoy life for a while.

Torrio, in turn, sent for a young guy he had met while engaging in unsavory activities around the Brooklyn Navy Yard. Al Capone was just twenty-one at the time of his entrance to Chicago. He was a graduate of New York's Five Points Gang, an organization he had joined shortly after matriculating from the fourth grade of the city's public school system.

He had worked as a bouncer and in the course of his duties sustained three vivid slashes across his face, the longest of which ran from his chin to the corner of his right eye. He was, as a result, already known by the sobriquet that would follow him through his career—Scarface.

It would follow him at a discreet distance because no one ever called him that within earshot. Or within any other kind of shot, for that matter.

Capone already had been investigated in relation to two murder cases in New York and his boss, Frankie Uale, figured this was an opportune time for him to begin an extended stay in the Midwest. He went to work as a bartender at the Four Deuces, on S. Wabash Ave., for $75 a week and found that he and Torrio were two minds in accord.

Prohibition had come in and opportunities abounded. But Colosimo was reluctant to grab them.

"We got the whorehouses," he said in a meeting with his two bodyguards. "We got the gambling. We don't need that other stuff."

A few days later Big Jim was dead, shot in the back of the head by unknown assailants. And the Chicago that would be linked inextricably with the roaring twenties was about to take shape.

Torrio already had put together an organization of suppliers and transporters of strong drink. Bootleg liquor was flowing in an almost unimpeded wave across the border from Canada to Detroit. So many motorboats made the illegal crossing that the Detroit River was popularly called the Whisky River.

Torrio made alliances with the Detroit gangs, including the Purples and the Little Navy, and the product made its way by truck to his network of speakeasies on the South Side. He was perfectly content to remain in the background and let the flashy, beefy Capone be the front man.

Capone was seventeen years younger than his mentor but moved quickly to a position of equality with Torrio. He thrived in his new hometown. Chicago already had acquired a reputation for civic corruption unmatched in America. While its boosters called it the city that most perfectly mirrored the character of the nation, others saw in its violent, seething streets a nightmare image of a place that had lost its moorings.

Payoffs to politicians and police were standard practice long before Capone arrived. He simply systematized the proce-

Library of Congress

dure and made sure he was its chief beneficiary. He owned its mayor, Bill Thompson, through a gift of $250,000 in campaign contributions. The blustery Big Bill, who threatened to punch King George in the nose if he dared visit his city, turned the other way when it came to Capone.

Torrio had much greater ambitions. Chicago was too unwieldy to control completely. The organization required a smaller unit of government to have in its pocket, and the suburb of Cicero answered nicely.

Actually, the strategy was not much different from that of industrial magnates who frequently placed their factories in small communities to give them control of taxing authority. Capone had another sort of business in mind, but to him it was all the same.

"Everybody calls me a racketeer," he once complained. "I call myself a businessman. When I sell liquor it's bootlegging. When my patrons serve it on a silver tray on Lake Shore Drive, it's hospitality."

Capone seized control of Cicero in 1924 by strong-arming the opposition into submission. Gang members cruised the streets on election day, beating up voters, and in some cases kidnapping them until the polls closed. County judges sent police into the city and gun battles raged in Cicero's streets. One of the victims was Capone's brother, Frank.

But the Capone ticket won. By maintaining control of the South Side he now had expanded his reach beyond the grasp of anyone in Chicago with any bright ideas about reform.

He set up offices at Cicero's Hotel Hawthorne and, in Chicago, at the Lexington Hotel, on S. Michigan Ave. at 23rd St. His organization now included thugs who would go on to succeed their boss and control Chicago's rackets for another forty years, including Anthony Accardo and Sam Giancana. His most talented aide, Machine Gun Jack McGurn (whose real name was DeMora) was credited with twenty-two homicides.

The take out of Cicero alone was estimated at $100,000 a week. But Capone and Torrio were thinking large. They now decided to move on Dion O'Banion and muscle in on the North Side.

In the world of Chicago gangland geography, this was a grievous breach of protocol. The city had been fairly divided among them and seemed to contain enough goodies for all. O'Banion, a former choirboy, ran a florist shop on N. State St. from which he directed all illicit liquor activities in his sector. Even his flower business was lucrative. He had provided $20,000 in floral displays for Frank Capone's funeral.

One Chicago journalist wrote: "He not only furnished flowers, but provided the corpses."

But Torrio knew that a significant part of O'Banion's liquor supply came from hijacking South Side trucks. Despite the impressive collection of firepower in the North Side crew, including noted gunmen Bugs Moran and Hymie ("Let's go for a ride") Weiss, Torrio felt he had to retaliate.

Having done business with Capone, O'Banion felt nothing was amiss when some members of his organization entered his flower shop in November 1924. While one of the visitors clasped him in a handshake, the others chopped him down with automatic weapons.

O'Banion's death was a turning point. From that point on, a fairly orderly process turned into a war of all against all. By the time it was over, five hundred bodies had stacked up in Chicago's streets, a level of urban violence that wouldn't be reached again until the drug wars of the late 1960s.

O'Banion's funeral was one of the legendary affairs in Chicago's mortuary history. Enormous floral wreaths filled the chapel, in a display that would soon become the custom of the place. It was Torrio who caught the attention of the North Siders, though. He turned up for the services in an Inverness cape and silk opera hat. This was over-the-top behavior for the normally reticent Torrio and his enemies quickly decided that his hand must have directed the killing.

The response came quickly. Two months later, a machine gun sprayed Capone's car, parked near a restaurant at South State and 55th Street. He had just vacated the vehicle and when he surveyed the damage, which included a wounded driver, he promptly placed an order with General Motors for a bulletproof, armor-plated, seven-ton Cadillac.

From that time on, Capone rarely traveled freely around Chicago. He remained in his various headquarters, closely guarded as a medieval fortress, or moved about surrounded by a brigade of gunmen. When he attended public events, he did it with several rows cleared in all directions. He was a prisoner of the violence he had set loose.

Torrio went down on the doorstep of his home with five bullets in his chest and part of his jaw torn away. It was supposed that Moran, who perfected the technique of drive-by shootings, oversaw the hit.

Torrio recovered but the incident seemed to rob him of his taste for combat. "I'm through," he told Capone in 1925. "It's all yours, if I can get out of this city alive."

He fled to New York and then to Italy to await developments. His nickname had once been "Johnny the Immune," because he kept in the background, avoiding both law enforcement officials and rival mobsters. But there was no immunity anymore.

The O'Banion gang next turned on the Genna Brothers, allies of Capone, killing three of them in the space of six weeks in May. There was some suspicion, however, that Capone himself arranged for the departure of the final two Gennas, eliminating a powerful set of rivals. When two star ex-employees of the Gennas, John Scalise and Albert Anselmi, joined Capone, that seemed to confirm the shift in loyalties.

The Cicero headquarters was attacked, and, in response, Weiss was machine-gunned just across the street from O'Banion's old flower shop. Lucky Luciano, paying a visit from New York, was shaken by this. "It's a real goddamn crazy place," the future organizer of Murder, Incorporated, told associates. "Nobody's safe in the streets."

Nor was there safety in New York. Capone's old buddy Frankie Uale was killed there, presumably upon directions of his former protégé.

As his rivals left the scene, Capone emerged as a towering public figure. There had never been anything like him in America. He commanded a private army, was a known killer, and one of the best known celebrities of the 1920s, right up there with Babe Ruth. The public ate it up.

He ran charities, bought the Boy Scouts tickets to football games, posed for photographs with members of the Chicago Cubs, opened soup kitchens. His estimated income was $100 million a year from liquor, brothels, gambling, and dog tracks.

The famous Untouchables, led by Eliot Ness, were far more famous thirty years later when they had their own television show. As an actual threat to Capone, they were regarded as not much more than an annoyance. Few contemporary reports mentioned them, and while they did manage to smash up several of his distilleries they never accumulated the evidence needed to indict him under the Volstead Act for liquor violations.

Much of the press, in fact, treated Capone as a likable lug, just another Chicago big shot playing complicated political games. The papers loved to speculate on who was up and who was down in the gangs, covering it like an election campaign.

"I give the public what the public wants," he told a sympathetic interviewer. "I've given people the light pleasures and all I get is abuse."

To forget his cares he bought a home (under an assumed identity) on Miami Beach's Palm Island and spent much of the winter working on a tan. That's where he was on Valentine's Day, 1929, when he finally seemed to overstep the bounds.

The massacre in the garage on Clark Street ranks with the gunfight at the OK Corral in American folklore. It has passed into legend, depicted repeatedly in the popular culture as one of the defining moments of a particular era and place in our history.

Historians have called Capone the last of the great American gunslingers and the destruction of Bugs Moran's gang the culminating act of a classic tragedy. Maybe that's a stretch. But murdering seven at one blow did raise the bar a bit.

Capone saw Moran as the final obstacle. No one ever was apprehended for the shootings but it was suspected that Scalise and Anselmi were involved, along with some imports from Detroit's Purple Gang.

They arrived at the garage, Moran's distribution center, shortly before 11 a.m., dressed as policemen. Moran's associates were used to occasional roustings as the cost of doing business and, registering boredom, moved to the wall to comply with shouted demands. That's where they died, cut to pieces by the rattling Thompson guns of two gunmen who got out of the phony police car.

But Moran was not among them. He had lingered over coffee in a neighborhood diner and missed Capone's valentine for him. The massacre only hardened his determination to carry the battle to the lord of Cicero.

May was an especially unpleasant month. Three Capone men were killed and, suspecting treachery, he summoned his favorite gunmen, Scalise and Anselmi, tied them to a chair, and beat their brains out with a baseball bat.

But by August 1930, Capone finally reached the summit, the undisputed king of Chicago's rackets. No one had ever climbed that high before.

His triumph was brief. The Depression was taking hold and there was less money to be spent for the "light pleasures." Capone's methods also had finally awakened a sense of outrage—in other communities if not Chicago. On a visit to Philadelphia he was arrested for carrying a concealed weapon and sentenced to ten months in jail. It was a humiliating comedown and he seethed at the indignity.

He was being pursued by an even more formidable enemy, though. The federal government was ready to strike. The word was that President Herbert Hoover himself wanted Capone taken down as a threat to American morals.

The raids on his warehouses were stepped up, trucks were confiscated, and a new tactic was tried. The feds charged his brother, Ralph Capone, and a top associate, Frank Nitti, with tax evasion. Only two mobsters ever were convicted of murder in Chicago courts in the 1920s. Capone had it wired. Judges took orders from him. But this crime of omission was successfully prosecuted.

Now the government was ready to take on Big Al himself. They turned to one of his accountants and with that information, in October 1951 Capone was convicted of twenty-two counts of tax evasion, fined $50,000, and sentenced to eleven years in prison.

Capone left the courtroom in shock, and seven months later he was taken to the Atlanta Penitentiary to start his time. He was thirty-two years old, architect of the greatest criminal empire in American history, and now it was over.

He had grown soft, fat, unable to withstand the rigors of prison.

The feds were in a vindictive mood and although he had done nothing to warrant it he was transferred to Alcatraz in 1934 as an incorrigible.

Younger prisoners, trying to make a reputation, roughed him up, insulted him to his face. One of them stuck a pair of shears in his back. Moreover, years of untreated syphilis started eroding his mental capacities.

Newspaper reports speculated that somehow he was still in control of the rackets from his prison cell. His former associate, Jake "Greasy Thumb" Guzik, discounted such stories. "Al," he said, "is as nutty as a fruitcake."

In 1939 he was released because of illness and spent the last eight years of his life at his Miami Beach estate, most of it in robe and slippers. A few of the old-timers came around to talk of better days. Most of them he greeted with incomprehension and was haunted by fears that gunmen were coming after him. He died of a brain hemorrhage in 1947 and was denied a requiem mass for his funeral in Chicago.

His grave marker says simply: "Alphonse Capone. My Jesus Mercy."

The last of his rivals, Moran, died in prison in 1957, in the middle of a twenty-year sentence for two small-time robberies in Ohio. A few months later, Torrio cashed out of a heart attack while seated in his barber's chair in New York. He was seventy-five years old and probably made out the best of them all. The Immune had known when to leave.

In a real sense, however, Capone has never left. Dozens of movies and television series have retold his story. There was even a number-one hit song in 1974 by the group Paper Lace called "The Night Chicago Died" that depicts a fictitious gun battle between the Chicago police and the Capone gang.

The joke was that Capone was eager to see one Edward G. Robinson movie "because he wanted to see how a gangster is supposed to act." But his life supplied the model for that.

The film *Scarface*, which shot George Raft to stardom, was based on Capone. And when Hollywood wanted to draw a parallel between the days of Prohibition in Chicago and the 1980s drug trade in Miami, it simply remade *Scarface*. It was still a good story.

In 1985 his old base at the Lexington Hotel was remodeled and Capone's vault was found in the basement. A huge national television audience tuned in for the live opening of the safe, which contained nothing. The Internal Revenue Service had filed an $800,000 lien on the property for Capone's unpaid tax bill just in case something had turned up. It might have been Big Al's last laugh at the feds.

At an auction of personal effects in 1992, someone paid $5,200 for a fish he caught in Florida sixty-three years before and $1,800 for a glass pitcher with his monogram.

Contemporary gangster movies concentrate on the mob boss as a businessman. But Capone was there before them, too. "I don't want no trouble" was his motto.

He was one of the seminal figures of the twentieth century, for better or worse. Probably worse.

THE SITES

Holy Name Cathedral The corner of N. State St. and Superior St. in Chicago figures large in the Capone saga. Dion O'Banion's flower shop stood on the northwest corner of this intersection. Directly across State St. is Holy Name Cathedral. It was while leaving this church in 1926 that Hymie Weiss was murdered on the orders of a highly vexed Jack McGurn, who thought Weiss had directed an attack on him in Cicero. The bullet holes on the cathederal's façade can still be made out.

Site of the Valentine's Day Massacre The garage where the Valentine's Day Massacre took place was torn down in 1967. Chicago was not especially eager to preserve historic monuments of this kind. The site, at 2122 N. Clark St., does have a memorial of sorts, however. Although the lot is now vacant, near the onetime garage wall seven trees were planted. They symbolize the victims of Capone's vendetta against Bugsy Moran. Although they were hardly models of civic behavior, history treats them with respect.

The Levee The focus of Capone's evil empire, in the Levee, is now a rundown part of the city, at the edge of the city's urban revival south of the Loop. If you drive to S. Wabash Ave., between 21st and 22nd St., you're at the heart of it. The Roma Café, where Big Jim Colosimo was murdered, stood at 2126 S. Wabash, and the Four Deuces, where Capone worked as a bartender, was at 2222 S. Wabash (hence the name).

Little Italy Any number of bars and restaurants around Chicago, its western suburbs, and rural Wisconsin claim associations with Capone. Some are even named for him. But most of these ties are tenuous at best, based mostly on stories told by aging relatives of the owner. One part of the city with an authentic relationship with Capone and his pals is the Little Italy section, centered around the 1000 block of W. Taylor St., on the near South Side. Several of the restaurants in the area have been in business since the 1920s and nearly all of them have stories to tell about the old days.

The Untouchables Tour The best introduction to the Capone legacy in Chicago is the Untouchables Tour. This highly entertaining two-hour bus trip presents local history and lore, complete with music, sound effects, and costumed guides. The tour visits all the sites associated with Chicago in the 1920s. It begins at 10 a.m., Monday to Saturday; 11 a.m. on Sunday; with additional 1 p.m. tours Thursday to Saturday and at 2 p.m. on Sunday. The adult fare is $25; children $19. It leaves from the corner of N. Clark St. and Ohio Ave. Reservations can be made at (773) 881-1195; www.gangstertour.com.

JOHN DILLINGER

He was just an American kid from the heartland, born and raised a Hoosier. He grew up in a small town and spent most of his adult life in prison. Aside from the nine months between October 1933 and July 1934, hardly anyone had ever heard of him.

But John Dillinger's impact on American popular culture is profound. The inspiration for dozens of movies and books, he is among the best-known figures in twentieth century crime. His wild cross-country battle with pursuing police agencies, his daring holdups and breakouts, his jaunty style—they put him right alongside Jesse James and Billy the Kid in the all-time pantheon of criminal heroes.

While their careers went on for years, Dillinger made his mark in a fraction of that time. He got big assists from semi-hysterical newspaper, newsreel, and radio coverage, especially from the publicity machine of the Federal Bureau of Investigation.

It made him the original Public Enemy Number One. How could the American public resist a title like that?

When he was gunned down in a Chicago alley, ending what was billed as the biggest manhunt in American history, the story was set in the largest possible type on the front page of every paper in the country. Many of them put out extra editions and could have sold more if they'd had the press capacity.

But he was no actor searching for a role, no singer on a stage. One contemporary described him as "only five foot seven and every inch was mean." Dillinger played for keeps and killed without remorse. Like Billy and Jesse, he was not worth a tear.

Billy was an orphan caught in a range war and Jesse was hardened by what he had seen in the Civil War. But Johnny had no such excuse. He grew up in

Popperfoto/Archive Photos

Mooresville, a quiet, rural community in the 1920s, now captured by the suburban orbit of Indianapolis.

His criminal career began in the most mundane way imaginable. He tried to hold up the local grocer, blew the job and wound up being sentenced to eight years in prison. He was twenty-one years old.

When he emerged in 1933, he was a tough little punk who wanted to get even with the world as quickly as he could. Prison had made him mean. It also put him in contact with young men of a similar stripe who would soon run with him.

There were few jobs in the America of Depression-torn 1933, and none at all for just released ex-cons. Within thirty-three days of returning to the outside, he held up a Marshall Field's thread mill in Monticello, Indiana, and then a sandwich shop in Indianapolis.

Before September was over he had robbed four banks in Indiana and Ohio, and wound up getting recaptured at the home of a girlfriend in Dayton. He was transferred to the jail in Pima for arraignment on the Ohio holdup and it appeared that the second phase of his criminal life was going to be no longer or successful than the first.

But on October 12, his old buddies from the Indiana penitentiary broke him out, beating the local sheriff so severely that he died later that night. Now Dillinger was involved in murder and the rest of his life was spent on the run.

Within a few days, the gang had gathered an arsenal of weapons and bulletproof vests by robbing two Indiana police stations. The first headlines appeared and the Indiana National Guard was called out to protect the citizenry from this menace.

But Dillinger already had gone to Chicago to hide out. There he met Billie Frechette, a part-Indian girl from Wisconsin, whose husband was spending time in Leavenworth as a guest of the federal government. She became his special chum.

He also had his first narrow escape. He had picked up a case of ringworm in the Pima jail and when he went to a Chicago dermatologist for treatment he walked into a trap. Dillinger escaped only after a high-speed car chase. The public was starting to think it liked this guy.

It was, after all, hard times and here was this Dillinger giving the banks and the cops an even worse time. He drove fast, he liked to wear snappy hats, and he had a habit of vaulting across bank counters—an athletic touch right out of an old Douglas Fairbanks movie. Inquiring minds wanted to learn more and the media was tickled to give it to them.

On November 20, Dillinger and his old pals from Indiana turned up in Racine, Wisconsin, driving a black Buick, and robbed the American Bank and Trust of $27,000. They escaped by using bank customers and employees, one of whom was wounded, as a shield.

But the Chicago police by now had formed a Dillinger Squad and were getting closer to him every day. One gang member was shot and another killed a cop in a garage shootout. By mid-December, Dillinger and Frechette decided to head for Florida. It was there he grew a mustache, a prominent feature in photographs of him. He also dyed his hair red to enhance the disguise.

Bored with the sun, Dillinger decided to head back to Chicago. On the way, he stopped off at the First National Bank, in East Chicago, Indiana, making a $20,000 withdrawal. He also was shot at nearly point blank range by a police officer. But the bullets could not penetrate his vest and Dillinger responded by killing the cop, the first death directly attributed to him.

With police in several states looking for him, he stopped off to see his father in Mooresville and then headed to Tucson to meet several other members of the gang. Now his luck turned very bad. A fire had broken out at the hotel where the gang had been staying and local firemen helped retrieve their belongings.

Back at the station, the firemen were thumbing through some magazines and saw the mug shots of the guys they had just helped. They alerted police, who arrived a few moments after Dillinger and Billie did. The whole bunch was arrested and while three states wrangled over who would get to execute him, Dillinger remained in the Pima County jail, giving interviews to national publications.

Indiana finally won the hot seat sweepstakes and Dillinger was flown back there on January 29, 1954. A thirteen-car, tight security police motorcade took him from Chicago's Midway Airport to the escape-proof jail at Crown Point, Indiana. He posed for cordial pictures with the prosecutor, cracked some jokes with the sheriff and then entered his cell, awaiting the legal proceedings that would probably end in his death.

He was arraigned for the murder of the East Chicago cop in February. Repeated requests by his attorneys for a transfer to Indianapolis were denied because security was so much better at Crown Point. Fifty guards turned up at the arraignment, at which Dillinger was shackled, and the trial was set for March 5.

Four days before that, Arthur O'Leary visited him in jail and smuggled in a special present that had been made for him by a German wood-carver in Chicago. It was a toy gun. (News reports of the time said that Dillinger had made the gun himself out of a prison wash-board. That's a good story, but it seemed that he did have outside help on the job.)

Knowing only too well that he would not hesitate to kill them, the guards backed off when he produced the pistol and allowed him to get away. For the next four months, Dillinger was the biggest story in America. He was already famous and the incredible jail break turned him into something like a super criminal in the public mind. Practically every week would now bring a new sensation in this run-ning story.

With the instantaneous communications of sixty-five years later, it seems inconceivable that Dillinger could have remained at large within the country for so long. But there was no *America's Most Wanted* flashing pictures on TV screens into the most remote corner of the country. There was no Internet or fax. A clever enough man could get lost in America, emerging just long enough to rob a quick bank or two and then disappear again.

Within a day he was in St. Paul, Minnesota, living in an apartment obtained by Billie, and putting together a new gang. This one would include a killer whose name would become almost as famous as the boss's, Baby Face Nelson.

They wasted no time. On March 6, they held up the Security National Bank in Sioux Falls, South Dakota. Nelson shot a motorcy-cle cop, human shields were made to stand on the running board of their Packard until they got out of town, and then they sped off with pursuing police firing futilely. They got away with $49,000.

But the next day, the Feds entered the case. By crossing state lines with a stolen car in his escape from Crown Point, Dillinger had vio-lated U.S. law. Now he had the FBI chasing him, too.

On March 15, it was the turn of the First National Bank, in Mason City, Iowa. But the haul of $52,000 was only about one-quarter of what Dillinger had expected and he also was wounded in the shoulder dur-ing the getaway.

He needed time to recover and returned to St. Paul, where he and Billie were living as Mr. and Mrs. Carl Hellman (the last name being a nice touch). But the landlady had her suspicions about them and by March 30 the FBI had the apartment staked out. The next day they banged on their door and demanded entry. Billie stalled, saying that she wasn't dressed and Dillinger then opened fire through the door with a machine pistol.

As luck would have it, a longtime gang member, Homer Van Meter, arrived at the apartment and he, too, started shooting it out with the police. Dillinger made a run for the rear door and while sustaining another wound, this one in the leg, he got away.

After getting emergency treatment for his leg, Dillinger and Billie made their way back to the family home in Mooresville for some down time. Incredibly, the FBI did not trail him there and Dillinger was able to have a final meeting with his father.

On April 9, they returned to Chicago. But FBI agent Melvin Purvis had been put on the case and he had a few ideas about stakeouts. They paid off quickly when Billie visited a favorite bar on North State Street and was arrested. She was taken back to Minnesota, charged with harboring a fugitive and sentenced to two years in federal prison.

By now, other members of the gang were getting picked off, too. Eddie Green was gunned down by the FBI in St. Paul. Herbert Youngblood died in a gun battle in Port Huron, Michigan. Harry Pierpont and Charles Makley, who were involved in the death of the sheriff in Pima, Ohio, were convicted and sentenced to die at the state prison in Columbus.

But Dillinger was still going strong. On April 15, he and Van Meter hit the police station in Warsaw, Indiana for a new supply of guns and were off again. After a brief stay in Michigan, they rejoined several other gang members at the Little Bohemia Lodge, outside Manitowish Waters, Wisconsin.

By April 20, ten of them were living in cabins. They relaxed, played cards, and seemed to be a group of pals and their wives, up from the big city to relax in the north woods. But Emil Wanatka, the lodge owner, was wary. He thought he recognized Dillinger. Moreover, the gangsters, as gangsters will, were getting pushy.

Wanatka's wife managed to get the word to her brother and he put in a phone call to Purvis in Chicago. By April 22, he had arrived at a nearby lodge with two chartered planes filled with fifteen agents.

They arrived at the Little Bohemia by 8 p.m., even after two of their cars broke down en route because of the cold weather. No one had warned them about the dogs, however, and when they started barking the gang knew something was up. They rushed out of the cabins, the agents opened fire killing a lodge employee, and the gang scattered on foot into the night.

Eventually, Nelson was cornered at a nearby lodge. He started shooting, killed an FBI agent, wounded a local deputy, commandeered their car, and drove away. The others managed to steal cars and raced south with several police agencies in pursuit. John Hamilton, another of Dillinger's original cronies from Indiana, was hit in the back and died of his wounds five days later.

But once again Dillinger had escaped certain capture. The story just kept getting better. In the coming days, he was reported in locations all over the country and pressure grew in Washington, D.C., to come up with some results. The raid had been a blunder and J. Edgar Hoover felt his agency had been made to look ridiculous. He didn't like that

Dillinger actually had gone to deep cover outside Chicago. His associates contacted a plastic surgeon, and on May 27 he underwent a procedure to alter his facial appearance and remove his fingerprints with acid. The results were mixed; some said they looked ridiculous and others simply horrifying.

Nonetheless, Dillinger still had enough charm to pick up a new lady friend. Polly Hamilton later said she'd met a man named Jimmy Lawrence at the Barrel of Fun nightclub in Chicago, and even though his face was kind of lumpy he seemed like a nice enough fellow. They celebrated his thirty-first birthday together on June 22, the day he was named Public Enemy Number One by an infuriated Hoover.

Eight days later, Dillinger, Nelson, and Van Meter robbed the Merchants National Bank in South Bend. A police officer died and Van Meter was severely wounded. Moreover, the take was a paltry $4,800. Things were turning sour.

Dillinger had no idea how sour. Hamilton lived in a rooming house with a Romanian immigrant named Anna Sage, who faced deportation for running two brothels. This was not a good time to be facing repatriation to Romania and Sage now saw her chance. She recognized Jimmy Lawrence as Mr. Public Enemy, and on July 20 she made a call to the police officer in East Chicago who was involved in her arrest.

She was assured that the deportation could be fixed if she delivered Dillinger. Two nights later she called back, telling him that she and Hamilton planned to accompany him to a movie at either the Marbro or the Biograph.

Purvis ordered stakeouts at both places and at 8:15 p.m., the three of them were seen entering the Biograph. The film was *Manhattan Melodrama*, a gangster epic with Clark Gable and Myrna Loy. By the time they emerged at 10:30 p.m., the place was surrounded with federal agents and five officers from East Chicago.

Purvis lit a cigar, the signal that Dillinger had been spotted. With the sort of instinctive sense that marked his career, he realized immediately that he was in danger. He broke away from the two women and started to run towards an alley south of the theater. Five shots were fired at him as he fumbled in his pockets for the two revolvers he was carrying. One of the bullets, probably from the gun of Agent Charles Winstead, hit him in the back of the neck and exited through his right eye.

He was dead where he fell. Several passers-by upon hearing who the dead man was dipped their handkerchiefs or the tips of their shoes in his blood. Dillinger was officially pronounced dead at a nearby hospital, and two days later the body was taken by hearse back to Mooresville.

On July 25, he was buried in Maywood, Indiana, at the Crown Hill Cemetery. To prevent the body being disturbed, his father ordered the gravesite lined with three feet of concrete.

"He was the personification of ferocity and he was as elusive as quicksilver," wrote the *Detroit News*, in a fairly typical editorial summation. "With his trigger finger on a machine gun, Dillinger sprayed death and made his contemporaries in homicide, Clyde Barrow and Pretty Boy Floyd, seem like minor leaguers."

Anna Sage was celebrated as the "Lady in Red," the color she was wearing when she walked out of the Biograph, and passed into folklore as his fatal betrayer. Van Meter was shot down in St. Paul in August. Nelson met a similar fate in November. Makley was killed while trying to break out of prison and Pierpont was executed in Ohio.

"I don't smoke very much," Dillinger once told an interviewer. "And I drink very little. I guess my only bad habit is robbing banks."

Shortly after his death, the movie *Petrified Forest* was made with a gangster role that made Humphrey Bogart a star. Many critics observed that he seemed to model his character on Dillinger.

So it began, and really has never ended.

THE SITES

Crown Point Jail For about twenty years, starting in 1975, several Dillinger admirers maintained a museum filled with memorabilia about him that had been gathered from across Indiana. It was located in Nashville, Indiana, a picturesque arts and tourist village in Brown County, just a few miles from his birthplace at Mooresville.

But with the death of its co-owner, the collection was crated up and shipped across the state to Crown Point. Exhibitors felt that this was a more appropriate venue because of its connection with his famed wooden gun jailbreak in March 1933. The original jail still stands in this county seat and plans call for the Dillinger museum to reopen there, late in 1999.

It will feature his death mask, old newspaper accounts of his career, part of the teller's cage from a bank he held up, items belonging to the family and keepsakes from his funeral.

Crown Point is 47 miles southeast of Chicago, by way of the Chicago Skyway and Interstates 90 and 65. The jail is located at 212 S. Main St. Call (219) 769-4788 or (800) 255-5253 for the opening date, hours, and admission prices.

The Biograph Theater The Biograph Theater is now a national historic landmark and is still going strong. Even without the Dillinger associations it would be worth seeing as a vintage movie palace from the great age of the silver screen.

The Biograph is located on Chicago's near North Side, at 2433 N. Lincoln Ave. A plaque on the south exterior wall of the building marks the place where he died.

The Little Bohemia Lodge The Little Bohemia is still in business as a bar and restaurant in Manitowish Waters, Wisconsin. A museum displaying mementos of the Dillinger gang's brief but violent stay here, in April 1934, including the original bullet holes in the walls, is part of the attraction.

The restaurant is on U.S. 51, just south of the resort town and about go miles north of Wausau. It usually opens on the last weekend in April and operates through December. Call (715) 543-8433 for hours.

BONNIE PARKER AND CLYDE BARROW

The car had remained in storage for fifteen years, unseen and almost forgotten. The 1934 Ford Fordor Deluxe Sedan had once been displayed on the front page of every newspaper in America, along with the blood-spattered interior and the few dozen bullet holes in the chassis.

It had toured the country for a while and was an attraction at a Cincinnati amusement park for twelve years. But interest waned, and in 1952 it went into storage. The world didn't seem to care anymore about the cautionary tale of Bonnie and Clyde.

But in 1967 this pair of long dead, small-time gas station bandits and cop killers suddenly became stars. Arthur Penn's stunning motion picture, starring Faye Dunaway and Warren Beatty, made Bonnie Parker and Clyde Barrow bigger than they ever were back in the 1930s.

To the America of the Depression years they were one of a series of fast-driving, gun-toting outlaws who emerged from the economic desperation of the times. Across a band of states from Texas to Indiana, they seemed to fulfill the sublimated wishes of the jobless and hopeless. They drove fast and robbed banks.

They were Public Enemies. From pulpits and editorial offices around the country,

Archive Photos

Americans were told they threatened the nation's moral fiber. But they seemed to be having a lot of fun doing it.

One after another they all met their fates, gunned down by the G-men or less exalted local police officers. Then the Depression ended and the country moved on to new threats and new dramas.

In the late 1960s, however, with America going through a cultural upheaval, it became chic to be an outlaw again. The resurrected

Bonnie and Clyde tore across the movie screen in their old cars, accompanied by jaunty bluegrass banjo music, reminding those too young to remember what great fun the 1930s had been.

The grainy nostalgia of the Depression Era Southern Plains was captured masterfully. The concluding slow motion ballet of death, with the two stars jumping like bloody puppets as their bodies are pumped full of bullets by lawmen, was regarded as cinematic artistry.

Of course, the characters on the screen were nothing like the two killers who actually died in the old gray Ford. The *New York Times*, in an uncharacteristic (for 1934) burst of colorful prose, described Barrow as "a snake-eyed murderer who killed without giving his victims a chance to draw. He was slight, altogether unheroic in physical appearance and was dangerous only when cornered."

His paramour fared little better. "She was a fit companion for him, a hard-faced, sharp-mouthed woman," said the Times. To which the *New York Herald-Tribune* added in an editorial: "Society is glad that Louisiana rubbed them both out yesterday."

They were believed to have committed thirteen murders, most of them policemen and guards who were shot down before they knew what hit them. The rest were either bystanders or unarmed store clerks who had the bad judgment to offer resistance.

Former Texas Ranger Frank Hamer led the pursuit that tracked them over thousands of miles of highways and back roads. He finally set up their fatal ambush in Louisiana and seemed to feel genuine regret about the way things turned out.

"I hate to bust a cap on a woman, especially when she's sitting down," he said at the time. "However, if it hadn't been her, it would have been us."

Bonnie had a gun across her lap and a half-eaten bacon and tomato sandwich in her hand when she was killed. Hamer, however, came across as the bad apple in the movie and his estate sued the film company. They must not have understood cinematic artistry.

During their crime spree, Bonnie got the lion's share of notoriety. Although Ma Barker was leading her band of thugs at about the same time, female killers were still a novelty.

Most media descriptions of the time concentrated on a report that she smoked cigars. In recent years, when such behavior by women is regarded as unspeakably sophisticated, it seems odd to fasten on that aspect. But cigar-smoking by a woman in the 1930s was seen as proof of unnatural instincts. It seemed to make her reputation as a killer more comprehensible.

As it turned out, the report was an error. Bonnie never touched the stogies. But it's always something with those newspaper people.

She had been born in a small town in Texas in 1910 and liked to serenade her Sunday school class with "She's a Devil in Her Own Hometown." When her family moved to Dallas, she was drawn to acting and got work as a shill for politicians trying to draw a crowd.

Her name fit her perfectly. She was less than five feet tall and weighed ninety pounds. Some of her biographers report, however, that her sexual appetite was voracious and that Clyde was not always the man to fill it. So for most of their time together, a third member traveled with the gang as an added gun, in every sense of the word.

Bonnie married at sixteen, but things just didn't work out. Roy Thornton was unfaithful and also got himself sent away for five years for robbery. She was working as a waitress in Kansas City, in 1930 when she met Roy Hamilton, another small time gunman. That liaison would lead her to Barrow.

Clyde's family owned a Dallas filling station, but he and his brother, Buck, preferred holding them up. Contemporary reports spoke of his "whining drawl" and general shiftiness. But Bonnie's mother was willing to meet him halfway. "He had what they call charm, I think," she said. "I could see why Bonnie liked him."

Both Barrow boys went to prison for car theft in 1930. Clyde walked away after being made a trusty but was picked up in Ohio and sentenced to fourteen years. He served less than two before being paroled by Texas Governor Ross Sterling. It was this lenient policy towards prisoners that prompted Hamer to resign from the Rangers.

It seemed that Hamer had a point. Two months after his release Barrow killed a shopkeeper in Hillsboro, Texas, shooting him in the back. In August he was in Oklahoma where he and a friend turned up at a dance drinking whisky out of a paper bag. When a deputy sheriff told him to put the booze away, Barrow shot him down.

The friend was Hamilton and the two of them had become a team. In October, a seventy-year-old butcher in Sherman, Texas, was their next victim. Barrow shoved a gun against his abdomen and the man made the mistake of trying to shove back.

It was sometime after that killing that they made it to Kansas City and Clyde met Bonnie. Although she was supposed to be Hamilton's girlfriend, that arrangement didn't last long. By December, he had split and Bonnie and Clyde were on their way to glory, stealing a car in Temple, Texas, and killing the owner when he protested too much.

The next seventeen months of their lives was an endless road trip of bad behavior. They were constantly on the move, exchanging one stolen car for another, holding up something whenever they needed money. They were soon joined by Buck Barrow and his wife, Blanche, and a teenaged Texas gunman named W. D. Jones, who also served as Bonnie's boy toy.

In the first half of 1933 they killed four more men, all of them officers of the law, in Texas, Arkansas, and Missouri. But by this time Hamer was leading the pursuit. On July 19, he trapped the gang at a motel in Platte City, Missouri, just north of Kansas City, but they managed to shoot their way through a cordon of police.

Five days later, however, they were caught again in a wooded area near Dexter, Iowa. This time Buck was wounded three times, captured in his underwear, and died of his wounds a few days later. Blanche was sentenced to ten years in the state penitentiary. She survived to see the movie made about the gang and was quite fond of Estelle Parsons' portrayal of her, "although she should be able to get better roles than me."

The Iowa shootout also convinced Jones that it was time to resign, although many years later he said that he still admired Barrow. "His badness wasn't just badness—it was fear," he said.

Six months passed while Bonnie and Clyde decided to stay undercover. Then in January 1934, they turned up at Huntsville Prison, in Texas. For reasons that have never been adequately explained, they helped Hamilton and four other prisoners break out. One guard was killed as Clyde covered the escapees with a stream of machine gun fire and Bonnie drove the getaway car.

Hamilton, showing there were no hard feelings, went his own way and was recaptured a short time later. But a young Louisiana escapee, Henry Methvin, joined up with Bonnie and Clyde, filling the varied roles of the departed Jones. This turned out to be a bad error.

The gang took the lives of three more policemen in the next three months and it was apparent that Barrow had developed a pathological hatred for all law enforcement officials. This made Methvin extremely nervous.

In May, the three of them went to Louisiana so that Methvin could visit his family. During the visit he managed to make contact with police and alerted them as to where they could find Bonnie and Clyde.

In the predawn hours of May 23, 1934, a posse of lawmen under Hamer set up an ambush near Gibsland, Louisiana. When orders to stop were ignored and Barrow began to back the car up, the officers opened fire. More than fifty bullets hit the Ford and its two occupants.

Police found $507 on Barrow's body. In the backseat, amid machine guns, rifles, pistols and ammunition, were a saxophone and some sheet music.

The bodies were returned to Dallas for burial. Despite Bonnie's repeated requests that they be interred together, her mother insisted on separate services and graves in different cemeteries.

"Her mother promised that she would bury them together," said Clyde's only surviving sibling, Marie Barrow, in 1997. "But then she didn't do it. I guess she thought Clyde had taken Bonnie off and got her killed. You know how mothers feel."

More than 50,000 people turned out to view the two bodies. The Associated Press reported that Bonnie was "clad in a blue silk negligee and her hair was freshly marcelled. Her nails again were tinted, as she had worn them for two years since she began her fast life with Clyde." She was twenty-four years old.

Bonnie's mother had the following epitaph carved on her daughter's stone: "As the flowers are all made sweeter by the sunshine and the dew, So this old world is made brighter by the lives of folks like you."

Historian John Toland insisted, in an article written shortly after the movie was released, that most of the droll and clever actions attributed to Barrow in the film were actually traceable to John Dillinger, a far more likeable killer.

But the movie did wonders for the old car in which the pair was killed. From a price tag of zip in 1967, the car increased in value, over the course of two auctions, to $250,000 in 1988. When Marie Barrow decided to put up several other items for sale nine years later, including her brother's bullet-riddled shirt, they fetched $187,000 more.

The most money Barrow ever got in any one robbery was $3,500.

THE SITES

Whiskey Pete's Casino Both the death car and Clyde's memorabilia were purchased by Primmadonna Resorts, Incorporated, and placed on permanent display at Whiskey Pete's Casino, outside Las Vegas.

The car was originally owned by Ruth Warren, of Topeka, Kansas, who bought it new in 1934 for $835. Clyde was a stickler for first-rate vehicles and this one came equipped with an 85-horsepower V8 engine.

The story that he had written a personal note to Henry Ford praising the speed and durability of the cars he made has also been attributed to Dillinger. The Ford Motor Company public relations staff in 1978 found a letter attributed to Barrow in the corporate archives.

"While I still have breath in my lungs," it said, "I will tell you what a dandy car you make. I have drove Fords exclusively when I could get away with one. For sustained speed and freedom from trouble, the Ford has got every other car skinned, and even if my business hasn't been strictly legal, it don't hurt anything to tell you what a fine car you got in the V8."

As an endorsement you can't improve on that, even if there is no way of proving its authenticity.

The car was stolen three weeks before the two fugitives were killed, but when Mrs. Warren turned up in Louisiana to claim it, local officials demanded that she fork over $15,000. She finally had to obtain a federal court order to pry it loose from the sheriff's grip. She sold it to a carnival for $3,500, and then it was resold for $14,500, before languishing in a warehouse for fifteen years.

Besides Clyde's bloody shirt, some of his personal weapons are also on display at Whiskey Pete's. The casino is located 35 miles south of Las Vegas on I-15, at the California state line. Like all Nevada casinos, it is open 24 hours daily. Free admission. (702) 382-4388.

The Ambush Site The marker at the site of the ambush that took the lives of Bonnie and Clyde is on Louisiana 154, south from I-20, at Gibsland. It is about 45 miles east of Shreveport.

Ted Hinton, one of the lawmen who took part in the ambush, said in 1969 that they had just about given up waiting for the two outlaws to arrive, thinking they had received a bad tip.

"If he'd been thirty minutes later, we'd have been gone," he said. "But I had a job to do and I did it. As far as I know for a fact, I never killed anyone." When asked how it was decided to stop firing at the car, Hinton said: "Everybody ran out of shells."

BUGSY SIEGEL

There is a story told about Meyer Lansky, financial genius of the Mob. While living in retirement in Miami, he enjoyed watching a television mini-series about himself and some of his oldest and dearest pals, including Benjamin "Bugsy" Siegel.

Siegel was depicted as a thug and a leg-breaker. "The people who made that ought to be sued," said one of Lansky's indignant friends.

"Why?" he replied. "In real life he was worse."

Lansky would have known. He and Siegel had been friends since they were teen-agers and formed the Bug-Meyer mob.

In recent years, Siegel has been depicted in pop culture as a dreamer of dreams, the man who created Las Vegas but ran into some unfortunate cost overruns along the way. When his creditors called in the debt in 1947, with two bullets from a .30 caliber rifle through his head, it was regarded as a sad ending for one whose worst sin was bad planning.

The reality was much worse.

Before he reached voting age, his record included arrests for rape, hijacking, extortion, robbery, assault, narcotics violations, bookmaking, and, oh yes, murder. Time actually spent in prison, however, was minimal, even though it was an open secret that he been deeply involved in two hits that propelled Lucky Luciano to the top of the New York Mafia.

He was also famous for his violent temper, which earned him the nickname he despised.

Siegel was fifteen years old when he teamed up with Lansky, who was then nineteen. They both came out of New York City's teeming Jewish neighborhoods with aspirations of a much better life.

Library of Congress

According to writer Robert Rockaway, who interviewed the few Jewish mob leaders who made it to their declining years for his book . . . *But They Were Good to Their Mothers*, Lansky indignantly denied that the Bug-Meyer gang actually went around harming people.

They merely hijacked vehicles for illegal liquor shipments in the 1920s and also provided drivers and a little bit of muscle if things went wrong.

"We were in business like the Ford Motor Company," Lansky said. "Shooting and killing was an inefficient way of doing business. Ford salesmen didn't shoot Chevrolet salesmen. They tried to outbid them."

But veteran New York cops remembered a different version of events. They recalled, instead, a violent organization and Siegel as a man who took a personal hand in messy things, who enjoyed inflicting pain.

As Luciano began his rise to the top of the New York mob, he struck up a partnership with Lansky and Siegel. The first fruits of this association blossomed in 1931 at a Coney Island restaurant called Nuova Villa Tammaro. Luciano lunched with his boss, Joe Masseria, and afterwards excused himself to visit the men's room.

In his absence, a car pulled up, carrying in it a future who's who of the mob—Albert Anastasia, Vito Genovese, Joe Adonis, and Bugsy. In a matter of bullet-filled moments, Masseria was the ex-boss of Luciano.

A few months later, the last remaining overlord, Salvatore Maranzano, was shot to death in his office above Grand Central Station. No one was charged with the crime, but it was understood that the job had been contracted out to Siegel and his colleagues.

The two hits filled Luciano with gratitude towards Siegel, and he was soon trusted with many delicate assignments. The one that intrigued Luciano most was the unfortunate situation in California. There was too much competition there and Luciano thought it was counter-productive to kill each other over turf. He felt that a simple consolidation would do wonders to improve cash flow.

So in 1937 Siegel was prevailed upon to leave his family and well-guarded suite in the Waldorf Towers and move to Los Angeles. It was an arrangement made in heaven. With his snappy wardrobe and good looks, Siegel was a natural fit.

Using the muscle of local mobster Jack Dragna and some liberal grease for the local authorities, Siegel was soon in control of the book-making and narcotics industry in California. He was especially friendly with actor George Raft, who apparently helped Siegel beat a felony bookmaking charge by the simple act of perjury.

It was then that he began to think of expansion. World War II was over, prosperity was in the air, and just across the Nevada state line gambling was legal. With a nearly invisible population base and a mining industry in free fall, Nevada had liberalized its divorce laws and legalized gambling in 1931. While editorialists decried the state as a moral cesspool, the money started rolling in.

Siegel was a frequent visitor to Las Vegas and was appalled at what he saw. Here, just a few hours from the huge Los Angeles market, was a place with unlimited potential being run by a bunch of small-timers. There was little more than roadhouses, two Old West theme hotels (El Rancho Vegas and The Frontier), and second-rate casinos.

What Siegel proposed was to build the country's most luxurious hotel-casino, out on the highway south of the city. His New York associates were decidedly unenthusiastic. They saw Vegas as a desert hick town. But he returned east and with the assistance of Lansky sold his concept to the mob hierarchy.

But the timing was wrong. Early construction estimates doubled because of postwar shortages in steel and copper. Besides, Siegel's vision kept expanding. Before long he was millions in the hole, writing bad checks to the construction company and in trouble so deep that even Lansky could barely save him.

Still, his Flamingo Hotel opened on December 26, 1946, with Jimmy Durante, Xavier Cugat, and Eddie Jackson heading the bill. But bad weather and equipment failures turned the gala opening into a fiasco. By the end of January, the Flamingo shut its doors.

He managed to get it reopened by March, but soon his partners began suspecting that Siegel was skimming. His girlfriend, Virginia Hill (whom newspapers of the time delicately described as "a former dancer and heiress"), was off in Europe on shopping trips and for the life of them his associates did not comprehend where she was getting the money.

On June 20, 1947, they acted upon their suspicions. As Siegel sat in the living room of a Beverly Hills home leased by Hill, reading an early edition of the *Los Angeles Times*, seven shots came through the front window. Five of them missed, but two blew horrific holes through Siegel's face.

It was a clear violation of his often-quoted dictum that one should "live hard, die young, and leave a good-looking corpse." He was forty-two years old. When his estate finally cleared probate, seven years later, it contained just $15,000.

Los Angeles police astutely figured that this was a mob hit. Sixteen months later, the Beverly Hills chief of police stated he knew who the killers were "but the persons involved are so big we can't go out and give them the bum's rush."

He said he needed a little more time to gather corroborating evidence. The world still waits. No one was ever arrested for the shooting.

After Siegel's demise, one of his New York friends, Moe Dalitz, was sent in to take charge of the Las Vegas operation. It was under his guidance that Siegel's dreams were realized and the Strip became the biggest moneymaking machine in mob history.

The massive, glamorous, themed hotels that line the Strip today exceed even Bugsy's dreams of avarice. Dalitz lived long enough to see the current round of expansion, although he was seriously wounded in an attempted hit at the construction site of the Mirage Hotel in 1986.

He survived that but three years later, while in the intensive care unit of a Las Vegas hospital, he was poisoned by an orderly who was paid $100,000 for the job. The mob operative who hired him was acquitted.

The Sites

The Flamingo Hotel Who says there is no sentiment in Las Vegas? Although the final remnant of the original Flamingo Hotel was torn down during an expansion in 1993, they still remember Bugsy. A historical marker bearing his likeness and crediting him with building the place has been placed near the hotel's wedding chapel. It is located behind the main swimming pool.

The hotel also issued a 50th anniversary commemorative chip honoring its founder in 1997. The Flamingo has grown larger than Siegel ever imagined. It now has 3,642 rooms and features genuine Chilean flamingos on the grounds. Moreover, the hotel's main showroom is named Bugsy's. Although Siegel hated that name, he probably would have been touched by the gesture. Then again, maybe not.

The Flamingo is located at 3555 S. Las Vegas Blvd., near the center of the Strip. (800) 933-7993.

Castillo del Lago Castillo del Lago was the name of the hilltop Spanish-style mansion that Siegel used as a gambling casino for the mob in the late 1930s. It still stands at 6342 Mulholland Dr., the road that runs along the crest of the Hollywood Hills. The best way to reach it is from the Barham Blvd. exit of U.S. 101, the Hollywood Freeway, to eastbound Mulholland. A hiking trail follows the ridge of the hills just below this castle, and that is the best vantage point from which to see it.

ALCATRAZ PRISON

Tough? You have no idea how tough this place was. There was even a period when the first warden of Alcatraz, James A. Johnston, allegedly made the inmates wear other people's underwear.

Johnston was convinced that cigarettes were essential in a prison for incorrigibles because they had a calming effect. Unfortunately, the budget he was given from the Federal government did not make adequate provision for the purchase of tobacco.

So Johnston bought smokes out of his underwear appropriation. This, however, left his prisoners in a somewhat exposed condition. That's when Johnston's true brilliance was revealed. The prison also did the laundry for the nearby U.S. Navy base. So Johnston simply held the underwear for an extra week, issued them to the inmates, and then relaundered them before sending them back to the Navy.

From the day it opened as a federal prison, in 1934 until its closing twenty-nine years later, tales of Alcatraz fascinated the American public. They still do. More than any other prison, the Rock symbolizes the true wages of crime-stark, silent isolation with no way out.

U.S. Attorney General Homer Cummings, who served in Franklin D. Roosevelt's first administration, was asked to come up with the answer to the problem of where to send the penal system's hardest cases. Cummings considered one of the Aleutian Islands, off the coast of Alaska, and even Fort Jefferson, in the Gulf of Mexico, off Florida, which had been used as a prison during the Civil War. Then he hit upon Alcatraz.

Newspapers quickly called it "America's Devil's Island," referring to the infamous French prison off the coast of Guiana, in South

Richard Frear/Golden Gate National Recreation Area, National Park Service

America. This irritated Cummings. These were the most notorious prisoners, who defied all rules of behavior, and Cummings thought their punishment was humane when compared with that of Devil's Island.

"It represents the ultimate in isolation," said Cummings. "And yet, oddly enough, it lies in the very midst of the busy, hurried life of the San Francisco Bay region. . . . These men are conscious hourly of the hum of life about them. Life is so near, but liberty so far."

That was the crowning irony. Separated from one of America's greatest cities by deadly riptides, 42-degree water temperatures, fog and patrol boats, the inmates had ample opportunity to reflect upon what they had given up.

But Cummings indignantly denied that the place was a Devil's Island. Those who were incarcerated there, he pointed out, brought it upon themselves by their actions in other prisons.

There were rules of silence, yes, but they were not absolute. During rest periods and while working in the shops, the men were free to talk. But not during meals or between cells or anyplace else where conversation would be "confusing and disturbing or threaten discipline."

Inmates could have visitors and receive mail and magazines. But those were privileges, said Cummings, and would be withdrawn if rules were broken. Since the enumeration and explanation of the rules ran to something like fifty typewritten pages, breaking one was fairly easy.

There were church services on Sunday but attendance was counted as recreation time and subtracted from the total to which the prisoner was entitled.

But the food wasn't bad. That was another of Johnston's dicta. Prisoners who ate well tended not to cause trouble. So the meals were hot and a prisoner could order a larger portion if he chose. Penalties for wasting food, however, were stringent.

Too much waste, in fact, could land a man in solitary, where those who started fights, assaulted guards, refused to work, or tried to escape also wound up. The food in those cells consisted of kitchen scraps drenched in beet juice and served in a paper cup.

While federal regulations limited time spent in solitary to eighteen consecutive days, the Alcatraz authorities sometimes took a man out for a few hours and then sent him right back in. The record was three hundred days in a row.

The motion picture industry has made much of such conditions. The film *Birdman of Alcatraz*, made the year before the prison shut down, depicted Robert Stroud as a tormented victim of the system, whose only comfort was the birds he studied. His crimes, however, were not dwelled upon.

Stroud was sentenced originally in Alaska in 1909 for the stabbing death of his sweetie's former boyfriend. Seven years later, he killed a guard at Leavenworth and was given the death penalty, a sentence commuted to life in solitary by President Woodrow Wilson.

Stroud used the time to make himself an expert on bird diseases and in 1937 published the most complete work on the subject ever written. But his repeated applications for parole were turned down and Stroud became increasingly vehement about gaining release. This earned him a transfer to Alcatraz and separation from his beloved birds in 1943.

Stroud remained on the Rock for sixteen years, until being moved to a medical facility in Springfield, Missouri. He died there in 1963, after being in prison for fifty-four years. But the fact that he killed two men is generally forgotten in the sympathetic treatment of "The Birdman."

Escape from Alcatraz, a Clint Eastwood film of 1979, concentrated on checking out. Thirty-six prisoners tried it over the years. Fourteen died in the attempt and nineteen were quickly recaptured. The film concentrated on Frank Morris, who led the only breakout that may have been successful. At least, no bodies ever were found and none of the three men were recaptured.

Morris, along with John and Clarence Anglin, made their run in June 1962. They dug holes in the back of their cells into a utility corridor that ran behind the block. Then they ascended three stories through the ducts to the roof, forced their way through a vent and splashed into the bay on a raft made of inflated raincoats.

Only the raft was ever found.

Even in the 1990s, long after its days as a prison were over, the film *Murder in the First* explored issues raised by the harsh methods Alcatraz was run by fifty years before.

It is hard to remember sometimes that officials here were dealing with bad guys, not movie stars. Al Capone was the best-known inmate (detested by other prisoners, who called him "The Wop with the Mop"). This is where his health began to fail from the syphilis that would eventually kill him.

Many others were big names in the crime annals of the forties and fifties but are almost forgotten today. Alvin Karpis, whose endearing nickname was "Creepy." Machine Gun Kelly. Bobby Sherrington, a good friend of John Dillinger. Counterfeiter Whitey Lewis. The kidnappers of millionaires, Harvey Bailey and John Waley.

Obscurities now. But in their time they made headlines and Warden Johnston felt one of the functions of the prison was to strip away their individuality. "We get the super criminal, or at least those with super ego," he explained in 1937, "and our job is to deflate that ego."

He didn't much believe in rehabilitation, but if some of that occurred, that would be all right, too.

Johnston had been a reform-minded lawyer when he was hired by California Governor Hiram Johnson to straighten out the state's prisons. He came up with a system called "examination, classification, and segregation." It ranked prisoners by degree of nastiness and sent the worst of them to Folsom. Enacted by California in 1917, it became the model applied to the federal system and Alcatraz.

To the Spanish explorers who first saw the Rock it was hardly a forbidding place. It was covered with pelicans and so was given the Spanish name for that bird, "Los Alcatraces."

The federal government fortified the island in the 1850s and used it as a detention center for Californians who opposed the Civil War too vocally. It was taken over by the U.S. Army in the second decade of the twentieth century and was used as a military prison. Most of the cell blocks were built during this time. German aliens were incarcerated there during World War I.

On June 19, 1934, the Department of Justice took it over. It usually housed fewer than four hundred inmates, and by 1963 the annual cost per prisoner had soared to $48,000 a year. "At that price, they could have put us up in the best hotel suites in San Francisco," said Karpis.

Attorney General Robert Kennedy looked at the figures and agreed. He ordered Alcatraz closed.

For the next six years, the island was left empty, with no clear plan about what to do with it. A group of Native American activists came up with their own plan and landed an occupying force on Alcatraz in 1969, declaring it to be property stolen from the Indians.

They held on for eighteen months, saying that they wanted to turn the place into a cultural center But when fires were set in some of the buildings and tourist boats were fired on with slingshots, the Feds moved an assault force onto the island and cleared the Indians off.

Two years later, in 1973, Alcatraz reopened as a tourist attraction and remains one of the most popular sights in the San Francisco area.

THE SITE

The Rock A good part of Alcatraz's notoriety is the fact that it is clearly visible from almost every part of the San Francisco bayfront. Telescopes along Fisherman's Wharf and the Embarcadero trained on the island bring its forbidding walls into clear focus.

It is now part of Golden Gate National Recreation Area and is administered by the National Park Service. Boats leave from Pier 41, Fisherman's Wharf and visitors are led on a walk through the blocks, to the cells where some of the Rock's most infamous criminals were held. Rangers lead the tours and a small museum highlights the history of the prison.

Some advance planning is necessary because the tours are so popular that during the summer months it is next to impossible to get same-day tickets. Tickets can be ordered one month in advance (although two weeks is usually ample time, except for holidays). (415) 981-7625; www.alcatrazcruises.com. Tickets must be picked up at the departure dock and there are no refunds. From October through April, tickets can be ordered only two days in advance. Boats leave at 9:30 a.m., 10:15 a.m., and then every half hour until 4:15 p.m. in summer. The last trip is at 2:15 p.m., rest of year. Fare and tour fee is $6.75; those over sixty-five $5; children under eleven $3.50.

BIBLIOGRAPHY

Beebe, Lucius and Charles Clegg. *U.S. West: The Saga of Wells Fargo*. New York: E. P. Dutton, 1949.

Bowers, Claude G. *The Tragic Era*. Boston: Houghton-Mifflin, 1957.

Boyd, Thomas. *Simon Girty: The White Savage*. New York: Minton, Balch, 1928.

Brooks, Juanita. *The Mountain Meadows Massacre*. Norman: University of Oklahoma Press, 1991.

Brophy, Patrick. *Bushwhackers of the Border*. Nevada, Missouri: Vernon County Historical Society, 1980.

Carpenter, Frank G. *Alaska*. Garden City, New York: Doubleday, 1923.

Castel, Albert. *A Frontier State at War: Kansas 1861–1865*. Ithaca, New York: Cornell University Press, 1958.

Connelley, William E. *Quantrill and the Border Wars*. Topeka: Kansas State Historical Society, 1909.

———. *Wild Bill and His Era*. New York: Press of the Pioneers, 1933.

Cromie, Robert and Pinkston. *Dillinger: a Short and Violent Life*. New York: McGraw-Hill, 1962.

Daniels, Jonathan. *Ordeal of Ambition: Jefferson, Hamilton, Burr*. Garden City, New York: Doubleday, 1970.

Davidson, James West and Mark Hamilton Lytle. *After the Fact: The Art of Historical Detection*. New York: Alfred Knopf, 1982.

Dimsdale, Thomas J. *The Vigilantes of Montana*. Norman: University of Oklahoma Press, 1953.

Dorson, Richard M. *America in Legend*. New York: Random House, 1973.

Dykes, Jefferson C. *Billy the Kid: The Bibliography of a Legend*. Albuquerque: University of New Mexico Press, 1952.

Evans, Marie. *The Hanging of the Columbus Villa Raiders*. El Paso, Texas: Bravo Press, 1990.

Fuller, Robert A. *Jubilee Jim: The Life of Col. James Fisk, Jr.* New York: MacMillan, 1928.

Gard, Wayne. *Frontier Justice*. Norman: University of Oklahoma Press, 1949.

Goodrich, Thomas. *Bloody Dawn: The Story of the Lawrence Massacre*. Kent, Ohio: Kent State University Press, 1991.

Hatcher, Harlan. *Lake Erie*. Indianapolis: Bobbs-Merrill, 1945.

Havighurst, Walter. *River to the West: Three Centuries of the Ohio*. New York: Putnam, 1970.

Horan, James D. *The Authentic Wild West—The Outlaws*. New York: Crown, 1977.

Jackson, Joseph Henry. *Bad Company*. New York: Harcourt, Brace, 1949.

Keleher, William A. *Violence in Lincoln County*. Albuquerque: University of New Mexico Press, 1957.

Kobler, John. *Capone*. New York: Putnam, 1971.

Lake, Stuart. *Wyatt Earp: Frontier Marshal*. Boston: Houghton-Mifflin, 1931.

Lefler, Hugh Talmage and Albert Ray Newsome. *North Carolina*. Chapel Hill: University of North Carolina Press, 1954.

Love, Robertus. *The Rise and Fall of Jesse James*. New York: Putnam, 1926.

McDonald, Forrest. *Alexander Hamilton*. New York: W. W. Norton, 1979.

Middlekauff, Robert. *The Glorious Cause: The American Revolution, 1763–1789*. New York: Oxford University Press, 1982.

Monaghan, Jay, ed. *The Book of the American West*. New York: Simon and Schuster, 1963.

Morris, Edmund. *The Rise of Theodore Roosevelt*. New York: Coward, McCann and Geoghegan, 1979.

Myers, John M. *The Last Chance: Tombstone's Early Years*. New York: Alfred A. Knopf, 1950.

O'Connor, Richard. *Bat Masterson*. Garden City, New York: Doubleday, 1957.

Parmet, H. S. and M. B. Hecht. *Aaron Burr: Portrait of an Ambitious Man*. New York: MacMillan, 1967.

Pound, Arthur. *Lake Ontario*. Indianapolis: Bobbs-Merrill, 1945.

Preece, Harold. *The Dalton Gang*. New York: New American Library of World Literature, 1964.

Rascoe, Burton. *Belle Starr*. New York: Random House, 1941.

Rosa, Joseph G. *The Gunfighter—Man or Myth?*. Norman: University of Oklahoma Press, 1969.

Sonnischen, C. L. *Roy Bean: Law West of the Pecos*. New York: MacMillan, 1943.

Steinberg, Alfred. *The First Ten*. Garden City, New York: Doubleday, 1967.

Stember, Sol. *Guide to the American Revolution*. New York: E. P. Dutton, 1974.

Stern, Philip Van Doren. *The Man Who Killed Lincoln*. New York: Random House, 1939.

Tratzer, Cliff and Steve George. *Yuma Prison Centennial*. Yuma, Arizona: Rio Colorado Press, 1980.

Van Doren, Carl Clinton. *Secret History of the American Revolution*. New York: Viking Press, 1941.

Vestal, Stanley. *Queen of Cowtowns*. New York: Harper, 1952.

Waters, Frank. *The Colorado*. New York: Rinehart, 1946.

———. *The Earp Brothers of Tombstone*. New York: Clarkson N. Potter, 1960.

Wellman, Paul I. *A Dynasty of Western Outlaws*. Garden City, New York: Doubleday, 1961.

Weyl, Nathaniel. *Treason: The Study of Disloyalty and Betrayal in American History*. Washington, D.C.: Public Affairs Press, 1950.

Wymore, Jack B. *History of the Jesse James Bank Museum*. Liberty, Missouri: published privately, 1997.

In addition, the original *American Guide* series, published by the Works Progress Administration, was especially useful for the states of Arizona, Kansas, Missouri, Kentucky, and New Mexico.

I also relied upon the files of the *Detroit News* for contemporary journalistic accounts of the careers of John Dillinger, Bonnie and Clyde, Bugsy Siegel, and Al Capone.

INDEX